THE BIG BOOK
OF
WIT AND LAUGHTER

Other publications by Peter Cagney/Bevis Winter:

Humour

The Treasury of Wit and Humour
Peter Cagney's Second Treasury of Wit and Humour (*Thorsons*)
Comedy Scripts for Tape Recordings (*Queen Anne Press*)
From Gags to Riches
Comedy Sketch Album
Panorama of Patter
The Gagmaster
The Comedians
Show Laughs
Cavalcade
Sad Laughter (*Mortimer*)

Novels

Darker Grows the Street
The Gallows of Rome
No Diamonds for a Doll
Murderers Make Mistakes (*Renown, New York*)
A Noose of Emeralds (*Bourgey, New York*)
Hear The Stripper Scream
The Night Was Made for Murder
The Dead Sleep for Keeps
The Dark and The Deadly
A Grave for Madam
Next Stop—The Morgue
Sleep Long My Lovely
Little Red Monkey (with Eric Maschwitz)
Let The Lady Die

Plays include:

Leave It To Laura
Make It Murder (with Jack Last)

The
Big Book
of
Wit and Laughter

Peter Cagney

WOLFE PUBLISHING LIMITED
10 EARLHAM STREET LONDON WC2

ISBN 72340496 8

PRINTED IN GREAT BRITAIN
BY EBENEZER BAYLIS AND SON LTD.
THE TRINITY PRESS, WORCESTER, AND LONDON

Contents

Contents

AUTHOR'S INTRODUCTION

THE BULK OF the material specially edited for this new book is an accumulation of items which were written in the course of preparing shows and comedy routines for a large number of celebrated entertainers in radio, television and variety, as well as performers in other branches of show business (such as the brisk world of clubland).

As there are several hundred personalities involved I apologise for not listing them, either alphabetically or in order of importance. In any case I have no wish to apportion degrees of renown in such a complicated profession as that of Entertainment. Suffice to say that I have always relished the prospect of creating comedy dialogue and situations, and derived the greatest satisfaction from knowing that the material would eventually provide laughter and enjoyment for audiences in their millions, through the various media of performance and production. The performers apply their stylised techniques and individual personalities to the scribe's raw material and are in effect the middlemen between writer and audience. I have been fortunate, in this way, to make many long-standing friendships with a galaxy of the world's funniest and most amiable people. It is with this in mind that I dedicate this new volume to all my 'clients'—each will know in his or her heart that my appreciation is fulsome and sincere.

Since publication of my earlier books in the *Treasury of Wit and Humour* series, I have received hundreds of letters from public-speakers, toastmasters, masters of ceremonies and similar raconteurs, expressing their views on the usefulness of these volumes as a source of ideas to embellish their talks with entertaining material. All these, too, I thank sincerely.

The third category of people to whom I owe my thanks are those in closer proximity to the mechanics of the exercise—who co-operated with the sorting, selection, compiling, checking, typing and indexing; or with good advice and moral support.

I am confident that this new volume will be equally useful to all those people who are called upon to climb a stage or a speaking-platform and entertain their customers or their guests.

For all speakers, the construction of your material can be simplified considerably by reference to the detailed subject-index at the back of the book. Once your basic theme is decided, all you have to do is scribble down all the complementary subjects and trace them through the index. For example, if you are speaking on the theme of 'education' you will find ample comedy covering this general field by turning to such index references as School, Children, Teachers, College, Howlers, Teenagers, and so forth. It is a good idea to go through the index and note all potential associations, since the cross-references might suggest

7

additional lines which can be built into your talk. This could provide you with far more material than you may require, and give you plenty of scope to effect some critical editing.

Of course there are many other applications for the book, too. It is a sound source of anecdotes for the party wag, a sedating volume for bedside reading, an ideal 'dipper' for convalescents and the perfect good-humoured companion on long journeys.

Several hundred of the included items are entirely new and previously unpublished or unproduced as they were written into the work as it developed, to enlarge some of the categorised sections.

PETER CAGNEY, 1972-3

PRE-ESTABLISHED COPYRIGHT

Quips,
Gags
and
Patter

1

The boss said: 'Let's talk turkey' and we spent the next hour gobbling at each other.

2

She confessed that she had told him a little white lie ... he wasn't really the father of their seven children.

3

Adam looked at Eve angrily when she came home three hours late and said: 'You've got to stop this gossiping'.

4

Everyone was singing around the camp fire. Except me. It was me they were burning.

5

They call her Bakerloo Barbara—she's always getting squeezed in the tube.

6

Money talks, said the dumb blonde.

7

Tomorrow we expect the patter of tiny feet in our house. I'm going to chase my mother-in-law to the front door.

8

After combing the hills for twenty years unsuccessfully looking for gold, he returned to California and became a Hollywood hairdresser. Still using the same comb.

9

The firm I'm working for is now under new management. The boss got married.

10

When the government debated the Obscenity Law it is significant that one of the parties got out a three-line whip.

11

Last month Alice Knott was the victim of a take-over bid. Some guy tried to pull off her sweater.

12

Mumbjibu was having dinner in a fashionable Congolese Cannibal Restaurant when he angrily called the pygmy waiter to his table and asked: 'What is this foreign body doing in my soup?' The waiter said: 'It sho' looks like the Australian crawl'.

13

Marian has just bought something that proved much too tight for her. A bubble car.

14

Norman Finglinger was dismissed from the Club last week, for cheating at cards. You can tell what sort of man he is—he was playing Solitaire.

15

Yesterday I was at a club where they play the new game—Poor-Man's Poker. The best hand I held was two Western Credit cards, a Barclay card, an American Express and a Diner's Club.

16

Single women who demonstrate for a man's salary ought to realise that millions of married women already get it.

17

Men—if you are fed up with golf and want a counter-attraction why not try Miss Wilkie who serves in the pro's equipment shop?

18

It is perfectly true that there are more ways of skinning a cat but obviously it has to be another cat.

19

Harold is not only a drunken driver, he even sleeps tight.

20

A wife is a woman who acts like a sponsor, talks like a spinster and carps like a censor.

21

When Matilda goes out for a walk at night, all she has to exercise is caution.

22

If you know what's what you stand every chance of getting into *Who's Who*. If not, you could very well end up in *That's That*.

23

A celebrity is somebody who, after two brief appearances on TV, makes a beeline for the V.I.P. lounge.

24
That character who is constantly binding about the permissive society and urging censorship of everything from corn flakes to cauliflowers has just come up with a new bright idea. Now he wants it made compulsory for babies to be born wearing clothes.

25
One of the players in the local football team must have had a real big night out on Friday. On Saturday it took him a lifetime to reach his goal.

26
Then there's the pop singer who made a comeback; he's so old he can remember his last trophy—a gold cylinder.

27
Irish news report: 'Yesterday in an accident involving two taxis, injuries were sustained to eight Englishmen, fourteen Scotsmen and an Irishman, the poor bhoy.'

28
We know an Englishman with such an aggressive jaw and such a stiff upper lip that he has to eat through a straw.

29
A northern comedian was attacked by a bunch of hooligans who roped his hands, tied his feet and corded his ankles to his neck. There was no gag used—the comedian didn't think it was time to be funny.

30
She sent her husband out to trim the front garden hedge and half an hour later caught him resting on her laurels.

31
You can tell how poor he is; when his tube packed up he couldn't afford to replace it . . . and that was only toothpaste.

32
After a fortnight's experience of married life, a girl sued for divorce. She told her solicitor that she had given her husband the best fourteen days of her life.

33
A deadbeat used to be a wastrel; now it's a pop song.

34
We know a printer who makes a good living producing blank visiting cards for people who wish to remain anonymous.

35
She always keeps small change in her purse: panties, bra and two pairs of nylons.

36
There's a club in Wales where comedians sometimes tell double-meaning jokes to people who don't even get the first point.

37
We heard the other day about a schizophrenic patient who asked his psychiatrist if he could have two couches because he felt crowded.

38
At a big party in a crowded London ballroom a sloshed newspaperman accidentally tipped a full glass of Martini down Twiggy's cleavage. He tried to apologise but her manager said: 'Oh, never mind; it's nothing'.

39
Uneasy lies the head that weds a crone.

40
The top priority of many a movie actress is to have two main features on release.

41
An anthropologist studying human behaviour in the back seats of cinemas has formed the conclusion that mankind is still groping in the dark.

42
If Stella can't find the right button she just sews up the buttonhole.

43
After a year of hard struggle, many a man realises that all he has to show for it is a calendar with the numbers struck out.

44
There are at least twenty-seven Hollywood actresses who always keep a piece of the wedding cake for their divorce lawyers.

45
Harry bought a new Japanese camera with a shutter-speed of 1/10000th of a second. It was the only way to get a picture of his wife with her mouth closed.

46
We live in a world where ten per cent of the people are capitalists and all the rest lower-caste.

47
A hypochondriac is a person who has every disease under the sundry ailments.

48
A fish-fryer named Scoothby has just retired a wealthy man. It was the oil he found on his property that put him in the chips.

49
At six a.m. every morning the fisherfolk of a small Dorset coastal village can be seen heading for the beach, mussel-bound.

50
As one political commentator insisted, Parliament is a place where bird-brains assemble and talk is cheep-cheep.

51
Yesterday I saw on the M1 a car old enough to be paid for. It was such an ancient banger that it didn't have front and rear registration numbers —just upper and lower plates.

52
A coward is someone who had always been quick-quitted.

53
A good motorist is one who can study a large-scale road map without playing an accordion.

54
Only one sort of man successfully marries for money. A preacher.

55
Most of the troubles of society are man-maid.

56
Only the hot dog feeds the hand that bites it.

57
Don't get worried if your wife starts talking to herself. She might be a ventriloquist.

58
When Sam's mother-in-law starts lecturing him it's like looking into the jaws of death *and* the teeth of disaster.

59
A husband who lets his wife rule the roost is just plain chicken.

60
A man was in a clinch on the sofa with his girl when there was a knock on the door. He angrily shouted: 'If that's opportunity, go away—I've already got one.'

61

A pungent theatre critic began his newspaper piece: 'At the last-night opening of Derek Holt's new play . . .'

62

Jack told his mates: 'I had a smashing dream last night! If it comes round, don't miss it.'

63

There are many things we should not see, but there is nothing we should not hear. That's why we have lids on our eyes but not on our ears.

64

If you are a well-preserved, successful academic banker, going to bed early will make you healthy, wealthy and wise.

65

An early bird is not such a catch if you catch her before she's had time to do her daily paint-job.

66

A party organiser is someone who pours drinks to mix people.

67

There was complete silence in the Woodbridges' house last night. Mrs. Woodbridge was speaking her mind.

68

Moira was on her second honeymoon in Brighton so she stopped off at the post office to mail a view card to her first husband back home.

69

Sam took his small gluttonous son on a fishing trip and after he'd found a good spot by the lake and organised his tackle he asked the kid to hand him the tin of maggots. 'What tin of maggots?' asked junior.
    'There's only one—with the—what's that in your mouth?'
    'Dad—I thought that was spaghetti!'

70

Rugby songs are Indian love limericks.

71

Frustration is trying to slam a revolving door.

72

In entertainment circles, black magic is ace, king, queen, jack, ten of spades.

73

The smaller the world gets, the more expensive it is to mail a letter across it.

74

Some politician once said: 'You can't fool all the people all the time'— but you don't have to. Just fool the majority and your party can stay put.

75

Man is still the noblest creature, despite having the knobbliest knees.

76

Roger is so impoverished even mosquitoes don't bother to put the bite on him.

77

Equality is what *causes* all the troubles of mankind. If the man-woman ratio wasn't 50-50 but 75-25, the world would be a happier place; provided the 75 were women.

78

All women think about is love, but men are different. All they think about is women.

79

A bachelor is a man who can have any wife he pleases.

80

A gentleman is someone with such good manners he never treats a guest like one of the family.

81

Bookmaker: The wizard of odds.

82

The Eskimo wife came in from the snow with a fresh roll of paper for the igloo and said to her husband. 'I've just seen the doctor. Soon we will be hearing the chatter of little teeth.'

83

What *can* you give to a man who has everything, apart from an envious glance.

84

How did he know he was going to be a dad? A twittering bird told him.

85

Husband to wife: 'When we were courting you said we were made for each other and ever since then you've been re-designing me.'

18

86

Overheard at the hairdressing salon: 'You can tell what a marvellous cook she is: her husband works at the circus as a sword and fire eater, and he eats out.'

87

Ulster is divided into two categories: the ones with the brass, and the rhythm section.

88

An orphan of the permissive society is a miss-begotten child.

89

The Russians are building a bungalow on the coast near Leningrad. It's for the tourist trade.

90

Antique furniture is all that modern stuff you ordered by the time you've finished paying off for it.

91

Last week they had to re-open the railway station at Boynebridge which was closed down two years ago. A late train showed up.

91a

Said the suspicious wife to her husband, late home from the show in which he did an illusion act: 'All right! Whose is that hare on your shoulder?'

92

The police car whizzed down the main street with the siren screeching. She'd been arrested for starting a commotion outside a cinema.

93

A sailor who was shipwrecked was left with only his trousers, his shirt and a tablet of soap so, he got washed ashore.

94

Pity the tiny sparrows on a spring morning—their little bills are all over dew.

95

Pharaoh's daughter was the world's first speculator. When there was a rush on the bank she got a little prophet.

96

If you see a dog running down the street with a can tied to his tail you can bet something is bound to a cur.

97

Mini skirts help most girls to get up them stares.

98

To a barber *all* bald-headed men are smooth customers.

The Corn Exchange

99

'They tell me in Mexico you can get three pounds of sugar, a pound of coffee, a quart of whisky and a wife for three dollars.'
  'I'll bet it's rotten whisky.'

100

'He's a tight one, you say?'
  'Tight? He wouldn't give a beggar a bite if he owned the Sandwich Islands.'

101

'Have a cigar?'
  'No thanks—I've given up smoking.'
  'Well, put one in your pocket for tomorrow.'

102

'I drink about fifty cups of coffee a day.'
  'Doesn't that keep you awake?'
  'It helps.'

103

'Never saw such a crowd at our church before.'
  'New minister?'
  'No; it was burned down last night.'

104

'I am chilled to the bone.'
  'Why don't you put your hat on?'

105

'What was the first thing the grasshopper said after it was created?'
  'Lord! You didn't half make me jump.'

106

'Why is a lady's girdle like a dust cart?'
  'Because it goes round and gathers the waist.'

107

'Well, back from visiting the top pop idol? How did you find him?'
  'Brushed the hair aside and there he was.'

108

'I don't like the new motorway signs.'
  'What do they say?'
  'Don't hug the soft shoulders.'

109

'There's a patient outside who says he has a split personality, doctor.'
  'Show him in, and find me the impact adhesive.'

110

'Have you a cigarette?'
  'Lots of them, thank you.'

111

'Terrible links, caddy, terrible!'
  'These ain't links—you got off *them* an hour ago.'

112

'What do you think would go well with my purple and green golf socks?'
  'Kinky boots?'

113

'You've been watching me for three hours. Why don't you try fishing yourself?'
  'I ain't got your patience.'

114

A meetless day means there'll be no tally-ho.

115

Marriage—the supporting life.

116

For breakfast in bed he had two rolls and a couple of turnovers.

117

My Dad was a toy manufacturer. Three feet tall, and Mom had to wind him up every morning.

118

I see that Paramount Studios are going to make an epic film called 'The Great War'—Raquel Welch was turned down for the lead role. Flat feet.

21

119
The way the cost of newspapers keeps rising, it will soon be cheaper to buy sixpennyworth of chips and read the wrapper.

120
The waiter served my dinner. I looked at the plate and said: 'Damn it, there's a dirty fat burnt bluebottle on my cabbage!' He shrugged and said: 'You didn't say you liked your flies underdone!'

121
My producer has joined the lunatic fringe. He came to rehearsal this morning with tassels on his turnups.

122
The only effective cure for knock-knees is to wear bow-legged tights.

123
Did you hear about the farmer who fed his old cow violet ink?—she mooed indigo.

124
The harder my wife works the more she has to show for it. She's a stripper at the Lido in Wigan.

125
If you want a holiday that's different this year, visit Greenland. You can best travel by B.O.A.C., but use their 'Go Now Pay Later' system, because that's the only class that gets parachutes. It's a wonderful country—full of God's frozen people. The President this year is a chap called Eski-moses. One word of warning—watch yourself in the ig*loo*— I got stuck there last Easter, frosted to the seat.

126
Violence is forcing me to stop watching television. Every time I switch it on the wife clouts me.

127
My sister was going past any Army Recruiting Shop last week and she saw the advert 'The Army Will Make You A Man'. She went in and ordered one.

128
I've not been well since I was in Spain. So I went to the chemist and asked for some Little Liver Pills. He said: 'Do you want the king-size pack?'

129
A girl was demonstrating brassieres during a lingerie exhibition, pulling and tugging hard to show how strong the elastic was, and half way through the performance her knickers dropped down.

130

They recently banned the screening of a new film by a London film society. It was an American production called 'Flesh'—a kind of updated production of the show 'Hair', closely shaved.

131

I wanted to drive down to Dorset quickly so I sent for an A.A. road-route. They routed me through Skegness to Manchester via Portsmouth, Sheptonmallet, Widnes, Aberdeen and Kenilworth, through Bournemouth and Filey. That's the last time I get my road routes from Alcoholics Anonymous.

132

My girl goes on a lot of protest marches. The other day she went to a plastic surgeon and had a kangaroo pouch grafted on to her stomach so that she could carry a bigger banner. When she got the bill it was headed 'Navel Estimates'.

133

I see the Prime Minister is reshuffling the cabinet. Maybe now I'll get a better deal.

134

Television programme controllers have to pass a special intelligence test before they get appointed. Anyone with an IQ above subnormal is automatically discarded.

135

The permissive society has resulted in 50 per cent of TV plays introducing a bedroom scene, often with the girl displaying cleavage right down to her toes. And the boy usually has trouble with his horizontal hold.

Oh Doctor

136

I was feeling seedy so I went to the local physician. I rang the doorbell and heard the strains of the musical chimes singing out: 'Nearer My God To Thee' . . . A maid came to the door and said the door was a bit tight—would I push? I hadn't got the strength to push so I rammed it with my bath-chair . . . The doctor was in his consulting room and the waiting room was full. Patients who had been dealt with were passed over our heads into a waiting hearse . . . He's supposed to be a good doctor . . . used to practise in the Australian bush—I don't know what he practised there but he's got a diploma signed by three kangeroos. When I got into the consulting room the doctor said: 'Just throw open that window there's a good fellow'. I said 'Will that do me any good?' and he said: 'I don't know, but I've been trying to open it for a week and I can't', I said: 'Why not?' and then he started to tell me how ill he was and showed me his various aches and pains. I said: 'Look, why don't you go and see a doctor?' and he said: 'I can't, I'm behind with my stamps.' After this preamble he sent me behind a screen and told me to get undressed. Twenty minutes later he put his head round the screen and said: 'I won't keep you a minute, Madam.' I said: 'Well, hurry up, I'm catching cold, I'm turning blue.' He looked at me and said: 'Your goosepimples have got goosepimples. That's remarkable.' Then he tapped my chest with his knuckles and broke two fingers. After that he tapped my knee with a hammer and I was so brittle, my leg fell off. I said: 'What am I going to do now, doctor?' He consulted a medical book and half an hour later found the right place. I said: 'Well—what do I do?' He said: 'According to the book, you limp ...' Then he said 'You're very pale ... what's the matter.' So I told him I'd had insomnia for months. He told me to go home and sleep it off ... Then he saw my red eyes and he asked: 'Did you have the television set on last night.' I said: 'As a matter of fact, I did.' He said: 'How did it fit?' ... I said: 'Never mind that, what can you recommend for my headaches? I want something for splitting headaches.' He gave me a prescription for razor blades.

Memoirs of a Moron

137
Only now can it be revealed that I was Adolf Hitler's nurse. I got the job through an advertisement in the 'Pigbreeder's Gazette'—from a couple who were expecting a baby. My wages were fifty pence a week, plus all the blood I could drink. His parents weren't sure whether to buy him a cot or a cage ... in the end they bought both. The baby stayed in the cot and the parents hid in the cage. Taking the baby for a walk was always difficult because he used to hide hand grenades in his napkins to fling at the frontier guards. At bedtime we always had trouble because the poor thing suffered from nightmares and would wake up screaming about angels, cherubs, fairies and Father Christmas. His favourite plaything was his doll. A small human skeleton. Although he was given one room to himself, by the time he was three and a half he had invaded the rest of the house, locked his mother in the cellar, and betrayed his father to the Income Tax authorities. He became devoted to music ... his favourite pieces being Rachmaninov's Prelude and Gloomy Sunday. He used to write clever little lyrics about starvation, death and disease. At the age of seventeen he was called up for the Army. His mother and father wept for days and days ... but their joy was soon ended; he came home on leave, filled with excitement as he told how the general had put a bayonet into his bare hands and sent him on a special job—in fifteen days he had peeled nine tons of potatoes. He was very glad to see his old nurse again and he showed me some poems he had written to me, in red. He explained that it wasn't really

ink—he'd got it by wringing dead rats over an old bucket. To this day I cherish the last gift he ever gave me, before I left him to make his own way in the world . . . a lovely floral garter . . . with his mother's leg still in it.

Holidays in Britain

138
I don't bother about looking for excitement on holiday . . . I'm satisfied just to sit on the beach and dream of the dames gone by. The last time I went on holiday I got into trouble—I played around with a girl old enough to be my wife . . .

Taking the wife along on holiday is a mistake I think. The only reason I take her with me is because she's so ugly I can't bear to kiss her goodbye.

She's really an oomph girl . . . when she sits in a deck-chair you can hear the framework go oooooomph.

While I was having a drink in the camp bar a ghost walked in and asked the barman if he had a licence to serve spirits.

Our chalet was a small place; the rooms were so tiny, some of the furniture consisted of drawings on the wall. There was hot and cold running water—it ran from the ceiling . . . There were twin beds in our room—but we didn't have twins.

When we were basking on the beach seagulls were flying over my head, and vultures over my wife's. Not far from us there was a beautiful blonde but she didn't look too good in dark glasses . . . so I took mine off . . . I watched her for a long time through my binoculars, she was lying on her stomach getting the colour back into her cheeks . . .

In the dining-room three hundred of us crowded round the tables. It was such chaos when the food was served. Everyone lunged at the big plate in the middle with a fork—I got my wrists stabbed four times.

The sort of people staying at the camp were a poor lot. In the restaurant there was a notice on the hat-rack which said: 'Watch Your Hat and Coat' . . . I spent so much time watching mine that someone sneaked off with my dinner . . . Mind you, for supper we had a meal guaranteed to tickle the palate . . . they'd left the feathers on the chicken.

The Money Game

Inflation has made everyone dishonest. Yesterday I was staying in a large hotel when the manager announced that they were trying to find the person who had lost a bundle of currency notes fastened with a rubber band. The man who'd lost the money applied for it, and the manager said they'd only found the rubber band.

You can never trust the modern bankers. Take my own bank for instance. Only yesterday I found out they've got more vice-presidents than depositers.

I'm all in favour of the medical protest against soiled currency. It's a known fact that germs breed on money. But I'm not worried—not even a germ could live on my salary.

I'm disillusioned by stockbrokers. There's one man who used to come to me twice a week and tell me about certain shares. He always promised me he'd get me in 'on the ground floor'. Yesterday he threw himself off a skyscraper roof.

The greatest financier the world ever knew was Noah. He floated a whole new company when the rest of the world was liquidated.

You can't get away from money problems. I remember how worried I was about my investments when I was in hospital last year. The nurse was taking my temperature and I asked her how it was. She said: 'It's 103.' I said: 'Okay. When it gets to 104, sell.'

A lot of our economic problems arise from labour difficulties. At a factory the other day, the men came out on strike. They wanted shorter hours. So the government is bringing in a decree shortening every hour to forty minutes. A local plumber fired his mate last night—just because the young fool remembered to take the tools on a job.

Business isn't too bad really. In my Company we're running about fifty-fifty. We got an order in the morning and a cancellation in the afternoon.

Swedish emigrants were among the earliest settlers in Britain. The other immigrants *still* owe money.

People are divided into two classes; debtors and creditors. A debtor is a man who owes money and a creditor is the fool who thinks he's going to collect.

Facing the Music

140

You may not think it, but I come from a very musical family ... All my relations were interested in music. Tuesday night was always a regular practice night for my family. I'd be playing the violin while my father slapped the bass ... Father was a great music lover, that's why he often slapped my bass ... At other times I used to play the piano, my mother played the glockenspiel and my brother was on the fiddle. He's been on the fiddle for years ... Even my great-grandfather was a musician ... He was one of the original members of that immortal trio —Old King Cole's three fiddlers. That of course was the very first three-piece band ... All they could play was three pieces. My father had a great number of musical friends. He even fitted a musical doorbell to our house, and if anyone wanted to visit us they had to buy a pound's worth of sheet music before they could get in. Of course I don't really play from music—I play by ear. As a matter of fact I learned to play by ear when I was with the orchestra of the Folies Bergère. To earn a little extra money, I used to help the cleaners clean up the theatre after every show. I was the one who picked up all the eyeballs.

Family Size

141

Have you noticed how married couples get to look more like each other as the years of happy marriage flow by? ... It's true ... My mother's moustache gets more like my dad's every day ... I led quite a sheltered life in my young days ... until the bus company tore down the shelter and dad had to buy a house ... My folks sent me to one of the nicest schools you ever saw ... that's because my father approved of good schooling and my mother also approved of good schooling ... so there I was ... at an approved school ... My teachers were quick to realise that I had a first-class brain: while all the other kids were moving up into class two and class three, I was still in the first class with my first-class brain. But here I am, all grown up and working. It was the war that put years on me. I'll never forget the day when the call to duty came ... I had to go down to Southampton, that's where the troopship was waiting ... My mother packed the bags and we travelled to the docks and on the quayside there were tears and laughter; then I kissed my mother goodbye ... and away she sailed.

Boarding House Blues

142

Last year I went to Shellbeach ... A lovely place ... Honestly, the beauty of that little town simply knocks your eye out ... As a matter of fact she knocked out two of my teeth as well ... The place I stayed at was a holiday camp ... a place where they were very careful about your health ... in fact they were so worried in case anyone got food poisoning that they didn't give you any ...

I met the manageress at the door ... she was a nice big blowsy blonde ... with peroxided hair, false eyelashes, fishnet nylons and four-inch French heels ... quite a homely girl ... if you like that sort of a home ... There was a dance in the camp on the first night and I danced with her ... she was wearing one of those off-the-elbow strapless gowns. During the tango I had to push her back into it five times ...

I got fed up with the place in the end and moved to a little hotel ... It was called a guest-house. The beds were so big! I found an old man in mine ... he'd been trying to find the way out for a week ... And the fleas! You never saw such big bugs ... they were so tough that if you weren't in bed by eleven they came downstairs to get you ... My room was right up in the attic ... and there were no lights up there ... it was so dark that even the bats were flying around with candles ...

But I was determined to enjoy my holiday ... I was a bit browned off, you see ... My girl-friend back home had given me grounds for a divorce, and I'm not married. I felt a bit lonely so I went down to the beach to see if I could find another lonely soul ... There was a beautiful girl sitting on the beach gazing at me with rapt attention ... That was the only thing about her that *was* wrapped ... I've got a fatal fascination for women ... usually they take one look at me and drop dead.

This is America — or Dragnet Meets Sunset Strip

143

Wednesday, August 15th, 3 p.m. Report comes through from the university ... It's my girl friend's report—she failed in physics, geometry and algebra. What a dame. She can't even talk algebra, and I speak it like a native. Another report comes in. It's from Highway Patrol ... Ten-four ... I wish it was ten-five, 'cos we always break for coffee at five past ten ... Still, there's a job to do, and I'm the man to do it ... It's a murder case.

A guy has been found in an uptown apartment; he has six bullet wounds in the back of his head, a dagger in his chest, his lips smell of cyanide, there's a rope pulled tight around his throat and he's bleeding from the stomach. The Chief suspects foul play ...

I leave headquarters and drive over to the apartment. Four blocks away I have to go back—forgotten the squad car ... The moment I see the corpse I'm sure of one thing ... Sal volatile is very good for a faint ... I wipe my mouth and get up ... I know straight off that the murdered man is dead—what's more, he was killed by an Italian. There's a venetian blind grasped in his right hand ...

28

His wife is sobbing her heart out ... nobody can shutter up. No? Very well. She's crying with a heaving breast and nobody can concentrate on the investigation. The fingerprint men are busy dusting powder. This is a fine time to take a bath ... The photographers are taking shots of the body from every angle ... The captain of detectives says to them: 'Okay, boys, that's plenty of the wife—now take pictures of the corpse' ...

I can see straight away that this dame is in a tight fix. The captain tells me to loosen the clinch ... I whisper to her to come down to my office and talk things over ...

Thursday, August 16th, 7-30 a.m. The dame comes breezing into my office carrying everything before her ... This is no longer Highway Patrol stuff—no 10-4 ... this is 42-25-36 ... She looks at my sergeant sitting at his desk, doing some filing ... he puts his nails down and stares at her ... I tell the dame that she's the obvious suspect and she looks like taking the rap for killing her husband ... She confesses that she only killed him because she didn't get a wrap—he bought his secretary a mink stole and his wife nothing.

I asked her why her dead husband hadn't given her a mink stole, too and she said it was because she refused to mend his socks ... She said: 'He didn't give a wrap so I don't give a darn.'

I tell her that we ought to go someplace to snatch some breakfast, and talk things over ... We go to Lindy's and she orders a table for two—and eats the whole table in four bites. This doll is hungry ... Then she says: 'Tuesday, I guess we'd better take a powder.' I say 'After what you just ate, you need a couple of powders ...'

We go straight back to headquarters and I sit her down in my office. On my knee ... I tell he she'd better come clean, so she gets off my knee and goes and has a wash ... When her face is clean I recognise her ... she's Annie McBean, gun moll for that big wheel of the Syndicate, Scarface Al Molone ... I figure she's trying to pull the wool over my eyes so I tell her to stop fiddling with her sweater and answer some questions ... I ask her six times, but she still says 'NO'.

I begin puzzling over why she is acting so strange. Then I realise she is hiding something down her bodice ... I say to her: 'Give it to me kid. Go on, give it to me,' so she hauls out a big automatic and shoots me clean through the heart. If my heart hadn't been in my mouth I wouldn't be here today.

I drop to the floor and she kneels over me ... I say to her in a faint whisper: 'Say, kid, is that a thirty-eight or a forty-four?' and she says: 'It's a forty-two, uplift model ...' I say: 'Are you going to confess to the murder, or finger the guy who did it?' And she says: 'Do you take me for a squealer?' ... So I get up and take her in my arms and she squeals ... I say to her: 'You may be a killer, but I could go for you in a big way ...' And she says: 'You don't have to go for me I'm still here.'

We walk out on to the office balcony. It's three hundred stories up, overlooking Mason Street. I wait for her to speak, knowing that sooner or later she is going to tip me off ... I fall three hundred stories to the sidewalk ... And there she is waiting for me outside the drugstore. She says to me: 'What kept you?' Then she says: 'I'm sorry about that, don't turn me in, I don't want to go to jail for ten years.' I tell her: 'Okay, so I'm pushed for time. Gimme a kiss, Baby.' She puts her cigarette into her mouth and gives me a burning kiss . . .

Then she says: 'Scarface Al Molone killed my husband. He didn't like the way he fixed his necktie.' I drag her back into the office and get the wires busy with a pick-up call for Scarface . . . The phone is ringing . . . ringing . . . ringing . . . So I get a towel and dry it . . . A message comes through . . . 'Scarface Molone seen heading due west on Highway 77 . . . block all intersections . . .' Annie McBean is sobbing her heart out again . . . they know that the cops will pick up her man . . . Sitting at his desk, my sergeant is idly blowing up balloons . . . making a lot of noise . . . He's blowing them up with dynamite . . .

The alarm is still on and Scarface is still heading west on Highway 77 . . . but the road blocks aren't doing any good because Scarface is crafty: he's heading west by wagon train . . . isn't standing for any nonsense from road blocks . . . 6 p.m. . . . Scarface has vanished . . . Annie McBean says: 'Looks like the dragnet muffed this one. If Al gets to know I spilled the beans, he'll slay me.' So we went straight back to her apartment and picked up all the beans and put them back neatly in their cans . . . Her apartment was cosy, luxurious, ultra-modern but very untidy. The corpse was still on the floor.

Annie rang down to room sevice and had them send up a charwoman. The charwoman dusted the corpse and went out again with a sneer on her face which made her look very beautiful . . . I carried Annie to the couch . . . Suddenly the French windows opened and a man came in with a gun. I know they were French windows because they had dirty pictures painted on them . . . The man had a scarf pulled right over his face: I guess the night had turned chilly. He leered at Annie and said: 'I'm gonna get you for putting the cops on my back . . .' He shot her eight and a half times . . . 'And now I'm gonna get you,' Scarface told me . . . His hand was in his pocket, holding something . . . he forced me to sit down . . . Then he sat opposite me and got a bead on my stomach . . . It was a jade bead, worth fifty cents . . . There were more beads on my forehead . . . Perspiration . . . I stared him out and he stared me out . . .

Annie crawled to the stairs and went home, still bleeding badly from the scratch on her arm where she'd dug in her fingernails in agony . . . Scarface pulled his hands out of his pocket, shuffled the cards and dealt . . . That night I won fifty-seven bucks on a straight flush . . . When the game was over, Scarface said: 'Okay, now say your prayers, mister . . .' So I said my prayers, and he tucked me up and put out the light and kissed me goodnight . . . Then I suddenly knew where I'd seen him before . . . It was Dad!

144
In 3000 B.C., the Lord gave to Moses at Sinai the Tablets of the Law. In A.D. 1968 in Rome the Pope had trouble with another tablet . . . the Pill.

145

At Oxford, Cambridge and Sussex universities they are studying the Bolshevik revolution; in Moscow university they are studying the student revolution.

146

In Ireland the Catholics are protesting about being subjected to injustices, and protesting about housing conditions and protesting about unemployment . . . there have never been so many Catholic protestants before.

147

According to the Egyptian Premier it is vital for the Egyptian population to be increased in order to ensure a continual intake for the army. Evidently there are not enough Egyptian mummies.

148

Hospitals are short of beds and the waiting lists grow longer. Every maternity hospital in Britain is being inundated with urgent advance bookings. Some men are giving as much as *nine months'* notice; even telephoning from bed.

149

Have you heard about the girl who trimmed the bottom of her shortie nightie with fur to keep her neck warm.

150

Israeli guerrillas attacked Baghdad Airport yesterday and destroyed eighteen flying carpets.

151

The population of China is now running at 700,000,000 people. Mao is introducing family planning. Soon we will have another billion Pekin-inis, and a lot more Chinese birds nesting.

152

The Meteorological Centre just issued their new long-range forecast. Fog, snow, sleet and thunderstorms will be prevalent—in Brisbane. That's as far as they can range until they get a new battery for the Antarctic weather station.

153

What a marvellous country Britain is! We have Free Trade, Free Enterprise, Free Love, Free Coupons, Free Health Service, Free Expression, Free Speech . . . Everyone is demanding more money to pay for them!

154

Our M.P. is a cool one—last Friday he told his wife that he would not be home over the weekend as he had to attend a conference in Brighton with his Foreign Secretary. He didn't explain she was his Latvian typist.

155

Enoch Powell telephoned his tailor in a state of anger and complained: 'Look, I ordered that new suit for my visit to the Palace when I dined with Her Majesty last night. And the zip got stuck. The brace buttons fell off and my trousers fell down and none of the pockets had any lining . . .' The tailor said: 'Oi, oi, I'm so sorry—I forgot my head cutter and three of my machinists are Jamaicans.'

156

Owing to the newspaper strike the other day my morning paper was only eight pages. It's ridiculous; have you ever seen the American papers? The *New York Herald Tribune* runs to 200 pages, is seven inches thick and weighs three and a quarter pounds. When the newsboy throws it in the doorway he doesn't shout 'Paper' he yells 'Timber!'

157

I must go now—I left something in the gas oven. My mother-in-law's head.

158

The Pope was lucky last week. He won first prize in the State Lottery. A honeymoon for two in Soho.

159

My uncle was stopped by the police while driving home last night. Before they gave him the breathaliser test they had to give him the kiss of life.

160

When the Privy Councillor visited 10 Downing Street yesterday to inspect the privy he was astonished to find a stack of Conservative leaflets there.

161

Oswald is convinced that Pan-American is someone who works in a U.S. hospital as an orderly.

162

They are having another economy drive in the National Health Service hospitals. Anyone with a temperature exceeding 108 has to be put in bed with a patient suffering from intense shock reactions, to save blankets.

163

A suspicious husband rushed home after a mysterious telephone tip informing him that his wife was having it off with Antonio. Eventually the searching spouse located his wife at the hairdressing salon being bobbed. The moral of this anecdote is: don't do anything to curl your wife's hair while she's trying to straighten herself out.

164
A pessimist is just an impatient optimist.

165
A Hollywood actor who is hopelessly in love with a desirable Hollywood actress can hardly wait for his turn to come round. Meanwhile the producer of an *avant-garde* one-man burlesque show on Sunset Strip found his Irish artiste drunk and unconscious up an alley, and he, too, is waiting for his turn to come round.

166
Sidney has always been generous to a fault. He buys expensive gifts for his nauseating wife.

167
A psychiatrist we avoid is one who told his patient Hank Foster that the beautiful belly-dancing showgirl he kept dreaming about was just a piece of mind.

168
The National Road Safety Association has issued a new booklet for motorists called 'How to Avoid Children'. A reviewer commented that the only merit the booklet possessed was the fact that it was cheaper than the Pill.

169
We live in stirring times. The well-known Texan sugar-daddy millionaire Hiram K. Sprunk II has just paid off attractive Rhoda Lushform with a lump sum. Evidently she wasn't his cup of tea.

170
Harold has a photographic mind. It's so dark and black in there you could develop a seven-reel movie.

171
A prisoner in court listened to the prosecutor's tirade and then pleaded ignorance. The judge asked the prisoner what he meant. Presumably he was even more ignorant.

172
For next term, the mature students of St. Phineas' College have to prepare a vacation piece on two Shakespearean classics—'The Rape of Lucrece', and 'Much Ado About Nothing'. Well, that takes care of that.

173
A home perm is when three adjoining couples on an estate practice wife swapping.

174

I'll say this for her—she was one of those girls who wasn't the least bit spoilt. I soon remedied that.

175

Punter: 'That horse looks very hot and tired. Did he win the last race?'
Jockey: 'Win it? He got this way walking to the starting gate.'

176

I'll never forget the day we got married. What a big wedding it was! The bride had more pages than a newspaper. And what a cake we had! Enormous. Everybody took a little piece home after the reception. My brother took two pieces home. One was a bridesmaid and the other had been a maid of honour. That was before my brother took her home.

177

I was watching TV last night and the worst wrestling match was going on that you ever saw . . . my girl won.

178

Then there's the comedian who goes to all the big variety shows at the leading theatres . . . just to hear what he's going to say the following week.

179

Psychiatrists are costing me a lot of money. Mine charges five guineas an hour. I was cracked when I started going to him—now I'm completely broke.

180

Uncle, to girl he hasn't seen for four years. 'Hullo Annie. Has your sweater shrunk or are you growing up?'

181

Advert: Post-war model wanted; must be good and fast. The advertiser got ten replies from blondes and six from redheads, but nobody offered him a car.

182

Advert: Wanted, furnished room for one lady with good south exposure.

183

I'm being trained by Micky Wood. He says he's building an idiot.

Great Musicians

184

What I'd really like to do is produce a great symphony or a cantata,

34

like Beethoven's Fifth. Beethoven's fifth was a girl—he'd always wanted another boy . . . My father was a composer. He was all for swing . . . That's how he ended up—swinging. They hanged him for murdering a piece of music. A little operetta. She was a telephone operetta. What a man my father was for the girls. He was always staring around to look at blondes. He developed a permanent twist in his neck and became the only professional musician to put the music-stand behind him when he played. He could play any instrument—picolo, clarinet, drums, French horn, bagpipes. He used to play the bagpipes by putting them on the ground and sitting down to them on a stool— that was because he started life as a dairy farmer. I can play any instrument, as well. I was once offered a job playing the organ at the BBC. You never saw such a big organ. It took me all my time to get it into my mouth, let alone play it. And as for the piano, I learned that when I was very young. My landlady had a boudoir grand. She often invited me up to her boudoir to play.

185
We have just learned that a well-known television interviewer left Heathrow last night en route to the North Pole. His assignment is to see if the chap who wrote 'I'm Sitting On Top Of The World' is still there.

186
Horace is eagerly awaiting Judgement Day. He's been appointed one of the referees for this year's Miss Universe Contest.

187
Literary Censorship: The deadly struggle between the Press and the Suppress.

188
We are advised that the interminably continuing story of Peyton Place will be suspended for two days on November 16th, while the maintenance men clear a flood of tears from the main street drains.

189
After a twenty-minute holiday to recuperate from the demanding pressures of Coronation Street, Ena Sharples and several others in the cast will be back on the screen tonight. The ravers return.

190
Pratulus, toastmaster to the Caesars, was probably the world's most overworked Roman orator. Whenever any Christians were being thrown to the lions, he had to do the after-dinner speech.

191
Advice to gimme-pig girls. If at first you don't succeed; cry, cry again.

Biological research problem. Does a square teenager attaining puberty develop cubic boobs.

193

Money is a very elevating commodity because a lot of jack can give you a lift.

194

Going to work yesterday on the Underground I was anxious to read the end of a report in the morning newspaper but it got off at Charing Cross.

195

Padded bras ? Bustboosters.

196

Adam and Eve instituted the first co-educational system.

197

Have you ever contemplated that the three traditional brass monkeys would be a complete flop at any contemporary cocktail party ?

198

The judge refused to convict the three coloured immigrants because he claimed that the prisoners were not as black as the prosecuting counsel painted them.

Horse Feathers
(extract from a novelette in a woman's journal)

199

She had pulled the wool over his eyes, and Benny looked pretty sheepish when he knitted his brows. He had always imagined that Irene couldn't say boo to a goose, but when he goosed her, she booed. But Benny didn't get down in the mouth: he simply ducked out and she didn't see him again for weeks. It dawned on her that he had cottoned on. Irene had done something wrong and Benny had found her out. In fact she was always doing wrong, and that's why she was always out. Miserably she sat at her bureau and wrote him a tearful note, using the sort of pen that writes under water; a weighted quill. In her tragic missive she openly confessed her promiscuous behaviour and its revealing repercussions. A shiver passed through her as she worked, so she pulled up the fur hem of her shortie-nightie to keep her neck warm. The secret was out. Slowly she took an envelope and licked it with the tip of her pink tongue. But the glue was too strong and now her lips are sealed.

200

If you build a better mouse-trap the world will beat a track to your door. If that fails, however, try clap-trap.

201

Circumstances alter cases. This means that if you are in comfortable circumstances you can afford a good lawyer to get you off.

202

The underprivileged countries will never get a fair deal as long as the big U.N. powers deal from the bottom of the pact.

203

The smartest prizefighter is the one who boxes on his knees to make sure he doesn't have so far to fall.

204

The son of the managing director doesn't need an extinguisher in his office because he's already fireproof.

205

You can tell what sort of a place we stayed at for our holidays last summer. A nuclear bomb fell on it and did £43 worth of damage.

206

We know a girl who is in very straitened circumstances; her figure is 34-34-34.

207

If you've ever wondered what a 'spoonerism' is, it's a schmalzy word you use on your girl friend when you're snogging.

208

Prevailing winds are what you experience when you have a fit of the burps.

209

Is it any wonder Irish gourmets are in a perpetual stew?

210

Adam and Eve were sitting in the garden wondering what to have for lunch when a servant came up and gave them an apple. Adam was annoyed by the interruption as he was busy leafing through a first edition.

211

Did you know that grouse and pigeons are game birds? Just for kicks they go around in braces.

212

They say that meteorological graphists are always hail and arty.

213

We've just been told where Solomon kept all those womenfolk of his . . .
It was in the Tower of Babel.

214

Geoffrey's mother-in-law always sleeps with her spectacles on because
she frequently has dreams about her son-in-law and likes to have a clear
view of his sufferings.

215

How to make a mountain out of a molehill. Take a small rumour and
keep adding dirt.

216

Florence has jilted her French count. While she admired his Gallic
artistry she couldn't tolerate his garlic taste.

217

His wife isn't at all athletic. Her only track record is for jumping to
wrong conclusions.

218

Husband, to wife getting dressed for the party: 'You look like an
unsolved jigsaw puzzle.'

219

At the wedding reception an envious rival toasted the showgirl who was
marrying a millionaire: 'Here's to Jackie, who worked attirelessly for
success and finally got a fat roll.'

220

'Do you know any political jokes ?'
    'Yes, several—Wilson, Heath, Brown, Foot . . .'

221

A health fad is someone who practises the daily dozen and the weekly
doesn't.

222

Said the husband to the wife as he started the car: 'Now if you see me
doing anything wrong, or feel in any way that my driving is causing you
apprehension or discomfort—just keep your big mouth shut!'

223

British Overseas Territories. Where necessity is often the mother of
intervention.

224

Pop statistics—a number of groups with a group of incomprehensive numbers.

225

Tommy wrote in his history notebook: Cleopatra was bitten to death by an aspirin.

226

Supermarket Sonic Boom: The cost of 50-pence worth of goods has now broken the pound barrier.

227

Georgina is not a girl to be easily conned but she was taken in by an unscrupulous girdle.

228

A shop steward who spent his savings on shares in his own firm now stands at the main gate whipping his mates to work.

229

Diplomat—someone who can successfully juggle three clangers, but plays safe by doing it on soft ground.

230

A lush is someone working his way from the bottoms up.

231

A friend asked Mrs. Cotter about the bottle of little pills on the table.
    'They're the tranquillizers for the twins.'
    'Oh! How many do they have to take?'
    'They're not for them—they're for me.'

232

His wife was sitting in front of the television set, tense and crying her eyes out, when Williams got home.
    'Good God!' he said, 'It's only the commercial for dandruff, woman!'

233

The male duck was building a very large nest near the foreshore. His wife said: 'Henry, we don't need such a big nest as this.' The duck said: 'Hush! It's not a nest. It's a hide, so we can watch that stupid ornithologist looking for us.'

234

She'd be going to church regularly if the vicar didn't keep staggering the date of the jumble sale.

235
Economic statistics show that wherever British finances look rosy it won't be long before we're in the red.

236
Economists are usually impoverished men. Rich men are too busy making money to find time to study it.

237
The pen is mightier than the sword, but no match for a waste-paper basket.

238
Education is something you start to acquire the moment you leave schooling behind.

239
If at first you don't succeed, try another bank.

240
Modern sales promotion has even invaded the barnyard. A hen who cackles is not merely advertising her own egg but also claiming that a duck egg is inferior because it's hard to quack.

241
He's such a confirmed egotist he even talks about himself behind your back.

242
Here's the latest in fire prevention methods. Give notice.

243
Alfred is going to the dogs, and the R.S.P.C.A. objects strongly.

244
The clothes she wears, such as transparent blouses, low-cut necklines and micro-skirts, are bought so that she can be seen in the best places.

245
At rehearsal the producer told the actress: 'We've seen everything else. Now—how about a display of emotion?'

246
A girl with circles under her eyes can usually blame the circles under her jumper.

247
A life of 'wine, women and song' will only leave you with gout, migraine and a sore throat.

248
The world is contracting due to supersonic jet aircraft, and our distant relations are getting too close.

249
Couched in those terms, an hour with a psychoanalyst costs five pounds.

250
The main advantage of free love is that it avoids an expensive divorce.

251
Few men get what they want but any wife will want what a husband gets.

252
What a man wants most out of marriage is to get out.

253
The doctor tells all his private patients not to eat too much. He thinks that, with the high cost of living, they might not be able to pay his account.

254
I know a Birmingham man who was unemployed for two years. So he bought a sun lamp and a turban and in three weeks he was working on the buses.

255
A word of warning to those intending to use the new civic baths . . . If you want to do the breast stroke, use your own breast.

256
She's had six children in eight years. Just because she can't tell margarine from butter.

257
Mr. and Mrs. Jones couldn't tell the difference between Vaseline and putty and all their windows fell out.

258
Now that capital punishment has been abandoned, the last of Britain's official hangmen has been pensioned off. So there goes the last of the big suspenders.

259
This morning my newspaper horoscope stated that I should be starting on a new cycle. Dead accurate it is—I'm having to sell my Rover and buy a bike.

260

I'll say this about her—nobody could ever fool my wife. She can't even be taken in by her girdle.

261

Every time I think I've got it in the bag, the bag breaks.

262

At a cosy little downtown underground restaurant last night me and the girl had two ducks. One to get through the entrance and another one to dodge the light-fitting. She ordered a cold salad and ended up with two lettuce leaves, a radish, a slice of cucumber and a tomato. I ordered something hot and they sent me the hat check girl.

263

I belong to the lunatic fringe. You know what a lunatic fringe is of course? It's when you have tassels on your toupee.

264

The latest road safety sign is a humdinger. It reads: 'Inward traffic keep left, outgoing traffic keep right, centre lane reserved for pile-ups'. You're all right on that road at night so long as you keep your gaze on the cats-eyes. I did that for twenty miles and discovered too late it was two tabbies making love on the tailboard of an articulated lorry. I finished up in a field on a new building site and me and the girl had to spend the night in the watchman's hut. He was a very good watchman —never took his eyes off us all night, except when my friend took off her shortie nightie; then his eyes left us: and rolled across the floor.

265

Not far from here they are establishing a new nudist camp. You can't miss it—the neon sign says: 'Nothing-To-Hyde Park'.

266

How to recognise a pair of Italian shoes. They pinch harder.

267

I play golf in the low seventies. As soon as it gets any cooler I quit.

268

On the summer cruise I took to the Med., all the lifeboats on board were strictly reserved for the 'Go-Now-Pay-Later' passengers.

269

My taxi driver charges a lot, but he doesn't mind if you spill cigar ash on his car carpets. He has a woman cleaner in three days a week.

270

Statistics indicate that half of all married couples are disillusioned and miserable. Mostly the husbands.

42

271

He's so wealthy, even when he sleepwalks he takes a cab.

272

A cop in New York last week uncovered a daring mischief. Her name was Marjorie.

273

A psychiatrist in London had such a busy practise that in the end he had to take patients a dozen at a time and lay them on double couches. Then he'd come back an hour later and find them all cured.

274

The weather was so bad, crossing the Channel, that the passengers were heaving more than the boat.

275

An artist doing comic press cartoons has just had a remarkable success with a new strip series. He got the idea watching his wife getting ready for bed.

276

My wife still has her own teeth. I know because I was with her when she collected them.

277

I surprised my wife last night with a new fur coat. She'd never seen me in one before.

278

The dentist said to the patient 'Do you want it out with gas ?' and the patient nodded, so the dentist got the blow lamp . . .

279

A new sports car on the market has no radiator—just a pedestrian perforator.

280

When she walked into the room, people turned, stared and held their breath. It makes you wonder how they can make perfume to sell at 4p a pint.

281

How lazy can you get ? My boss buys his chewing gum ready munched.

282

Moira has a tip-tilted bust. It points the way to the dump.

283

There she was, stripped to the waist, washing her smalls.

284

The question is *can* you have good clean fun in a communal bath?

285

She was wearing stretch tights that seemed to be suffering from fibre fatigue.

286

I don't think I shall give my girl anything for her birthday—she already has everything I need . . .

287

I can never travel on British Rail. They have first class and second class, but there's nowhere for me. I'm lower middle class.

288

Girls in tight jumpers and sweaters look very attractive, but take away their woolies and what have you got? Palmy days!

289

Look, this girl Agnes may not be a particularly good looking character but I could give you 39-24-36 reasons why I love her.

290

I've just joined a society that helps compulsive drinkers. They've made me Chairman of Alcoholics Unanimous.

291

I'm suffering from athlete's foot: my girl friend's brother is a four-minute miler, and yesterday he kicked hell out of me.

292

My girl's parents are in the fish and chip business. Every fortnight they take the fryer into the manufacturer's works to get the oil changed.

293

Giving up smoking is as easy as falling off a log. I haven't had a cigarette now for—let me see—six hours, eighteen minutes and thirty seconds.

294

A former beatnik repented and joined a monastery. It took the monks' barber a fortnight to give him a tonsure.

295

I went out with this girl named Eliza for a while. She was very fond of gin. In fact around Soho she was known as Breath-elizer.

296

I broke a big window in the bedroom the other day. Some girl threw a rocking-chair at me, and I ducked.

297

Saw a funny thing this morning—a well-built nun riding up the High Street on a small child's pedal cycle. Talk about vergin' on the ridiculous . . .

298

We were having dinner in one of those phoney restaurants where the lights are kept low to disguise the food. We sat there for an hour without being noticed and in the end my girl friend sent up a Very light.

299

A girl in the Salvation Army was presented with a navel honour last week. For fourteen years she had carried the large banner.

300

I know a poor chap who was so exhausted, his doctor gave him a large bottle of tonic but when he got it home he couldn't pull the cork out.

301

During an operation the short-sighted anaesthetist said to the surgeon: 'Should I give him a bit more air?' The surgeon said: 'I wouldn't— he's nearly on the ceiling already.'

302

I see the Prime Minister proposes to re-shuffle the cabinet, but there's still no chance of the public getting a fair deal.

303

A woman demonstrator was arrested last night. She was demonstrating for equal pay for strippers in a new Shakespeare production of 'As You Like It'.

304

A fisherman making himself a new net ended up with a net two miles wide and eight miles long. He'd forgotten how to cast off.

305

The old railway man gave his son some advice about women. 'Watch your points until you get a clear signal, then give it all the steam you've got and only stop by special request.'

306

It pays to advertise. My firm advertised for a night-watchman, and the same night they were robbed.

307

She certainly carries a torch for that bloke of hers . . . Every time it's foggy he makes her run in front of his car with a flashlight.

308
There's only one thing to say for the (Rolling Stones, Uglies, The Who, etc.) . . . They have some wonderful radio shows, but some lousy home perms.

309
She was so ugly that when she went to the doctor for a few days sick-leave he gave her an 'X' certificate.

310
My last girl friend was so ugly, when she walked into a room the mice used to jump on chairs.

311
She said she was saving herself for the right man, so I warned her that it's difficult to get rid of old stock when the new models come in.

312
Did you hear about the dumb bride who thought Wedding Rites absolved her from premarital wrongs.

313
I asked an eighty-year-old man if he and his wife kept up the battle of the sexes. 'No,' he said, 'we've decided it's a dead heat.'

314
My mate's wife complained to him about two birds perched on the garden fence. Mind you, I blame the birds. He told them to wait for him in the pub.

315
In a little village in Italy lived a monk who did the garden work for the Little Sisters of the Poor, and one day there was a terrible earthquake and he woke up next to a yawning abbess.

316
Then there's the sadistic school headmaster who planted his grounds with birch trees for posteriority.

317
The best cure for a nude exhibitionist is to send her home to get dressed and go to bed.

Notices of Note

318
'To Ethel and David Croopes, a fine son. Others please copy.'

46

'Lowest Prices for Local Fish. Our competitors can't get anywhere near them.'

'Girl wanted by wife of Naval Officer. Anyone with the right experience welcomed.'

'Owing to pressure of column space many births have had to be held over until next week.'

'Wanted adaptable cook capable cooking large county family.'

'Anyone wishing to go sick must make application at least three days before the Cup Final.'

'The Suggestion Box has been discontinued until the supervisor gets a larger one.'

'The population of Smidglehook has dropped by thirty per cent since Squire Hancock closed down the mill. In fact no children have been born in the village since his death.'

'New Grill Room now open adjoining bar. Continental meats a speciality. Come and see Mrs. Lennard calving.'

319
Two snooty women met for the first time since they had left Rodean. They talked about their families. 'My son Arthur,' said the Hon. Veronica Beancote, 'is now at Harrow. He's been there two years.'
The other one said: 'Mine's at the "Plough and Harrow" and if he isn't out of there by two o'clock we'll miss the first race.'

320
If you'd given as many people a piece of your mind as she has, you'd be stupid too.

321
She never bothered about local or national elections and she never voted because as far as she was concerned she never minded who got in.

322
Did you hear about the girl in Prague who was betrayed by a merchant banker, and had to have an abortion. It was just another cancelled Czech.

323
She played in the tournament at Windsor, then won the tournament at St. Andrews and finally the championship at Gleneagles. Within three months she had become the inter-course champion.

324

The professor was doing a demonstration for the class during his lecture on 'Sex and the Human Race'. Taking a deep breath he said: 'And now if you will go back to your seat, Miss Gregory, I'll get on to another subject.'

325

Did you hear about the cautious American? If his girl forgets to take the pill he takes a powder.

326

They were in action in the car on a secluded highway when the girl shouted 'Help! Help!' He said: 'Shut up, you don't need any help.' And she said: 'No, but you do'.

327

Never change your mind. It may be worse than the one you've got.

328

I've got a great aim in life. All I need now is some ammunition.

329

This girl, you see, practically threw herself at Sid. She meant to throw herself at Dave but she was drunk.

330

The solution to pollution is a social revolution.

331

The Londonderry Air would be a good tune but for the flying bullets.

332

I like flying. Yesterday for example, I had breakfast in London, lunch in Hong Kong, dinner in Tokyo, and luggage in Munich.

333

I'm going to sell my alarm clock. It scares the living daylights into me.

334

My new car runs on high-powered alcohol, and so does my Uncle Sam, who's known around town as The Sam Again.

335

One of the biggest financers in London was counting up his liquid assets the other day—two crates of brandy, four magnums of champagne and a cellar full of cooking sherry.

336

Uncle Harry has gone on the wagon . . . and taken a cocktail cabinet with him.

337
The man who denied paternity was merely practising his alibiology.

338
Mr. Notting always makes allowances for his family. He's paying two lots of alimony and three maintenance orders.

339
The size of the average young woman's ambition can be measured in cups.

340
The advantages of our sort of democracy is that you can say what you like—but there isn't much to like about our sort of democracy.

341
With graduates being disgorged from universities in ever increasing multitudes, it now takes an average of four years to get a degree and ten to get a job.

342
They say that a good story is always worth repeating, but it doesn't work for the husband who has three late nights out.

343
Popular glamour actress Paula Revere has just celebrated her sixth wedding anniversary. And six husbands are something to remember.

344
The human being is not as unique as anthropologists claim. Think how many hogs, pigs, cows, asses and bitches are included in the species.

345
American college. A place where they used to rub out the blackboard and where they now rub out the teachers.

346
I went to prison for something I didn't do. I didn't pay the fine.

347
A man visiting Japan made love to a lovely girl in the red light district. He had a thousand yen for her.

348
A girl who had four children and no husband insisted one day that their father should marry her—she got a sudden longing for a bit of iced wedding cake.

349
You know your stomach is in bad shape when bicarbonate gives you ulcers.

350
Then there's the grateful blind man who took his seeing-eye dog to a nudist colony.

351
There's a naval explorer whose passion is for tall scraggy women. He has a thing about sunken chests.

352
When they sent me a *Playboy* calendar, the envelope steamed itself open.

353
We know a man who has a racehorse worth fifty thousand pounds. He's the only horse in the world with a building society account.

354
There's a surgeon in London who is so positive he can save his patients' lives that he offers a money back guarantee.

355
Her father's a C.I.D. man: if she gets home after eleven he dusts her for fingerprints.

356
He was so drunk, the world went round him for eighty days.

357
A man went to the doctor complaining that he had an obsession and kept thinking he was a dog. The doctor must have thought so too, the way he took his temperature.

358
No wonder the contender won the championship—his opponent was the exact double of his mother-in-law.

359
I had a leading part in the show 'Hair'. I played Dan Druff.

360
A Russian went to the dentist for relief from toothache and when the dentist told him to open his mouth, he didn't know how to do it.

361
A motor mechanic visited a psychiatrist and the doctor told him to lie under the couch.

362
She wears deep-plunging necklines just to keep her boy friend on his toes.

363
The most efficient labour-saving device a woman can have is a padlock on her front door.

364
A Jewish gentleman and an Irish colleen had a very happy relationship, and some months later the girl gave birth to a Leprecohen.

365
I once started to import cheap cotton jeans for women from Hong Kong, but they tore so easily the bottom dropped out of the market.

366
I don't know what's the matter with Paula; ever since she started on the Pill she's been unbearable.

367
So that she won't be recognised at the Nudist Centre, Felicity uses a cunning disguise; she wears a black fig leaf.

368
There's only one word for those people who practice the rhythm method. Parents.

369
When he was in prison he had to be forcibly fed. Not because he was on a hunger strike but because the food was completely inedible.

370
My girl is very prim and proper. Last night I started to tell her a party joke, and in disgust she jumped out of bed.

371
All the famous men in Britain have their names inscribed in *Who's Who*, except in Birmingham and Brixton, where they are listed in *Who Dat?*

372
I've just got here, straight from a sickbed. My girl has a cold.

373
Chelsea is a wonderful part of London; one of the few affluent areas where a man can live like a queen . . .

374

We know a monk who always spills soup down his clothes when he eats. That's two dirty habits.

375

'Have you ever slept with a woman before?' she asked. 'Yes,' he said, 'and after.'

376

In utter frustration, after twenty minutes, she said 'You know, you'll never start a car with a flat battery'. So he said: 'It's not so much my battery as your flat headlamps'.

377

It was quite a while after they first met before Lord Camperton bought his girl friend a mink coat, and by that time she couldn't button it up.

378

Did you hear about the fat old maid? . . . she was trying to diet because she was dying to try it . . .

379

Yesterday I saw a Jewish person who hadn't been circumcised. Her name was Rita.

380

Did you hear about the rich and famous architect who had his house made on a hill? His wife divorced him.

381

And, contrary to popular opinion, it was not the apple on the tree that caused all the trouble; it was the green pair on the grass.

382

Poor Tina . . . when she had her baby, gosh how she cried and screamed and struggled and fought and bit . . . and that was only when she was conceiving.

383

It was one of those free-and-easy all-night parties. The most popular dance was called the Pony Trek—three times round the floor, and outside for your oats.

384

A furniture test to discover whether a woman is scared stiff or just frustrated. Let a mouse loose in the bedroom. If she jumps on a chair she's terrified; if she jumps on the bed, she's frustrated.

Miss Dumbelle's Interpretations of Familiar People and Things . . .

385 *SHOTGUN WEDDING:* A matter of wife or death.

386 *FREEMASON:* Someone who builds you a stone wall free of charge.

387 *CANARY:* A young bird born to succeed.

388 *ALCOHOLIC:* Someone like a piano; if he's not upright he's grand.

389 *PHILISTINE:* Someone who prefers to have the flower show covered on radio.

390 *FATHER TIME:* Someone who is a great healer but no beauty specialist.

391 *CHART TOPPER:* A vocalist with a very rich voice.

392 *AMATEUR CHURCH ORGANIST:* Someone who frequently forgets to let his right hand know what the left is doing.

393 *BARREL ORGANIST:* Someone who only plays music by Handle.

394 *RED BERET:* Someone whose memoirs provide a down to earth story.

395 *AGITATOR:* Someone whose vocation is provocation.

396 *CROQUETTE:* A teeny weeny dinner service.

397 *PIÈCE DE RESISTANCE:* A restaurant steak.

398 *MARRIAGE:* The condition that makes the world go ruined.

399 *ADAM:* Someone who prayed to the Lord to make him a woman.

400 *SECRET WEDDING:* A union in which both parties keep mum about their past.

401 *PUNCH DRUNK:*   A gatecrasher going too oft to the party bowl.

402 *TOUPEE:*   Bareskin headgear.

403
Any girl who doesn't take the Pill is practicing licence without medicine.

404
An indignant husband confronted his wife when he got home from the local pub. 'Evadne, what was the big idea of letting George Parker know that you have a 49½ bust?' She said: 'I'm sorry, Jack, but *I* didn't *tell* him. It just slipped out'.

405
I don't know whether I'm being unjustly suspicious, but me and my wife have just moved down to Bournemouth from Edinburgh, and we still have the same milkman.

406
I took my wife to a fancy dress ball last week. I went as an old flower girl. She went as an old flour bag.

407
At the weekend we went to that new cosmopolitan restaurant in West Street. We had a mixture of international dishes—from China, Italy, Israel, Malawi . . . The Malawi dish was Yam and eggs . . . And have you ever tried eating boiled-beef-and-spaghetti with chopsticks? My wife finished up with tomato ketchup down her skirt, birds-nest soup over her dumplings and two French fries up her nose.

408
You can lead a horse to water, but Dean Martin always had an armed escort.

409
My wife bought me a new necktie for Christmas and it was so horrible I've had to grow a beard.

410
She's not like a female woman at all—more like Boris Karloff in drag.

411
She's so intelligent. Yesterday she went to the butcher and asked him for half a dozen lean Karati chops. And the butcher spent half an hour in the deep-freeze cabinet *looking* for some.

412
Last week the Government brought out a devastating new White Paper, running to 560 pages, all concerning 'The Permissive Society in Britain in the Seventies'. Within an hour of publication MGM had bought the screen rights and cast Liz Taylor, Raquel Welch, Diana Dors and Vanessa Redgrave as four nude Cabinet Ministers.

413
I once sent away to a bodybuilding company for some chest developers and it took me six months to develop my chest from 32 to 34. On the other hand my wife sent away to Kaysers for some chest developers and did the same trick in two minutes.

414
Faith is what we all need. Faith like my father-in-law's got. Bald as a coot he went into a chemist's shop and bought a bottle of hair restorer and some scissors. He doesn't like hair in his eyes.

415
My wife made some rock cakes for tea. To avoid wasting them I spent all Sunday in the garden building a rockery.

416
She's always looking for bargains so when she saw a food mixer advertised at 50p she sent for it. She got a swizzle stick.

417
She had a long run in her stockings yesterday. Some sex maniac chased her through the woods.

418
The Prime Minister's last visit overseas was to the President of France. At the airport when he landed, the Police, Navy and French Army gave him a twenty-one gun salute. Everyone missed.

419
The Labour Government built nearly as many houses during their term of office as Winston Churchill built in his youth as a bricklayer.

420
Fred tried hard last week, but he could not get through the iron curtain . . . not Russia—his girl friend's house—she'd built a wrought-iron fence.

421
Scientists tell us that the air is so full of filth, we shall all die early. And it's not just the radio and television either—some newspapers are as bad.

422

Advertising experts insist that most advertisements on TV for chocolate bars use them as phallic symbols. This is a case for the Race Relations Board.

423

I went to visit my psychiatrist as usual yesterday, but it was different. He said to me: 'Good morning. Lie on the floor, will you . . . My receptionist and I are using the couch.'

424

A farmer's labourer in Norfolk has just invented a new process. He crosses Rhode Island Reds with buck rabbits and gets instant poached eggs.

425

She wore some lovely perfume. You know what perfume is? It's a smell that fights back.

426

The manager of the new club is so mean—anything to save a penny. He's got two strippers doing the cabaret—tassel dancers. But he's moved the tassels and replaced them with cocktail-shakers, so that he can sack one of the barmen.

427

She sprays toilet water behind her ears: I don't know what she'll do when she's had the cistern fixed.

428

My wife has a memory like an elephant. And why not—she's got a shape that goes with it.

429

She wears black-topped stockings in memory of all her male friends who have gone aloft.

430

Do you realise that all the arguments about a population explosion are completely false. Take Brighton for instance. The population has not changed over the past ten years. That's because every time a baby is born there, a man leaves town.

431

Polyester padding—the answer to a maiden's pair.

432

Her husband is reading a whodunit. It's his wife's diary.

433
I suppose you've heard that Ariel and Radiant have biological action?
But then again—who *hasn't*?

434
You all know what happened to the enemies of Israel in the Bible? The
modern Egyptians are luckier. When a patrol of Egyptian commandoes
attacked an Israeli-held town in Sinai, the Israelis only cut off their
retreat.

The British Working Man

435
He makes his living on Social Security. He draws unemployment pay,
sick benefits, supplementary Social Security to pay the rent; gets
credit for his health stamp card and is supplied with free dinners
through the meals-on-wheels service. A woman from the WRVS calls
daily to make his bed and do the charring, and every Friday he gets a
hamper from the Red Cross, and argues with them because they won't
give him Green Shield stamps with it. A Voluntary Hospital Service
car picks him up every Thursday and takes him to the Family Planning
Department of the local hospital where he gets his free pills. The
Housing Department provided him with a larger council house because
he needs an extra bedroom for the au pair girl, supplied by the International Red Cross Overseas Voluntary Youth Service, and they also
subsidise his TV payments and fitted him with a new aerial. He gets
all his reading matter from the free library, and drops by there each
afternoon to catch up on the daily papers. He gets a free three-week
holiday each year through the auspices of the Cold Research Centre.
And he spends his spare time writing letters to *The Times* complaining
about the government, demanding that the retirement age should be
lowered to 35. For this he uses a post office pen.

436
Evelyn has made her husband an equal partner in matrimony. He's the
doormat and she handles all the money.

437
Psychiatrists say that women should show more imagination. He's
forgotten what women look like these days because what they show
leaves very little to the imagination.

438
An inmate of one of the better-known asylums in Germany has just
received an accolade. Orange flavour, with ice. He got it for writing a
new signature tune for the institution, which will be featured on Israeli
television. The title? 'Gott Rest You, Jerry Mentalmen'.

439

Look here; when opportunity knocks can the neighbours be far behind?

440

Millions of people in this intemperately-climated country talk about the weather, but nobody does anything about it. Except Oswald. When it snows he stays in bed and reads a pornographic novel.

441

Hilary is the worst driver on the links. She hits nothing. But wait until she gets behind a steering wheel.

442

You can tell what a hustler he is; he even puts his wife's living bra on his income tax form, as a dependant.

443

Ludo. The money you put into the slot at your convenience.

444

If you want to join the Guards do it at the start of the week. You are bound to be a little short by Thursday.

445

And fellows, if you want to join the Wrens, you'll have to climb over a fairly high wall—their quarters are in a converted penitentiary.

446

Pedestrians, if you are feeling low and run down, remember that life is what you make it. Assuming you can make it.

447

Report in a local newspaper: Johnny Hippleburke, a student at St. Solomon's College, was reprimanded by his headmaster for sleeping in school. Coincidentally so was the French teacher, Miss Yvonne Vermir.

448

Simone, the stork, who has been laying a lot of scrambled eggs lately has been told by the curator to kneel down before delivery. Simone replied that saying her prayers wouldn't help.

449

Book review: The author of this lengthy dissertation displays a remarkably keen sense of vivid imagery. If he imagines that people will read his rubbish.

450

A British brain-teaser: If you buy a pair of knickers labelled 'Empire Made', were they made in Rome in A.D. 387?

451
With the Church considering revoking the celibacy code, some snags seem to suggest themselves. For instance, when one priest has to go for confession to another, will it be more of a man-to-man talk?

452
The sewage pouring out into the sea from coastal towns is visible proof that we live in an effluent society. In some resorts, nothing clears the beaches faster than a gentle sea-breeze. Every day the Irish bogs get closer and soon most of the Cross-Bog Steamers will be wedged solid in the channel.

453
Ladies: Would you like to make yourself a new maxi dress? It's so simple. Just climb into a sugar sack, and kick the bottom out. To shape it up, just tie a nylon cord around your waist and stick your bottom out.

454
Divorce is much easier under the new legislation; which is wonderful for couples who can't stomach each other any more.

455
Memorandum: Nature will never take its course if she hasn't got that sort of a nature.

456
He didn't have much fun as an infant in infancy but he's making up for it as an adult in adultery.

457
The boss said to him: 'We've never had a man of your calibre in this firm—so you're fired'.

458
She used to work at the local mattress factory but they sacked her for lying down on the job.

459
She told me she was starving and I said I never made love on an empty stomach.

460
My wife went out and bought a topless mini-dress. We *used* to call them belts.

461
You know what sex drive is, don't you? It's the journey from your place to *hers*.

59

462

Trying to win the pools is as frustrating as trying to find a transvestite in a nudist camp.

463

There she was at the launderette, washing out her smalls in an egg cup.

464

The best film anyone could see on a TV set today is a film of dust.

465

I'll never forget the time I appeared at a Royal Command performance. Prince Philip told me to belt up.

466

I went to a tea party given by Madeline Smith, with four other guys. We sat down and she said: 'Who's going to pour?' and I said: 'All of us; but let's get tea over first'.

467

When I parked my Rolls Royce outside the club some cheeky kid came up and said: 'I wish my Dad could afford a car like that!' and I said: 'So do I!'

468

My wife was slicing the bread for breakfast when she cut her finger. I went over, took her in my arms and cried like a baby. That's one way to get salt in a wound.

469

Jack goes to the club wearing a very loud tie and a muffler.

470

Last night in Salford a burglar's house was broken into and he was attacked by an old maid.

471

Have you ever met a sporty blonde who had two challenge cups?

472

We hear that Lady Maltravesty is expecting a baby following a course of heir-conditioning by his Lordship.

473

In Toronto, a pretty English girl visitor complained to the authorities after an incident involving a mounted policeman.

474

Whenever there's a collection for charity, Jock is the first to put his hands in his pockets.

475
Yesterday a mail plane passed over our house followed by a pigeon carrying the P.S.

476
Our au pair girl didn't come down to breakfast yesterday because she was under par.

477
When I boarded the crowded tube train yesterday I thought British Rail had decided to brighten up the carriages by fitting them with thick-pile carpets, but then I realised we were all standing on two girls in fur coats.

478
People say London gets smoggy, but it's even worse abroad. In Los Angeles there are thousands of teenagers who haven't yet seen their parents.

479
When my mother-in-law was ill in bed I wouldn't let my wife feed her on calve's feet jelly—it was too much like cannibalism.

480
The hotel was very full but after bribing the manager he fixed me up on the seventh floor . . . a rug on the landing.

481
She said as she died that if her husband was unfaithful to her memory she would turn in her grave. Up there she is affectionately known as Revolving Dora.

482
I must surely have the smartest lawyer in the country: last week I was booked for parking near a zebra crossing, and he got me off with fifteen years in the Scrubs.

483
Stella has a great idea to avoid being searched by Customs as she flits around the world. She has a frontal-nudity passport photograph.

484
The ticket collector at Basilworth is in hospital with a pair of fractured wrists. Some joker came through his gate and handed him a London 'phone directory instead of a ticket.

485
You never have to pick out the best people nowadays. They usually volunteer.

486

He's such an expert on women he often has to take a day off.

487

I read somewhere that the lobster frequently has a crab for his mate. George must be another lobster.

488

Mrs. Proctor told her teenage daughter that she would never of thought of doing some of the terrible things that girls do nowadays. And she regretted it.

489

When little Charlie was frightened by a bang, he hid behind his mother's skirt. Standing on a bar stool.

490

When that newsworthy teenager Violette Spriggette pleads to stay out until midnight it becomes a matter of mind over mater.

491

Always be suspicious when your boss pats you on the back in a manner reminiscent of swatting a mosquito.

492

Sylvia models swimsuits but nobody considers that she is entirely wrapped up in her work.

493

Playing the field is like taking pickled onions from a fresh jar. Once you've got over the first one, the rest come easy.

494

A woodworm we know is always going on picnics. He loves eating out of doors.

495

Horace always treats casual visitors as he would his own family. That's why they usually make excuses to leave early.

496

Maria will never lend you any money but she's always good for a touch.

497

We know a chap who is paying his wife £50 a week maintenance money . . . for her doctor, plastic surgeon, chiropodist, alienist, electrolysist, health store, chemist, hairdresser, beauty parlour, masseur, sauna baths, the vet . . . And she's still a wreck.

498

Nature study query. How many swallows make an alko?

499

It matters very little that your face is not your fortune. Just ensure that it's not your misfortune.

500

A bird in the hand is not quite as good as a bird in two hands.

501

Moira is a very very shy woman. She blushes when she tells you she's 28—because that's 12 years shy.

502

Young modern vocalists of the folk genre don't sing the old songs any more. The comparisons would be malodious.

503

Most young couples don't get married quickly these days because they're still waiting for a divorce to come through.

504

An unemployed trades union official sued a football club because he was injured when watching one of their matches. Apparently he fell off the clock tower.

505

Man has now been proved to be a worm. He wriggles along in life until some chick grabs him, and he ends up on the hook.

506

Oswald's mother-in-law went much too far yesterday. To the Himalayas, thank God.

507

There was a new play on television last night that had a very happy ending for a change. Half way through, the tube imploded.

508

The vicar organising the ceremony said: 'Who giveth this woman away?' so the bridegroom turned quickly, stared at the rows of young men in the front pews and snapped: 'He ain't talking to you lot'.

509

Scientists inform us that anthropoid apes were completely incapable of making musical sounds. He was not, of course, referring to contemporary soul singers.

Then there's the couple who live in Mean Street—they were too stingy to buy an alarm clock so they had a baby.

Making Ends Meet

511
The cost of living is so high that the next step is for the Government to collect everyone's wages, and give them a voucher each week for a bottle of water and a bread roll . . . I'm not so worried as some people because I've got my money safely tied up—in an old sock . . . I wouldn't be in this financial mess if it wasn't for my dependants—a wife, fourteen children and twenty-six Civil Servants . . . I'm having all my new suits made without cash pockets because there's no point . . . When I say all my suits, I really mean my working suit and my Sunday best—I get the money to pay for the instalments on the everyday suit by pawning the Sunday best from Monday to Saturday—I haven't yet worked out a system for paying for the Sunday suit—but every Sunday I sit in church and pray for my tailor . . . while he sits in church and prays for the man who sold him the cloth that he hasn't paid for . . . I wonder who prays for the sheep ? They haven't been paid for the wool.

512
She was always wary of visiting her boy friend, a writer, when he was in a working mood. Because he always prosed in the nude.

513
Then there's the international golf champ who had a wild night out the day before his wedding because he wanted to try a few practice puts.

514
There was a time when she would have given him the shirt off her back, but it's all off now.

Dining Out

515
We went to a very ritzy restaurant, so exclusive that before you can get in you have to open the door. They have an 18p cover charge to keep out the riff-raff. I told the waiter I was hungry enough to eat a horse and he said I'd come to the right place . . . Even the gravy was tough— it bent my fork . . . I started off with a double Scotch—that's an ordinary Scotch that makes you see double. My girl said she couldn't dance, so she stood on the edge of the floor and clapped me as I danced by myself. The prices for dinner were graded. For 120p there was à la carte, and for 125p you got the horse thrown in. A guy next to me was dancing with tears in his eyes. His girl was sucking an onion. I asked

my girl to marry me and she said I'd have to ask her father first. When
we got home I asked her father, but he didn't want to marry me either.

516
We met a world traveller who will never forget the last leg of his intrepid
trip. It belonged to a redhead named Shirley.

517
Joey had a pet hog whom he called Porkus, because it spoke pig-Latin.

518
The nurses call the incubator in the premature baby intensive care unit
'the womb with a view'.

Holy Deadlock

519
The joke about Beryl is that she weighs fourteen stone and yet when
she got engaged she started a *little* bottom drawer. People were always
asking her to get married; especially her mother and father and her
younger sister . . . Nobody would have her; in fact it took her parents
all their time . . . Beryl and Tom courted under ideal conditions: the
moon was out, the stars were out, her mother and father were out . . .
and so were her teeth . . . Her vital statistics are 38-32-43 . . . and that's
only her face . . . They say that Tom was hugging and holding her tight
one night for three hours before he realised he'd only got hold of her
arm . . . They want to go to Paris for the honeymoon because Tom's
seen pictures of the Folies Bergère and now he wants to see it in the
flesh . . . They've broken off their engagement several times but Tom's
always had to make it up because he can't get the engagement ring off
her finger . . . Beryl's mother is looking forward to the wedding—it's
a long time since she had a good cry . . . Tom's friends are looking
forward to it too—it's a long time since they had a good laugh . . .
Maybe he loves her because he's a butcher and spends so much of his
time around cattle . . . The first time Beryl took Tom home, her father
was so pleased he told Tom to feel like one of the family and treat the
house as if it were his own . . . so Tom sold it . . . With the money he
bought a crate of whisky and went wild with a pack of loose women.
The rest he just frittered away . . . After that he promised he'd never
look at another woman, and he had the bulb taken out of the roof light
in his car.

520
There's a story going round Chelsea that one of the inhabitants has
just decorated his bathroom and installed His and His towels.

521
A synonym is a word which you use when you don't know how to spell
the other one.

522
Marriage—a very expensive method of gaining a woman for nothing.

523
Then there's the girl who said 'I do', and some months later had to get married.

524
We know a man in Mansfield who took a mistress just to break the monogomy of life.

525
A bull-dozer is someone who keeps falling asleep during a political talk.

526
My girl said she was throwing me over for her new boy friend who was a doctor. She raved about him. I said: 'What's this character got that no other doctor has?' And she said: 'Warm hands'. In view of her infatuation I thought I'd go and consult him myself. He had a reputation for leaving no gallstone unturned, and it's said that he once took out a Royal appendix—to dinner. Mind you, he had worked nights to help pay his way through school—the local poker school. He had so little money that when he first started his stethoscope was on a party line.

527
The modern brassiere was invented in 1789. It was the answer to a maiden's pair. Men were quick to see that this new garment had its good points. It saved an area of inflation from spreading. Worn in conjunction with plunging gowns, the brassiere gave the impression of two bald-headed men peering over a net curtain. Small-busted women were still dissatisfied and demanded something more outstanding for their figures. So 'falsie' pads were added to the original garment. Stuffed with cotton wool not only do they make figures better but in cases of emergency can be used for swabbing major injuries. So, girls, why not take your husband with you when you go to the next bra sale at your local store, and let him have a look around?

528
She insisted that she couldn't take money from a perfect stranger which only proves that he was far from perfect.

Miss Dumbelle Thinks That . . .

529 Caged birds are four topless showgirls trapped in a lift.

530 Political asylum is the House of Lords.

531 A lightning conductor is a speedy Pakistani bus-ticket dispenser.

532 Above par is anyone else working for the firm.

533 Population explosion is heir pollution.

534 A free agent is an escaped spy.

535 Piles of work are what the standing committee does.

536 An antiseptic is someone who genuinely believes.

537 Bully Beef is when you ill-treat a steer.

538 Party politics is just block bluster.

539 Bridle rein is a wedding day shower.

540 A cabaret club is a weapon used to discourage rotten entertainers.

541 Gear lever is a nudist getting ready.

542 Fly specks are aeronautical goggles.

543 A baby doctor is a three-year-old neurosurgeon.

544 An *affaire de cœur* is a dirty dog.

545 Allegro means a line of chorus girls.

546 Windblown means flatulent.

547 A hand laundry is a wash-basin.

548 Copper plate is the licence number on a police car.

549 Deisel fitter is a coloured salesman in an underwear store.

550 A booby trap is the snapper on a bra.

551 A junk shop is when someone grasses on an addict.

552 A theatre angel is a prudish actress.

553 Wild honey is a blonde raver.

554
When they first got married they used to have a quickie before dinner.
Well, they still do—he has a Scotch and she has a small gin.

67

555

Sadie is not only a tough woman, she's also a champion. She can whip any man in the house.

556

This space is leased by the Mutual Assurance & Accident Corporation to advertise their remarkable new accident policy. Only last week one of our clients met with an accident that broke his neck and fractured his pelvis . . . immediately he received £2,000 under his Mutual Assurance policy. Just think—next week it might be YOUR lucky turn . . .

557

A bachelor is a cheap chiseller who is cheating some good woman out of her maintenance payments.

558

We know a financier who had a spot of trouble with two negotiable blondes.

559

A miracle happened in the sheik's harem in Dour-en-Slyme the other week. The sheik had to fire a unique eunuch.

560

A wolf is a fellow who treats all women as sequels.

561

There's a lot of talk in town about Andrea and Phyllis who have been bosom friends for years.

562

Have you noticed how often a divorce can give two people a splitting headache?

563

Showgirl—a dancer who brings home the bacon a strip at a time, from a theatre where the belles peel.

564

Bitch. An underdog.

565

A hot sandy beach is a place where the peeling is mutual.

566

'Is it true,' a visitor from Britain asked a French gendarme, 'that the men in your *Sûreté* office have the slogan *cherchez la femme*?' 'But of course,' replied the gendarme, 'But only on their own time.'

Outdoor Sports and Other Minor Injuries

567
The other day I went fox hunting for the first time: thrills galore: over hill and dale, across swamp and ditch; between the trees and over the gateposts. It was such fun, next time I'm going to take a horse with me . . . I've given up backing horses, and three bookmakers have threatened to sue me for maintenance . . . I once backed a horse in Africa that won by a short head . . . it turned out to be a giraffe . . .

One horse at the races last week was such a cert I put everything I had on his nose . . . and it rolled off . . . But the next race was better. I backed Fancy Free, a ten-year-old filly. It used three legs to run with and the other one to trip up the rest of the field . . .

In the 4-45 I backed a cab-horse because my tipster said he'd walk it . . . Trouble was the other horses ran. I can always find my way back to the Tote—they keep a light burning for me in the window.

One day I went out fishing . . . There's nothing to it. I put a worm on my hook and threw it into the water . . . I tugged and tugged and struggled as the line was wrenched in my hands; yessir, that worm certainly put up a fight . . . Then a chap came along and told me that fishing was banned. I didn't argue with him. I could have licked him with one hand tied—but he wouldn't let me tie his hand . . . I decided to take up shooting.

I took a 12-bore rifle and thirty rounds with me. Thirty rounds of toast come in useful when you get hungry. But I didn't shoot anything except one mad dog. And he wasn't mad until I shot him.

Television Lines

568
They call it a TV medium because so little of the programmes are rare or well done.

569
Television is doing great things for education. Every time my wife switches it on I go into another room and read a book.

570
A large family of immigrant Pygmies who rented a colour television set complained to their landlord that there was no bathroom.

571
I sometimes wish that there was something on TV between the test card and the little white spot at closedown.

572
We used to deport old lags to Australia; now it's old TV movies.

573
One old Western movie re-run was so old that Tom Mix was riding a dinosaur and Maureen O'Sullivan swung to and fro from a cactus tree.

574
The best show of the decade was a play called 'Cathode Go Home'.

575
There are so many Miss World contests and other beauty competition programmes that television sets are being called boobie tubes.

576
A chap in Fulham spent over £300 on a colour TV set and all he can get is 'The Black and White Minstrel Show'.

577
The big problem with colour television is for the commercials. When they show adverts for washing powders, the whites come out yellow and the other colours run.

578
A television set is just an electronic window-box.

579
They call TV favourites 'stars' because they come out at night and fortell the past.

Portrait of a Late Lothario

580
A dirty old man is one whom the years are outstripping, and who would rather be out doing a little stripping himself.

581
He's a kindly sort of chap. When he stays at an hotel he insists on helping the chambermaid to make his bed, or gets the hall porter to help him make the maid.

582
He waits outside stage doors for the chorus girls, and puts on his very charming paternal manner. Asks one of them if he can be her father while she's working in town . . . For all he knows he probably is.

583
He says that he's very rich and he can show her a good time. When midnight comes around he says that's as good a time as any.

584
He asks her to call him her Sugar Daddy because she stirs him, and every time he makes advances to her he gets a lump in his throat from old memories.

585
He asks her how she'd like to travel with him in foreign parts, and a few hours later books a room in some Italian hotel in Soho.

586
He takes her to see an *avant-garde* production and sits there looking at the showgirls; picturing how they might look with clothes on.

587
He asks her how she would like something warm next to her skin, and she has visions of a very lush mink coat. But that's not what she gets.

588
He's young in heart and likes every night to be Christmas, with stockings hanging over the foot of his bed.

589
He's never stumped for inspiration: if a girl seems a little aloof, he mixes her a gin and anti-freeze.

590
He tells his girls that although he's old enough to be their father, he feels like a youngster.

591
If a girl tells him she's in financial trouble because she spent more than she could afford on this new evening gown, he offers to help her out.

_____

592
He shaves twice a day. Says he's got a five o'clock shadow. That means that when he goes out at five o'clock, his wife shadows him.

593
It was a very high class hotel with a very considerate staff. At dinner the head waiter said as he served me: 'Watch the soup, cock—it burned my thumb.'

594
I guess I speak French like a native. In Paris last week I asked the way to an hotel and got directed to a thatched kraal.

71

595
My wife and I have a perfect understanding. She told me yesterday that she wouldn't be home as she was spending the night with a girl friend. I knew she wasn't, so *I* did.

596
Sometimes the political situation was so complicated that Edward Heath never knew which course to take. So he just headed S.S.E. and hoped to make land by nightfall.

597
Two Moslem gentlemen in Birmingham decided to do a bit of wife swapping—and it was like the rush hour at Central Station.

598
The plate was coming along the row of pews in church and was passed to my dentist, Gerald Fishbeizer, who swiftly relined it.

599
Deborah has a very restless figure: it keeps going in and out.

600
Of course George knows there's a population explosion. Who do you think lit the fuse?

601
The best things in life are three: a drink before and a cigarette after.

602
Sheik Abdul the Dimmed used to ride into the village and pick up any good-looking girl who happened to be hanging around. Then someone gave him a gramophone for a present, and the sheik hasn't been in the village since. Seems he broke his pick-up arm.

603
There was once a sheik who loved animals. He bought second-hand garments from Lollobrigida to keep his dromedary warm in cold weather . . . Now he's got a camel with the warmest humps in Araby.

604
It's a nuisance, that old custom in the desert of girls having to wear a veil. One sheik carried off a woman to his tent, and when he had her in his power he dragged away the veil, and still couldn't see her face because of her beard.

The Dolly Scene

605 I bought my girl a piece of lingerie for her birthday . . . and that was her first slip.

606 She went into the store to buy a new bra and the saleslady said: 'What bust?' She said: 'Nothing—the old one just wore out'.

607
She's just got a new job with a bookmaker . . . modelling betting slips.

608
All modern fabrics are synthetic . . . nylon, terylene, orlon, acrilan. All of them made by man . . . And so are the women who wear them.

609
Her new lingerie set was made from parachute silk. At bedtime she just stands by the bed, counts three, and bales in.

610
She dresses down-to-the-see-this in slips. He's what you may call a strap-hanger . . . but he prefers shoulder straps.

611
The other day while opening a Lingerie Store in Oxford Street, my girl fainted. Ambulance men carried her out into the street, two abreast.

612
She's a pin-up girl. Everything she wears is so outsize she has to pin it up.

613
She's flat chested. Keeps taking her chest into different flats.

614
For her seaside holiday she packed all her bitch-wear.

615
I had a job as a vanman for a cleaning firm. Spent all day going around picking up women's dresses.

616
She shed tears for a fur coat . . . but she had to shed more than tears before she got one.

617
She had lots and lots of glamour, then one day she washed her sweater and it stretched.

618
She went upstairs to throw on a dress . . . and practically missed.

619
She went into the maternity department and the salesgirl said: 'Excuse me Madam, your slip is showing'.

620

She was wearing a dark brown slip with a white lace collar. She looked just like a small beer with legs.

621

She's an Olympic champion. Expert at the hop, strip and jump.

622

I only ate the rubbery steak at lunch to avoid having rissoles for supper.

623

He's an aerial photographer. Spends all day taking pictures of radio and television aerials.

624

Taking pictures with an underwater camera he once got a mermaid down on the sea-bed.

625

He's a chap who's always worked hard and finally come out on top . . . He's gone bald as a coot.

626

He took her home, they sat on the couch, and he leaned across and started to mix some drinks on the small table. She whispered: 'I'm drunk already, don't pour me too much'.

627

Goldbar's Pink Cold Cream is greasier, messier, smoother. If you use it all over don't forget to nail your panties on.

628

Commercial TV—that's the infallible way to sell stuff that nobody wants to people who can't afford to buy it . . . My wife was so eager to run down to the local store to lay in a stock of a new detergent that she forgot she was still wearing her pyjamas . . . Ever since then she's been saving the coupons from cigarettes and buying furniture for our bedroom with them—for 10,000 coupons you get a wardrobe, and so on. . . . We have a lovely bedroom now, but we can't use the lounge—it's so full of cigarettes.

629

She uses Helena Rubenstein lipstick, Goya vanishing cream, Elizabeth Arden rouge and Patti Page mascara. You should just see her—she looks like Max Factor.

630

She was so hungry, he ordered her a martini with eighty-four olives.

631
Russian lecturing on Marxism: 'If I have two cars, I give one of them away—this is the principle of Marxism, of Leninism, of Communism. If I have two bicycles, I give one of them away, if I have two dogs, I give one of them away, if I have two blonde girl friends . . . anyone want another dachshund?'

632
Brand X toothpaste will give you teeth like pearls . . . and Pearl's teeth come back from the dental mechanic tomorrow.

633
I used to have a job dusting old men out of the girls' dressing room at the Hippodrome.

634
They used to think I was a heavy drinker because I could down eighteen double whiskies in one evening. You should see my old man—he spills more than that down his dickey. One night we went out and painted the town red. The next night we gave it a second coat.

635
She worked for one fashion photographer who was so shy he used to take pictures of her in the nude and paint in the undergarments afterwards.

636
She may have had flat feet, but she made up for it above the waist.

637
The new Hollywood horror flick was so terrible that Alfred Hitchcock fainted in the Odeon.

638
I gave up regular work because I was in a dilemma. The place where I worked was a madhouse. If I arrived too early, the boss made me pay rent for the waiting time, and if I got there too damn late he fined me.

639
I spend all night playing stud poker . . . with four horses from the National stud.

640
Out in South America last year I mixed with a really tough bunch of miners. When we went to the barber he didn't use an old-fashioned electric razor. He used a blowlamp.

641
Ten years ago I had an uncle who was arrested in Texas for rustling. They gave him a suspended sentence. The lynch mob hung him.

642

My psychiatrist has two couches. I lie on one having my mind investigated while he lies on the other and has a Swedish au pair girl massage him.

643

It costs me more to park my car at meters than it does to run it.

644

I must cut down my smoking. It's such a habit I'm never without a cigarette in my mouth. This morning I lathered the end of a filter-tipped and shaved it off.

645

The stork has been to Horace's house again. Well, the stork brought the baby, but it all started originally with a lark.

646

Britain Today . . . What kind of a democratic country are we living in, folks? I'll tell you. Britain is a nation of shopkeepers, shoplifters and shop stewards.

647

There's an aunt of mine in Canada who has given birth to seventeen children. I tell you, the woman is stork raving mad!

648

Me and the wife have opened a new joint account at the bank. Yesterday she raced me down there and beat me to the draw.

649

Saw an odd sight when I was in Algiers last summer. Went into a queer Arabian night-club and saw people dancing sheik to sheik.

650

My brother's an idiot. He spent three weeks trying to invent a new style shoulder strap for topless dresses.

651

Early marriages among students have created fresh problems for some universities. A new college in the north has half solved the problem by issuing an edict. From now on married girls must either live with their husbands or else make other arrangements with the caretaker.

652

Angela Korminski has just passed her examinations as a masseuse. Prior to this she worked for the council and served on a number of local bodies.

76

653

A new movement in California is called the Free-Bees. They are a kind of emancipated hippie. They believe in free love, free speech, freedom from work, and handouts. Their flowered caftans are made from parasite silk.

654

Caroline is a nice girl who advertises in Soho showcases that she is prepared to model for nude artists.

655

Britain is cagily considering changing over to driving on the right. As a matter of interest it seems that the change is being made gradually. Many motorists anticipated the new law long ago.

656

The aristocracy still put a lot of emphasis on good *breeding*. Poorer people have many other interests.

657

If Dad goes missing for a couple of days don't get worried: he's probably just still looking for somewhere to park the car.

658

Joe's smart. He speaks fourteen languages. George is smarter. He keeps his mouth shut.

659

'Come on kids, let's have a day out in the country.' 'Great, Dad! Germany, Poland, or the Sudan?'

660

She said to her alcoholic hubby: 'I won't ask you to come straight home from the club—but don't stagger too far away.'

661

'Where's our John?' 'He's out in the car.' 'Good. Now all we have to do is find out where the car is.'

662

Some men are here today and gone tomorrow but she's got one who's here today and gone tonight.

663

Yesterday Fred livened up the anniversary party by not going.

664

A donkey has no need to talk. Politicians usually do it for them.

665

We all know that women can do without men. But what can they do?

666

The accent may be on youth but the stress is on the parents.

667

The best thing to do quickly is nothing.

668

A lot of couples are husband and wife, but not each other's.

669

When Adam said to Eve 'Let's get married,' she replied 'Who'd have us?'

670

He's just joined the A.A.—Adulterous Association.

671

When a feller gives a girl the key to his flat she doesn't know what she's letting herself in for.

672

Yesterday the chap from next door came round to borrow a little sugar. My wife followed him eagerly.

673

He takes his girls to a small country cottage. It's the little retreat where he makes advances.

674

He's so thrifty he even stops his watch to save time.

675

The poor are the best-off people. They have everything to gain and nothing to lose.

676

Even a most philanthropic woman won't give away her age.

677

For his birthday his wife bought him a novelty ash-tray, shaped like a hearthrug.

678

A man has opened a fish and chip parlour in Park Lane. You get your order wrapped in the *Financial Times*.

679
There's a new detergent that's so strong on the whitening process that they have to give a free packet of dirt with every carton.

680
There's so much fighting going on in Northern Ireland nowadays, all the restaurants serve the potatoes in their combat jackets.

681
I see George has landed a plum job in the city. He's working in a jam factory.

682
He still can't get used to being a nudist. Whenever he eats in the colony restaurant and is served by the best-looking waitress he gets gravy stains down his ribs.

683
She went to the hairdresser to have her coif straightened but what she heard from an adjoining cubicle curled it again.

684
She always bought a certain brand of toilet soap because she'd read that it made bigger bubbles.

685
They call it colour television because if you can't afford one you see red and turn green with envy.

686
He used to be a small-time nicker, but now he's king of the undie-world.

687
They promised the lovely young starlet a big build up but all she got was a padded bra.

688
He bought one of those new 3-D television sets, and every time Raquel Welch turned round to talk to Michael Caine, she switched the set off.

689
There's a new type of bank robbery now. Their charges.

690
She used to put his dinner in the oven for him when he was due home late, so he bought her a pressure-cooker. Now she leaves his dinner on the ceiling.

691
One thing about an auction sale—no matter what you buy you get a lot for your money.

692
You can be excused if you look at a camel from a long distance and imagine it's a cow lying on its back.

693
Everything is so big in Texas: any girl with a bust less than forty-two feels inferior . . . so the cowboys say.

694
She was so scrawny, when she worked as a bubble dancer in a soap opera she slipped down the plug hole.

The Hippie People

695
He has so many flowers in his hair he doesn't suffer from dandruff but he has permanent hay-fever.

696
Two British hippies who couldn't wait to get to San Francisco had themselves sent by Interflora.

697
A group of flower people were arrested by the police in San Francisco. They were not put into jail. They went into the glasshouse.

698
Two married hippies were so wealthy—having sold a million copies of their latest disc, 'Tramp, Tramp, Tramp Through the Tulips with me' —they were able to afford their own personal gardener.

699
A Trappist Monk decided to take up transcendental meditation in India. He came back playing a guitar that had no strings, and doubled on a sitar.

700
The San Francisco Metropolitan Museum had just added a new room to the institution, containing some of the Hippie Relics. They include a safety-razor, a bar of soap, two aerosols of deodorant and a jar of weedkiller.

701
A tubby young flower girl entered the park wearing a badge which stated: 'Never Mind Oxfam—Feed Twiggy'.

702
There's a racketeer in San Francisco working a new form of confidence trick. He sells L.S.D. to hippies and when they are ready for a 'trip' he flogs them an airline ticket home.

703
Then there's the flower-power lad who arrived back home singing 'I Left My Harp in San Francisco'.

704
One hippie went to have a look at the exhibits at the local flower show and he was so fully tattooed with blooms they gave him first prize.

705
A party of hippies got fed up with the city and left 'Frisco to take a ramble through the Arizonian desert. On the way they were ambushed by a party of Sioux Indians. The Sioux gave one look at those fourteen mops of hair, threw their tomahawks in the air and fled.

706
A group of hippie guitarists sang a medley of their folk songs. Their folks sued them for libel.

707
Hippie leader Fred Tomkins from Brixton keeps his hair in a cloche.

708
One hippie lay for so long in the sun his kaftan wilted.

709
Irene came home from San Francisco boasting that she had just become engaged to a bunch of carnations.

710
One hippie spent an hour lying in the grass with a flower-power girl from Brooklyn. He admired her floral hair-do but didn't think much of her Dutch bulbs.

711
Albert walked to Paris to get a psychedelic experience. He thought it was a six-day bicycle race.

712
There was one terribly poor young hippie who couldn't afford to buy any flowers so he decorated himself with seeds. He spent six weeks in the rain and was absolutely mad when they came up cauliflowers and sprouts.

713
A flower-power girl had a baby and when her mother asked questions about it she explained that the stalk brought it.

714
The international emblem of the Flower-Power Men. Narcissus.

715
Andrew met a party of foreign girls in San Francisco. He spent some time cross-pollinating with a girl from Norway.

716
In the park there was a very bloody battle between French and British hippies and American hippies. They were arguing against war.

717
A well-known pop group went to visit an Indian Mystic in Bombay. They were very impressed and wrote an article in the *Bombay Times* all about it. This so impressed the population of India that Mrs. Gandhi is now doing a pop-song programme on Delhi radio.

718
Reporters thought that there was a serious riot going on in San Francisco when they saw a patrol of police officers playing fire-hoses on the crowd in the park. It turned out that it was just a bunch of hippies being watered.

719
Did you hear about the cowardly hippie? He went around bragging that he was on drugs. And showed an empty aspirin bottle to prove it.

720
Marcus O'Reilly believed in going the whole hog so he not only decorated himself with flowers but he also carried a big bouquet of Irish peonies. When he was interviewed by Alan Whicker on BBC-2 in colour television, the camera blew a fuse.

721
A young married hippie couple were proud of their children. Even the baby was on pot.

722
A vegetarian flower-power boy came from a family of very strict vegetarians who didn't believe in murdering plants, so he decorated himself with plastic nasturtiums.

723
One hippie was all dressed up in a flowered shirt sprinkled with yellow dandelions, yellow marigolds, yellow cornflowers and yellow roses. He wasn't *against* war—he was just yellow.

724
It's too bad for the hippie people. What's the good of believing in free love if you can't tell the boys from the girls?

725
One hippie youngster was arrested in San Francisco for assaulting a flower-power female. He said in his defence that he was not harming her. He was just playing she-loves-me-she-loves-me-not with her dress, which happened to be made of petals.

726
The reason why many hippies are in such a dirty, unwashed, condition is that the flowers grow better in that kind of soil.

727
A lot of girls in the park were wearing nothing but fig leaves. Clarence is going back quickly in the fall.

728
One girl was very attractive, with flowers tattooed all over her. There were two pansies at her breast. The police arrested them.

729
Iris was the most passionate girl, on the expedition. The leader used to keep her in the hothouse at night.

730
A tough Scots football supporter was walking along the street towards the Celtic ground wearing an enormous rosette when a hippie accosted him, winked and tried to sell him a reefer.

731
I've just bought the most fantastic 40 h.p. car. Fantastic for the 40 h.p. mean forty hire purchase payments.

732
Harry got a job in the security department of a nuclear research station. He's a Geiger counter-spy.

733
Alice's new cocktail gown is a wow. You should just see the law of gravity battling it out with the law of decency.

734
The Lapps don't think too much about hard labour. The average Lapplander works for five or six months and calls it a day.

735

There's the effeminate university graduate whose family had a long tradition in the Army. He joined the Cold Cream Guards.

736

A girl stopped me in the street and asked me for change for sixpence as she wanted to make an emergency call. I said: 'You don't need coppers—just go in the booth and dial 999.' She said: 'That's no good for the sort of emergency call I want to make.'

737

Outside an old church in Sussex there is an enormous sign which reads: 'Enter Here All Ye Faithful And Find Heaven'. Going closer one finds a smaller typewritten message reading: 'This door is kept locked on account of the draught'.

738

On television the other night the TV Cook said: 'And so you will find this very appetising chicken dinner sufficient for four, and furthermore you can make a very nourishing broth from the remains if you have an invalid in the house.'

739

Gladys's husband lacks vitality. She says he's not as good as he was once, although he's as good once as he once was.

740

The team's athletic coach was very disappointed with the condition of the goalkeeper who looked very washed out. He tapped him on the shoulder and said severely: 'And look, Sandy, I think you've been overdoing the push-ups a bit.'

741

Two friends decided to have a honeymoon in Bermuda. They went to the airline office outside which there was a big sign which suggested 'Fly United'. They tried it and got thrown off the plane.

742

The bride walked up the aisle looking cheerful, serene and expectant.

743

One person in every 2,030 is educated at a British university. So much for the future.

744

Then there's the dim furniture salesman who, when the customer asked about sectional furniture directed him to the bedding department.

745
An American movie producer went all the way from California to Rome to try and get a gorgeous Italian star named Selma Magnacia to appear in his latest production. But she wouldn't come across.

746
Lady Mainwaring was at Ascot to lead her winning filly 'Sonata Sal' into the enclosure. She was wearing a pink tulle frock trimmed with picot-edged frills, diamante sequins and a large picture hat. Which is a silly way to dress a horse.

747
At the Conservative conference this summer the girl shorthand writers were working all out in brief shifts.

748
I don't stand any nonsense from girls. Last night she said she didn't want to see me any more. So I shoved my head under the pillow.

749
They live a simple everyday existence. And his wife loves it.

750
David was out in the potting shed playing billiards with Cyril's wife.

751
A girl who had been arrested for street offences demanded to be legally represented and when the man arrived she said to him: 'I sent for you because we're sort of in the same kind of business, so as one solicitor to another . . .'

752
All morning she suffered with a nasty pain in her chest but by the afternoon she had shaken it off.

753
When the bride was taken ill in the honeymoon suite of a big Torquay hotel a doctor was called to her, while one of the maids gave the husband first aid.

754
A girl I know gave an address at a Salesman's Conference in Southend and later that night there were fifty men queueing outside her house.

755
The vicar asked the congregation to utter a special prayer for Suzy Grey. Then he dashed down to the betting shop and backed her in the 4-15 at Doncaster.

756

The Irish politician began his speech: 'There is something I want to get off my chest today that has been hanging over my head for weeks, and I'll be glad to put it behind me before we come to the end.'

757

One of our typists, Dora, made a mistake in the office today and the boss made her stay over and do it all again.

758

Trudy goes to all the charity dances. It's the only way she can get a partner.

759

I was a bouncing baby of eight pounds. I was born during a trampoline act in the circus, where my mother did a double act with the lion tamer.

760

He took his girl home and kissed her goodnight on the doorstep. She said: 'Why don't you kiss me on the mouth?'

761

Here is a word of warning for all people born under the sign of Capricorn—during the next few days don't let any complete stranger take out your appendix.

762

He's what you might call a hatchet-man for a psychiatrist: he chops people on the head to give them a split personality.

763

Do you want to hear a sick joke? Last night for supper I ate fourteen sausages, three plates of trifle, a jar of pickled onions, four grapefruit, a kipper, two helpings of spaghetti bolognaise, a pound of mushrooms, fourteen oysters and two rhum-babas.

764

She had beautiful long lush brown hair. Especially on her arms.

765

Fred bought a book on car maintenance. Very useful indeed. It has several footnotes, which is handy because Fred has seven feet.

766

Last summer I was astonished at all the kids on the beach. Thousands of them. I used to wonder where all those kids came from, but not any more. Last night I found out.

767
I once went out with a movie star who did a lot of Western films. She had a perfectly matched pair of lethal weapons.

768
His car is such a complete second-hand wreck, you don't get in through the driving-seat door. You just lie in the road and pull the car around you.

769
I love singing peppy songs. Last night I was going over a hot new piece in front of the microphone. The stage manager objected—she was his wife.

770
The first time I met her I knew for sure she was a real lady. It said so on the sign above the door she came out of.

771
My landlady said this morning: 'Do you know you owe me six weeks' rent? I haven't had a penny from you in months.' This afternoon I gave her a penny.

772
We eat like fighting cocks at home. All over the floor—feathers, blood, chicken bones.

773
The fleas we have are very tough. I sprayed the room with flea-killer last night and one of them brought up his bowl and asked for more.

774
What with all this recent soccer rowdyism among the home-team hooligans one referee I know had a lot of trouble last Saturday after the match. He couldn't get all 514 empty bottles into his car and so lost about £2·32 on empties. I suppose he might have put some in the boot, but that was filled with toilet rolls.

775
Now that the Transport Ministry has introduced the 70 m.p.h. limit, I'm going to have to sell my second-hand sports car. It will only do 27.

776
Last week the Unemployment Figures were up again, I see. Over 650,000 people were out of work. Mind you, 300,000 of them were just on strike.

777
An errant husband returned home blind drunk at 3.0 in the morning, crept as quietly as possible into the bedroom and held his alcoholic

breath when his wife stirred in her sleep, turned and murmured: 'Is that you, Fido?' What he did was bend down quickly and lick her arm.

778

Her name is Edna but all the men call her frequently.

779

He was one of the earliest Mexican settlers, Bicarbonato de Sodati.

780

My little boy came home crying from school yesterday. He said his teacher, Miss Sopwith, had had to punish him. I asked for details. Seemingly she had hit him so hard on his hand she had bruised her thigh. The day before he put up his hand in class to ask her a question, and she said 'No'.

781

Pop stars are very generous when they hit the big money, aren't they. Did you read that Tony Tornado bought his parents a £15,000 house and a £4,000 car out of the loot from his last disc? I'm the same, you know. I have just started to rebuild our local workhouse so that I can shove my old man in it.

782

His wife wanted to undergo some beauty treatment but he couldn't afford it. In the end he bribed a passing pickpocket to lift her face.

783

He came home with his arms full of nylons. His wife cried: 'Gee, Arnold, what lovely stockings. How did you know my size?' And he said: 'Shut up and put one on—you're driving the getaway car tonight.'

784

My wife is so suspicious she has spare eyes in the back of her head. So I admitted frankly that I'd been out with this other girl—and the tears ran down her back.

785

She told me she was going to have lessons in self-defence to prevent being assaulted in the street. I told her: 'Don't waste money like that. Your face is a kind of built-in self-defence.'

786

So the police took me along to the station where the police surgeon took a sample of blood for a test. They came back half an hour later and said: 'Well, you seem okay—it's negative.' I said: 'No alcohol?' They said: 'No blood'.

787

I thoroughly enjoyed life as a schoolboy. Mostly because my teacher Miss Ankers used to keep me in after school to teach me how to multiply.

788
I have a new hobby now, collecting wild birds. Do you know in one night I collected five from three dance halls.

789
I had dinner last night with a chap who hadn't seen a white woman for two years. He's a refugee from Brixton.

790
When my wife came home from her holiday in Spain I gave her a warm welcome. I set fire to her nightdress.

791
My wife's sister was on an assault course last night. Walking home from a dance.

792
She was wearing one of the sexiest dresses you ever saw. A pair of mink ear-rings.

793
I was educated at a high school. We seniors on the thirty-third floor had to wear parachutes.

794
One radio DJ is walking around with a black eye. It seems he got confused with the various BBC programmes and stopped another feller in the corridor and asked him: 'Are you One?'

795
Broadcasting pop music for 12 hours a day calls for a considerable number of discs, thus the quality suffers. One disc issued by a famous company is such a bad one, between broadcasts it has to be given vitamin injections.

796
Yesterday I was stung by an adder, in a supermarket. She totalled my order £5·25 too much.

797
There's a colour bar in George's house. They can't afford £300 for a new TV set.

798
Jack has invented a new gadget that can be used by beauty contest judges to check entrants for being fit to drive home. It's a breastalyser.

799
We've just found out why they scrapped the 'Music While You Work' programme. Forty per cent of the people in the country ain't working.

800

Now we know how the Russians managed to steal our plans for the topless dress. Philby took all the Foreign Office files with him to Moscow, labelled 'Topless Secret'.

Songs for Swinging

801

Songs for Swinging Chefs: 'Twenty-four Hours from an Ulcer'.
Songs for Swinging Met Officers: 'Take These Rains From my Chart'.
Songs for Swinging TV Series: 'There's a Peyton Place Somewhere'.
Songs for Swinging Boxers: 'I'll Close Your Eyes'.
Songs for Swinging Epilogue Parsons: 'Can't We Walk It Over?'
Songs for Sammy Davis: 'That Old Black Midget'.

802

Recently banned by the Board of Censors was a film adapted from a modern play in which were four acts and two scenes. All four acts were cut from the two scenes.

803

The craze for mini-skirts has spread to the Islands in the Sun. Last week hula girls in the Carribean were wearing skirts made from lawn clippings.

804

A waiter and a waitress who worked for four years in an Indian restaurant decided to get married. At the church, their fellow employees threw curried rice at them.

805

When Twiggy was working as a model for a brassiere firm, she had to wear the samples back to front over her shoulder blades.

806

Duff comedian. The only way he can get an audience is to write to the Pope and ask if *he'll* grant one.

807

We ate last night at a sea-food restaurant. Maggots, ragweed and dried mackerel.

808

A broken leg is nature's way of slowing you down.

809

My wife used to look a doll in those form-hugging cocktail dresses but she looks horrible now that she's fifty pounds older.

810

Then there's the medical student who did his housework in a mental hospital studying in the woman's ward. He was an expert on prefrontal lobes.

811

It's funny how fall-out looks much better on television, or on a Bunny girl.

812

I'm going to be late home, so would one of you please ring the house, If a gruff, gravelly voice answers—that's my wife.

813

At a private Hunt Ball in the heart of wild Middlesex, Cynthia won the spot prize twice. Every bachelor at the dance found the spot.

814

My mob in the army was the rottenest lot you ever met. Even the chaplain dodged church parade.

815

Did you hear about the belly-dancer who won a seat in Parliament and on her first day there put a swinging motion before the house?

816

A malingerer is someone who's not as cracked up as he's cracked up to be.

817

Civilisation is a world full of art treasures and unemployed artisans.

818

The Female Liberation Movement is a society of females who burn their bras not so much as a protest but because they don't need them anyway.

819

I saw a tired old couple at the discotheque last night. Then she slipped into the powder room and tightened the shoulder straps.

820

Did you see the newspaper report about that rich old man of seventy marrying a twenty-year-old girl? It said the bridegroom's gift to the bride was an antique pendant.

821

The lads called her 'Televera' because she never had much on at weekends, and she often gave repeat performances.

822

A psychiatrist wasted an hour treating a patient on his couch before he found out the chap was just re-upholstering it.

823

Ken Dodd is sponsoring a new mild cigarette made out of rope. It produces knotty ash. You also get it if you smoke hemp.

824

Most Parliaments come about through a chemical process. A fusion of hot hustling gas and statistical electrickery.

825

Statisticians can produce even more remarkably absurd figures than a cheap corset.

826

A wealthy bachelor is just a man who saved up religiously to get married and then minded his change.

827

Evolution is working well: the development of complete automation is slowly causing people to lose the use of their hands. By 1989 only virile men will be able to push the buttons.

828

Rings, in order of appearance. Telephone. Key. Engagement. Church bells. Wedding. Teething. Bath. Eternity. Wrestling.

829

We know a budding author whose work doesn't get much credit. The tradesmen prefer cash.

830

If your girl friend closes her eyes when you kiss her, she is probably day-dreaming about some matinee idol. You'd better find out who took her to the theatre yesterday afternoon.

831

Someone's just invented a special low stool. It's for getting condensed milk.

832

Have you heard the story of the Russian who rushed down Moscow High Street yelling: 'The Commissar is an idiot!' He was arrested and sent to prison for forty-five years. Five years for calling the Commissar an idiot and forty years for giving away a state secret!

833

After recent meetings in Bucharest at the Communist Corn Exchange it was decided that from now on no stamps are going to picture the Heads of State. The reason given was that some individuals would spit on both sides of the stamps.

834

Basil married a girl who had everything . . . including two sets of twins.

835

Matches are made in heaven—they only make firelighters in the other place.

836

Why go to all the trouble of dressing up to go out and see puerile third-rate films at the local cinema when you can stay right in your own parlour and watch rubbishy third-rate films on television?

837

And now the Government has adopted a pop song. 'The Best Things in Life are Free. Sex, Sin, and Social Aid'.

838

Her husband came home after a hard day's work and begged for his dinner. He was given fish. He turned to his wife and said: 'Fish for breakfast! Fish for lunch! And now fish for dinner!' He was so mad he was breathing through his cheeks.

839

A parrot broke out of his cage in a Trappist monastery one night and after being free for over a week an old peasant found him lying exhausted by the roadside. He picked him up and took him home. For months the peasant tried to teach the parrot to talk but the parrot couldn't. One day the parrot again broke out of his cage, picked up a pencil and paper, and wrote down: 'Pretty Polly!'

840

A delegation of farmers visited Tahiti to investigate the Hula girls' system of rotating their crops.

841

When a pretty young girl came to the door collecting for the Old Ladies' Home, Jack offered her his mother-in-law.

842

When they built the new prison, the architect's sense of humour really showed up. He put swing doors on the condemned cell.

843

'Waiter, there's a fly in my ice-cream.' 'I know sir. That's progress. If it's anything in food these days, they deep-freeze it.'

844

A publisher in London, says *The Bookseller*, has decided to re-issue very old novels, some of which were originally published in the sixteenth century. This is probably because this publisher has been watching the bookstalls lately and realises that many readers are interested in old pros.

845

Out hunting one day, an intrepid big game man was hiding behind a tree in the jungle when suddenly he realised to his surprise that there was something right behind him. He felt the lion's breath on the back of his neck. So he turned his collar up.

846

In the bright moonlight of that romantic night she whispered into my ear those three magic words that made me walk on clouds. 'Go hang yourself!'

847

I'm not really a gentleman but about one thing I'm very particular. I never use bad language before my wife. I let her get hers in first.

848

I'm a bit suspicious of our butcher. My wife gave him a pound note for half a pound of sausages and he gave her the change in horseshoes.

849

I sent my wife an expensive dinner service for her birthday. I crated it very carefully and then stuck a large label on it saying:' China, With Care'. It was sent to Pekin.

850

I nearly went crazy when this big beautiful blonde turned me down. My brother DID go crazy—he married her.

851

I've just been named as the correspondent in a divorce case. They won't be able to touch me. I can't even write.

852

I was the last customer late at night in a coffee bar. The waitress served me in a rather tired manner, putting cup and saucer down on the table so that the coffee sloshed all over. Sarcastically I said to her: 'Thanks, and what about a spoon?' So she turned off all the lights and sat in my lap.

853

I don't mind doing the dishes for my wife . . . after all, she helps me with the rest of the housework.

854

When I first married my wife I used to catch her in my arms: now I catch her with the secretary of the golf club. We're still like a couple of love birds—she's always flying into a rage and I'm moulting. One day I found my wife putting the baby on our radiogram because it had an automatic changer. At home we were a very big family; eighteen children used to sit down at our dining table for dinner, and we were so starving hungry that sometimes only seventeen got up afterwards. My mother refused to let me go and see the local nude show at the Alhambra in case I saw something I shouldn't see, but I sneaked over there one night, and I certainly did see something I shouldn't see . . . my father sitting in the front row . . . With his arm round a girl . . . and that took some doing because the girl was posing at the back of the stage. When he finally got home my mother was so angry with him she sent him to bed without any breakfast.

855

The other day my wife made me rock cakes. Suddenly as I was trying them for size, she came into the kitchen, bent down and picked something off the floor. 'Darling,' she said, 'You've broken my string of pearls.' I said: 'Pearls nothing—those are my teeth'.

856

As a safety measure the administrators of the American Space Exploration Programme (ASEP) are not going to pay their astronauts any salary. They want to make sure that the explorers are down and out.

857

There will come a day when the atom splits Man.

858

An interpreter is just a human hearing-aide.

859

Archaeologists dig down deep to find old memories. The common man just probes around in his attic.

860

A mother always knows what's best for her teenage daughter, but her daughter knows something better.

861

When a dolly girl goes out to hook a man, she knows exactly how to wiggle her bait.

862

Many writers owe their unusual success to genius. The genius of their publishers' ad-men.

863

Men are born to command. But then they spoil everything by getting married.

864

Autobiography is invariably obscene. No old man should strip off in front of the public just because he thinks he's a public figure.

865

George's wife has dish-pan hands, and her feet are too big, as well.

866

Every war in the annals of history could have been avoided if there had not been so many brave orators unfit for military service.

867

The fact is that you only want to get away from it all when you have nothing.

868

Edna has earned the love and affection of many musicians. They call her 'Strumpet Voluntary'.

869

The man who considers himself head of the household finds himself beheaded the moment a new baby arrives.

870

A bachelor is someone who doesn't believe in unions because the dues are too excessive and he doesn't want his pockets picketed.

871

There are so many social and psychological problems developing from life in high-rise flats and offices, it looks as though buildings will eventually design *us*.

872

Just as you think you have won an argument with your wife, you start to realise it's only half-time.

873

His wife could sleep through an earthquake; grandma suffers from a daily gin coma; the kids can never drag themselves out of bed after a late night out. Try raising that sort of family.

874

Isn't it remarkable how things generally manage to average themselves out? For instance if you go visiting and receive a cool reception, you can be sure of a warm farewell.

875

Modern paintings are all pretty much alike except that most of them aren't pretty, they don't fetch much, and they're not likeable.

876

We know an old village doctor who gets paid per hour, per visit or perhaps.

877

There's a new headache cure on the market but it's now so expensive due to inflation that ten minutes after taking one tablet you have a relapse which needs two more.

878

The British Industrial Trade Fair got off to a good start and we have already received one firm order: 'Get out!'

879

News from China: Four men who have been held inside a Pekin prison yesterday ended their seven day hunger-strike. They died.

880

Last week, a woman in Australia was hypnotised to enable her to have a baby without pain. This surely is a revolutionary development—she wasn't pregnant.

881

The other day, at an all-important peace conference, none of the world's leaders could agree. To break the deadlock the Russian and American delegates decided to have a working lunch. During this they worked out the perfect settlement. Then they argued over who should pay the bill.

882

With trembling hands he tore at her paper dress; then wiped his nose.

883

A stately home had so many visitors last summer, the lions started lighting fires at night.

884

Here are the latest temperature readings: London 49 degrees, Birmingham 41, Liverpool 40, Leeds 42. London now meet Liverpool in the final.

885

I see that the P.M. at the last election promised that he would lead us to the promised land. If Moses ever met the P.M. there would have to be another Commandment.

886

An English scientist took many years to develop his working robot. Last week it was ready to go on public view. The robot's first words were 'Where's the picket-line?'

887

Statistics state that during a normal day a bus-conductor will walk twenty-six miles. Why doesn't he catch a bus?

888

Fashions have gone mad recently. At a dog show in New York, a sex starlet arrived and we were dazzled by a figure-hugging gold lame gown, and large pearl ear-rings. That was the dog!

889

A school headmaster received a note from an angry parent. 'I'm extremely concerned about my son's report which I have just received. Not only has he got very low marks in all subjects, but he left your lousy school three years ago!'

890

Did you hear of the story about independent fleas who saved all their money and took a mortgage on an Airedale?

891

The centre-forward of a leading First Division club kissed his team-mate after scoring a winning goal. The manager, at the following week's match, announced their engagement.

892

Britain invented television and the Americans developed it.
Britain invented the jet and the Americans developed it.
Britain invented the film and the Americans developed it in Japan.

893

The difference between a sewing machine and a go-go girl is that a Singer has only one bobbin.

894

If you have to choose between wine and women, study the vintage.

895

She tried to tell him that she had a 42-inch bust but he couldn't grasp the point.

896

Irene came home with a nasty scratch on her thigh, caused by her American officer friend's good conduct medal.

897
The vicar told her to rectify her error but instead she horrified her rector.

898
Then there's the man who chanced to be in the powder-room in an hotel in southern Japan when the town was struck by an earthquake and the hotel collapsed. He thought he didn't know his own strength—all he did was pull the chain.

899
We planned a runaway marriage. Every time I called for her she ran away.

900
Last night I finally got my girl to say 'Yes'. It was such a relief: I'd been thinking I'd have to marry her.

901
Admiral Byrd would have been first to discover the Pole if one of his husky dogs hadn't beaten him to it.

902
Then there's the young amateur cricketer who scored ten runs in a match with the local women's C.C.—They were in the captain's stocking.

903
A husband and wife would not speak to each other except in the deaf and dumb language. One night when the husband came home rather late the wife let him have her raging anger, her fingers flying twenty to the dozen. Just as he raised his hands to answer her, she turned out the light.

904
'Do you cheat on your wife?' asked the psychiatrist. 'Who else?' answered the patient.

905
Some farmers' daughters go out every Saturday night and sow wild oats, then go to church on Sunday and pray for a crop failure.

906
One of the young secretaries had just returned from her honeymoon and was discussing it with the girls at the office. 'How did your husband register at the hotel?' one co-worker wanted to know. 'Fine,' the secretary said, beaming. 'Just fine!'

907
A young man met his ex-wife at a party and after a few drinks, he

suggested that they have another try at marriage. 'Over my dead body,' she sneered. He downed his drink, and replied, 'I see you haven't changed a bit.'

908
A bachelor is a man who believes in life, liberty and the happiness of pursuit.

909
'I hear that your doctor is a great humanitarian.' 'Rather. If he wants to spank his small son, he chloroforms him first.'

910
From Paris this season comes the latest thing in ultra-modern foundation garments for the most meticulous maiden. Filter-tipped brassieres.

911
I was introduced to a wonderful little blonde at the swimming baths last Tuesday. Twice I took her out. And she was awfully annoyed, because she wanted to go on swimming.

912
There was an old woman who lived in a shoe. She had so many children because she didn't know what to do.

913
Mary had a little bear, which thought her really kind. She always walked along the street with her little bear behind.

914
Another Bunny girl is in hospital. She got badly crushed—trying to play a piano-accordion.

The Eternal Female

915
The model girl at the fashion display was studied by the announcer: he felt the texture of the mini-skirt and her other bits of finery. The new boy friend took her to a Hunt Ball, where all the girls were experts. She once went out with a Japanese karate expert who had bought a new car—half way to town he put out his arm to turn right and chopped a Rolls Royce in half. Their new house was built by a sex maniac, it has Crittal windows, a double-breasted chimney stack and Diana Dors. When she was introduced to his grandfather the old man showed that he took an immediate liking to her—three days later he was fined for assault. She went with Henry to a holiday camp and the moment they got there they changed into something more comfortable; she changed into a brief mini-bikini and he changed into a frustrated lecher. Her

new boy-friend is rather sweet, tall, long, thin and wiry, a sort of male Twiggy with hairy legs. The weather was so hot the day they went to the lido, even the dogs were lying around with their buttons undone.

916

Things must be worse than the public realises—the first Hot Line call that the P.M. made to the President in Washington took place yesterday —and he reversed the charges.

917

Two stockbrokers met in a pub, and one of them was so distressed he was crying in his daiquiri cocktail; when his friend asked what ailed him he said: 'Damn it, man, how would *you* feel if you made a killing on the market, then went home unexpected and found *your* wife had gone public?'

918

A group of suburban couples decided to try the American society game of swapping partners. Two nights later one of the wives said to another: 'I wonder how the boys are getting on?'

919

I hear that a well-known artist in Australia has left Sydney and gone back to Adelaide. Sydney hasn't spoken to him since.

920

Little Albert, looking worried, came home and asked his mother 'Mom, what's sex?' Dutifully, if embarrassed, she went into a lengthy and careful explanation that took her most of the evening. When she'd finished Albert said: 'Heck, how am I going to get that all in on one line in my school questionnaire about the holiday cruise?'

921

A well-known musician I know has very catholic tastes in music— mostly rhythm and blues.

922

Did you hear about the enthusiastic muscleman who worked seven hours a day to toughen his muscles and died at twenty-five with hardened arteries?

923

A man went to his doctor and said: 'Doc, I'm worried; my wife stays in bed all morning chopping firewood.' The doctor said: 'It must be her nerves. Don't worry—just let her have her own way: when she's had enough she'll stop it'. The man said: 'That's all very well, but we've got gas *central-heating*.'

924
All my money is tied up—it's in trussed units.

925
My wife is using lots of reducing cream—it comes in pint-sized flesh-pots.

926
Four men snatched a 747 jet plane in transit from New York by Pan-Am: It seems Pan-Am were six payments overdue on it.

927
She was used as a model by Spillers for one of their shapes.

928
Preparations are now being made for Enoch Powell's state visit to Trinidad.

929
When a famous film actress had a new topless dress designed by an equally famous designer she had to go back fourteen times for a fitting.

930
He was so drunk when they gave him the breathalyser test, the balloon shot skywards and made ten orbits of the earth.

931
She's such a catty girl, when she sees someone in a mink coat she gets Thoughts of Miaow.

932
She thinks that a social drop-out is a girl whose bra breaks in a crowded lift.

933
I hear that Fred Gittins of the Rovers is being eagerly sought by Don Stevens, the manager of Bentham Athletic. He's been playing a pretty good game lately—with the manager's daughter.

934
You know what a girl is?—at eighteen months her parents try to get her out of bed and at eighteen years, into it.

935
My wife can just about manage on what I earn. My problem is—what am *I* going to live on?

936
Did you hear about the Indian fakir who went to the cobbler's and asked them to put a couple of dozen nails in his shoe?

937
Tom's wife is worried: she's just received a stick of real rock from her absent husband—with the name 'Dartmoor' written right the way through.

938
The other night I played strip poker with a blonde in her flat—we played for matchsticks because her father wouldn't allow her to play for money.

939
Last night I went to a reception to meet the four semi-finalists in the National Deer-stalking contest—three chaps and a reindeer.

940
A builder I know has had a great idea—he's building a new Slum Estate to rehouse the people who leave collapsing towers of flats.

941
In bed last night my wife was reminiscing and she said: 'I don't know about Christmas not being what it was; Santa Claus isn't what he was, either'.

942
It may not nowadays be considered deplorable to have promiscuous habits before getting married—but try not to block the aisle.

943
Before the bank manager fixed the amount of my last overdraft he tested me in his wind tunnel.

944
I said to this girl 'Look, what's Tom Jones got that I haven't got?' and she said: 'Do you want it in alphabetical order?'

945
She thought he must be a politician because he made a strange bed-fellow.

946
As the two men in the space capsule hurtled moonwards at 25,000 mph one looked worried—he turned to the other and said: 'I can't remember if I bolted the back door before I left home'.

947
On her engagement day, Lydia resigned from the Nudist Colony because she wanted to be married in white.

948
Sid took his family on holiday to Spain and spent the first day on the beach throwing shells at his mother in law—six-pounder 9mm. ack-ack.

949
Martha went to the butcher to buy some lights for her cat. The wretch is frightened of the dark.

950
All this terrible fear about the atom bomb and the new aluminium bomb and hot-lines between Moscow, London, Washington, Paris and Soho . . . it's got so when I stay at an hotel I'm even too frightened to ring for room service in case I press the wrong button.

951
The A-bomb worries me sick . . . I dread the day someone is going to yell 'Ay—Ay—look out here comes the bomb!'

952
Ever since he started going with that lady karate champion he's been speaking in a high-pitched voice.

953
A vicar went into a bookstore in Soho to get a copy of the *Church Review* and he accidentally dropped his half crown on the floor in the crowd, so he bent down to look for it and the man at the counter said: 'Did you want something,' and the vicar stammered: 'Yes, I'm trying to get something from under your counter,' and the shopkeeper said: 'Oooooh! I'm surprised at you!'

954
When his mother-in-law came to stay with them for a week, every night the husband used to bring the old lady a large packet of spaghetti; one night his wife asked why and he whispered urgently: 'Shut up, you silly woman, don't you KNOW your mother is this year's head of the Mafia—and if she ain't she should be.'

Soccer Riots

955
Eleven men took the field—the referee and his ten bodyguards. Then the home team took the field—chunks of it. In the face.

956
The away team kept turning the sods with their feet and many of the home team were injured.

957
It was a terrific game; the left-half kicked three goals in the first half and eighteen spectators in the second half.

958
Suddenly someone yelled 'Foul', and sure enough the ref found an iron horseshoe in the home captain's left glove. The ref sent him straight off the field, with a well-aimed judo throw.

959
The right-back was struck by a left hook and gave it right back.

960
The gate suffered that Saturday because all two fans were frightened to show up.

961
The groundsman still did all right—he got fourteen pounds back on the beer bottles that littered the pitch.

962
At half time the score was Home Team 5; Away Team 6 dead, 4 asphyxiated and 10 captured.

963
The fans were really out for the directors' blood—six of them needed transfusions.

964
On Monday their best player was sold to Aston Villa for five pounds and 130 Green Shield Stamps.

The Colour Problem

965
He's so dedicated to the cause of keeping immigrants out of Britain he won't even have colour television in the house.

966
He struck his wife when she ordered new curtains for the bedroom, in brown taffeta.

967
His servants are so scared of him that even his butler has sold his sunray lamp.

968
The other day he protested to Cadbury's because they were advertising chocolate on ITV.

969
On Friday two cannibals called round to his house with a large black pot and asked him to join them for dinner—as the main course.

970
One of them was a pigmy and he shouted to him: 'Get out of here you half-bred half-breed'.

971
For Christmas twenty West Indians clubbed together to give him a present—he is recovering in the Middlesex Hospital.

972
A Zambian diplomat sent him a pipe for his birthday—with a dart still in it.

973
He was very annoyed when a Pakistani Jew stopped him in the street and asked him where he could buy some kosher Kit-E-Kat.

974
The Asians can now take their hats off faster—they've invented a new jet-turban with vertical take-off.

975
One immigrant has made a fortune by inventing a new style golfing blouse for women—it's topless so that coloured women can improve their swing.

976
He keeps complaining that the only coloured man he ever liked was Al Jolson.

977
If his wife buys brown eggs, he makes her bleach them.

Modern Music and Musicians

978
The last time that guitarist had his hair cut his nurse changed his nappy at the same time.

979
He only wears his hair that long because he's growing his own G-strings.

980
Every time they go to London they get picketed by the Barbers' Union.

981
When they were in Zambia for a tour of the native villages, the villagers stood to attention while they played 'Hit It Jack, It's Coming Back', because they thought it was the national anthem.

982
An ape swung out of the dense jungle and shouted to the fellers 'Welcome Home'.

British is Best

983
At a meeting of the U.N. this week Britain was officially made the fifty-second state of the International Monetary Fund.

984
Before the Prime Minister set off to ask the Zurich gnomes for another overdraft, he stopped off at Istanbul and borrowed a Trappist monk's begging-bowl: he figured he'd get a better reply if he looked religious.

985
In March last year statistics showed that 650,000 Britishers were unemployed: that means 650,002 people were drawing pay for doing nothing.

986
The countries of England, Scotland, Ireland and Wales are said to share the same flag—the Union Without Jack.

987
Eighteen members of the Houses of Parliament Committee on Drug Offences sat round a table discussing new moves—they were the official dope ring.

988
MacDougall 'phoned a doctor and breathlessly reported that his baby had swallowed a sixpence. 'I'll be right over,' said the doctor. 'How old is it?' Replied the Scot: '1894'.

989
She was the only woman I ever knew who wore two uplifts. One in the usual place and one for the bags under her eyes.

990
It's all right boasting in the pub about having handkerchiefs to match your shirts, but you don't tell them you haven't got a shirt to your name with tails on it.

991
Then there's the nice young English girl who went out one night with a gondolier. But she wouldn't let him fondola in his gondola.

992
A girl buying a Valentine card said: 'Have you got one that will convince him how passionately I love him without committing me to any immediate proof?'

993
My brother-in-law is looking for a Polynesian girl because he's interested in Samoa.

994
'Yes,' said the old hotel porter to the new lad, 'You see plenty of sights in this job. I wish I had a quid for every woman I've seen wearing nothing but a surprised expression.'

995
It's been raining so hard this year—never stopped for five weeks. The curator at our local zoo is piling all the animals into an ark.

996
A woman said to the assistant in the hat shop: 'What I'm after is a hat that will give me some personality.' The assistant said: 'Lady, we are selling hats, not miracles'.

997
His missus says: 'When that young blonde fainted in the pub you couldn't get there fast enough to loosen the neck of her blouse and fan her with your hat, but when I fell my full length on the garden path the first thing you did was check to see if I had cracked your crazy paving.'

998
Tom's theatrical agent is so hard if you kicked him in the heart you'd break four toes.

999
Number seventeen million on the Red Chinese Hit Parade—'God Bless America'.

1000

A vicar I know proposes to campaign against those extra-long movie kisses. He says he was at the cinema the other night and the goings-on in the back row were terrible.

1001

Have you noticed how once again girls' dresses are getting shorter—at the top?

1002

And there's also a shortage of women. All those I've met this month have been under five-feet-two.

1003

Always put your girl on a pedestal, and then take the ladder away.

1004

Told that she would have to cut part of her act, the bubble-dancer decided to dispense with the bubbles.

1005

I had a nasty shock last week—a 45p latch-key cost me £25.

1006

I dreamt about Stella last night, so I had to go around this morning and apologise to her.

1007

A nit is a chap who takes a girl up the hill to watch the sunset and watches the sunset.

1008

If she's a wife she's at home but if she's always available she's abroad.

1009

Say when. Okay, after the Epilogue.

1010

For every conceivable occasion the Pill is recommended.

1011

You might say that Cyril is a flower with a weak stem.

1012

Her husband didn't leave her much when he died. No, but he left her quite a lot while he was living.

1013

You were in prison for some years weren't you. Did you like it? Not much. Just because I once hit a warder with a shovel the governor wouldn't let me attend choir practice.

1014
I like playing onesie-twosie on the cash register. You mean onesie for the boss, twosie for you?

1015
I kissed a girl in the moonlight but she wouldn't kiss me back. Why should she? What's so special about your back?

1016
What do you do when you see a handsome man? Well, I stare for a while and then I put the mirror down.

1017
Mary has said she will be my wife. Well it's your own fault for hanging around the house every night.

1018
Are you getting engaged to Sybil? I'm not sure. I've still got an option on Mavis.

1019
Later Sam went to the doctor to complain about his insomnia. He told the doc he was sure something was wrong because he kept waking up every two or three days.

1020
Has your new baby learned to walk yet? Not yet—he's still learning to drive the car.

1021
What kinds of sports do you like? I'm not fussy—blondes, redheads, brunettes.

1022
At least Florence dresses like a lady. I wouldn't know; I've never seen her dressing.

1023
I didn't say goodnight to Mary yesterday, when I left her. Why, did you have a tiff? No—by the time we'd finished saying goodnight it was morning.

1024
In one club they give special concessions to the poor old age pensioners —they can come in free if accompanied by their parents.

1025

I hear that Gerald and Mary are going steady. They've both joined the A.A. organization.

1026

My little boy worries me. He's developing class hatred. Communistic? Oh no. He just hates going to school.

1027

Do you understand French syntax? No. I didn't even know it was taxed.

1028

Tomorrow I'm going to a lecture on Anatomy. I hate organ recitals, myself.

1029

I hear they're teaching good manners to the cannibals in darkest Africa. One missionary has even had books printed; on the first page is the instruction: Never speak when you have someone in your mouth.

1030

My husband is the only man who has ever kissed me. Are you boasting or complaining?

1031

I'm not sure whether I'm in love or not. It's probably just inflation.

1032

Is it true that Ethel inherited her good looks? Yes, her father left her a chemist shop.

1033

What does Gladys' new evening dress look like? In a lot of places it looks like Gladys.

1034

Dick talks a lot of tripe. Yes, practically everything he says would make a modern song title.

1035

Did you hear about the celebrated stage illusionist who walked along the High Street and turned into a gents' toilet?

1036

They make a lot of fuss about these new-fangled lie-detectors, but I went and married one.

1037

I'm not in a very good state of health today. My wooden leg keeps bothering me. My wife hits me over the head with it.

1038

'Mary, don't forget to put the cat out' . . . 'I didn't know it was on fire.'

1039

The fat woman at the dance, shaking it all about in the okey-kokey.

1040

It's tall and thin and green and always faces north. It's a magnetic cucumber.

1041

My wife wanted a coat which was in the window marked 20 per cent off. It got it for 100 per cent off—I didn't buy it.

1042

In a contest to find the most popular Hollywood star, John Wayne and Gig Young were well placed and Raquel Welch was well supported.

1043

Girl in a certain fragile condition sings extracts from musical shows— including 'I am six months going on seven months'.

1044

A communist joker knocks on the door of his best friend's house and shouts 'Is Len in?'

1045

A Jewish convent is a sanctuary run by the Mother Shapiro.

1046

A month after Bill got married he had his visiting cards overprinted 'Under New Management'.

1047

To 'come the old acid' was once a term meaning to be objectionable but now it means pushing L.S.D. microdots.

1048

A man's best friend is frequently the stranger who runs off with his wife.

1049

A reform school is a kind of college where even the flies are thick.

1050

There is no mathematical formula which explains why a man who is the same age as his fianceé when they get married becomes five years older than her after ten years of marriage.

1051

A short while ago an Australian pickpocket was arrested and found to be in the possession of twenty-two baby kangaroos.

1052

A girl who gatecrashed a Fancy Dress Ball where her host was dressed up as a nudist, didn't know him from Adam.

1053

Holiday advertisements are exhortations for us to summer in the country instead of having to simmer in town.

1054

A psychic bartender is someone with a double interest in the spirit world.

1055

In Hampshire lives an experimental farmer who crossed an onion with a spud and got a potato with watery eyes.

1056

Jones went to an exhibition of very disinteresting and shoddy old ornaments which were boldly labelled 'Art Objects'. So did he.

1057

An advertising executive is someone who takes a coach tour of beautiful Britain and gets annoyed if the hoardings are concealed by trees.

1058

Flora McMintloch was singing loudly in ecstasy on the hotel balcony on the first night of their vacation. Her husband was arrested for beating his wife.

1059

If you wish to know how Webster came to compile his dictionary, it is a rather sad tale. He was constantly arguing with his wife and one word led to another.

1060

Who was the first man to use a cradle ? David, when he rocked Goliath to sleep.

1061

Littly Suzy went regularly to Sunday school and one day she brought a hand-mirror as a gift for the vicar. The vicar was very pleased at her thoughtfulness and asked if there was any special reason for the present:

Suzy said: 'Well, now perhaps you won't keep putting your collar on back to front.'

1062

The chap who learns by correspondence course is a very exceptional person. He's in a class of his own.

1063

A university lecturer was attacked and beaten up by eight thugs on the campus. A policeman, making his report, began to write down the evidence. 'You say you were set upon by a gang of hoodlums?' 'Please!' said the professor sternly, 'Hoodla!'

1064

Get yourself a brassy-bed-warmer for Christmas; and see how your wife reacts.

1065

When you feel too old and the night is still young, it's time to quit.

1066

Go-go girls . . . footloose and fanny free.

1067

Spanish lesson: *Mañana* means tomorrow. Pyjama means tonight.

1068

He met a girl while in the army. It was love at first sight. He only had a 24-hour pass.

1069

On a trip to Arabia I got back to the hotel unexpectedly from a visit to Cairo and my wife let out a terrified sheikh.

1070

It's terrible to marry someone for life and find out she hasn't got any.

1071

She has a heart as big as a whale. If I upset her, she blubbers.

1072

When I met Joyce in the pub she was resting on the counter, and you should have seen what she was resting.

1073

I met my wife at a night-club. It annoyed me a lot—she was supposed to be at home minding the children.

1074

A woman is someone who walks around all day in a light dress with a deep V-neck and then moans all night that she hasn't got enough of the blanket.

1075
Unless I stop kissing so many short girls, I'm going to get awfully round-shouldered.

1076
Question of the day? Instead of making ballet dancers prance around on tip-toe, why don't they just get taller showgirls?

1077
She knew she'd made a mistake marrying Sandy Mackintosh Ferguson —on their wedding night she caught him trying on all the old shoes tied to the car.

1078
Grandma leaned over the cot and said with tears in her eyes: 'Oh you luvverly little cherub you, you dark darling, I could eat you!' Kid sits up and says 'Yeah? With no teeth?'

1079
An ostrich at the zoo died of frustration after trying to hatch out a German army helmet.

1080
She has had a string of aristocratic boy friends, but on holiday in Basle she spent her last knight.

1081
How did the rooster cross the road? It jumped on a Rhode Island.

1082
If you suffer from insomnia, you should always sleep on the edge of the bed and you'll soon drop off.

1083
It was the impressionist's birthday so he did himself. He used to do bird impressions until his wife gave him a tin of worms for Christmas.

1084
'Some of my best Jews are Friends,' said the Quaker.

1085
How did you ever come to be in a profession like this?' he asked the blonde. She said: 'Maybe I was just lucky.'

1086
He spent so much money on Gina he had to marry her to get some of it back.

1087

A man in St. Albans wrote indignantly to his Council demanding a council house in a different area. He gave his present address as 22 St. Stephen's House, St. Mary's Lane, Church Road, St. Albans, and signed the letter William St. John Fareham, a confirmed atheist.

1088

A waltz wizard in Wigan has invented a woman with her bust on her back. It makes dancing so much more interesting.

1089

So do you know what it was Juliet said to Romeo on the balcony. She said: 'You piker—why didn't you get orchestra stalls?'

1090

A well-known comedian accidentally fell off a ship near Eddystone lighthouse . . . he almost drowned to death swimming round in circles to keep in the spotlight.

1091

It was a very poor drama . . . the audience was only in tiers because the seats are fitted that way.

1092

I played the part of Romeo in a repertory company once. Business was so bad I couldn't afford to shave, and after three weeks we had to change the play to *Othello*.

1093

She loved me from the bottom of her heart. There was no room at the top.

1094

Katie is the only girl I could ever love. The others wouldn't let me.

1095

My wife is suing me for support . . . I would not buy her a girdle.

1096

I know a girl who is absolutely prone to make mistakes. In fact that's how she makes them.

1097

Skiing on the slopes in Switzerland is marvellous—you just start at the top and finish on the bottom.

1098

If it weren't for the threat of fall-out there probably wouldn't be so many drop-outs.

1099

A new show which opened in London was so desperately appalling that one first-night critic sitting in the circle asked the guardsman sitting in front of him to put his busby back on.

1100

Poor Treadwell has gone to rest. He's got a job with a nationalised industry.

1101

If virtue is its own reward, why does our vicar keep collecting money?

1102

Lilian Mortlake is both an artists' model and a burlesque artiste. She told our reporter that she finds it very profitable to have two spheres of interest.

1103

A man living in Balham has just had terrible bad luck. It was probably because he struck three matches to light his cigarette lighter.

1104

Mrs. Lessing dresses to please her husband. She always wears her old clothes for eight seasons, and it delights him.

1105

Because she loves flying, lovely Monica Harris has joined B.E.A. as a hostess. She's quite sure that flying is strictly for the birds.

1106

Clubs are trumps. In 2500 B.C. the male used to say 'Shut up, you old witch, or I'll go for my club.' In 1980 the males will still be saying: 'Shut up, you old cow, or I'll go to my club.'

1107

The BBC is producing a new documentary programme called 'The Parliament People'. Our cultured cynic insists that it is just a ploy to counteract the popularity of ITV's programme 'The Comedians'.

1108

The strong man of a one-ring country circus billed himself as 'Hercules Junior', and was much put out when he heard that a local farmer had boasted he could break Hercy in two. He took one of the big white horses from the ring and rode out to the farmer's house. 'What kind of hooey have you been spreading about me, you runt?' he bellowed. The farmer didn't say a word. He just grabbed the intruder, hurled him bodily over the fence, and went back to his churning. Hercules picked himself up, and gazed ruefully at the farmer. 'Ain't you had enough?' called the latter. 'Or have you something more to say?' 'No,' said Hercules. 'But would you be kind enough to throw me my horse?'

1109

A young parson had taken for his text at his young men's class the parable of the Wise and Foolish Virgins. In conclusion, he said, 'Now, which would you prefer? The five wise virgins with the light or the five foolish virgins, in the dark?'

1110

The boss returned from lunch in a happy mood and called in all his staff to listen to a couple of jokes he had picked up. With the exception of one girl, everybody curled up laughing. 'What's the matter?' grumbled the boss. 'Haven't you got a sense of humour?' 'I don't have to laugh,' replied the girl. 'I'm leaving on Friday.'

1111

In Honington, a family of live-wire gypsies rented a store and attracted business with a sign reading, 'FORTUNES TOLD: £1; PSYCHO-ANALYSIS: 75p EXTRA'.

1112

The mental hospital patient walked up to the new superintendent. 'We like you much better than the last fellow,' he said. The new official beamed. 'Why?' he asked. 'Oh, you seem more like one of us.'

1113

An art enthusiast was studying an exhibition wall in a gallery and admiring in particular the beautiful miniature portraits. Another man came in, dressed in a very off-beat fashion, and started muttering under his breath as he moved from picture to picture. The bigger chap said: 'What's the matter? Don't you like these little masterpieces?' The bearded one replied: 'Huh, these little daubs leave me cold. I prefer the great big landscapes and seascapes that take up enormous canvas space . . .' 'Oh,' said the enthusiast, 'are you a *well-known* art critic?' 'No,' replied the other man, 'I'm a frame-maker.'

1114

Way out there in Hawaii the cult of the super-mini grass skirt has arrived with a vengeance. There's an enormous factory in Honolulu making them from shredded wheat.

1115

Medicine has made vast strides over the centuries but just the same when you're suffering from a common cold you're beyond medical help.

1116

Alfred has what you might call green fingers. He got them from smoking chlorophyllated menthol cigarettes.

1117

It was so hot in Cannes that year, visitors were eating bread rolls and sipping the butter through a straw.

1118

Cadburys are now feeding their dairy cows with chucky eggs to produce instant custard.

1119

George took all his five hundred pounds savings last summer and went to an Italian coastal hotel to get away from it all. The hotel took it all away from him.

1120

On a cruise around the islands he was very excited when he saw a lovely mermaid sprawled on a rock. The first time he'd ever seen a topless dress on a bottomless woman.

1121

Cyril was exploring virgin territory about four thousand miles up the Amazon when he ran out of food. Then he spied a little hut outside which a scrawny savage Indian was making himself some flat cakes. He bargained with the Indian and received four of the unappetising Yam pancakes in exchange for two Confederate Army silver dollars. He had gone on about four miles when he heard the Indian running after him, so he stopped and waited. 'Hey,' said the native, pushing something into his hand, 'You forgot your Green Shield stamps.'

1122

When they posted Private Collins to Combined Services Headquarters, he didn't like the uniform. It consisted of bell-bottom khaki trousers, a flying jacket, a camouflaged anorak, rope-soled white deck pumps, a striped jerkin and a busby.

1123

A poor Cockney boy who became a self-made millionaire decided to go back one day to have a look at his old school and revive memories. He came back with a terrific headache—all the pupils had welcomed him by banging their tin mugs against the bars.

1124

A girl went to her local police station and complained that every night when she went home from the public house where she worked as a relief barmaid, a strange man chased her down a long dark alley. The desk sergeant said: 'What makes you think this man is strange?' She told him: 'Well, every time I slow down, so does he.'

1125

An aggressive half-back was playing away one Saturday and became very upset when two of his goals were disallowed. At half time he went over to the referee and said: 'Say, ref, don't you think you should get yourself some glasses?' The other man said: 'Okay, and you'd better come along with me, because I'm only selling salted peanuts.'

1126

The psychiatrist said to his new patient, who seemed very ill-at-ease: 'Relax now, and just lie there on the couch. We'll soon find out what makes you tick.' The patient said: 'I don't really mind about the ticking, but I get worried when I chime the half-hours.'

1127

The magistrate said to the girl: 'Frankly I don't quite understand what you and your boy friend were doing in the park at eleven o'clock at night.' The girl said: 'We was just communin' with nature.' Said the magistrate: 'In pitch darkness?' The prosecuting officer said: 'It was a car park, your honour.'

1128

Thieves broke into a toothpaste factory and stole half a million tubes of toothpaste. They sold it to a receiver for £25,000: £50 for the paste and the rest for the lead.

1129

Young Lady Cynthia said sternly to her butler: 'Hawkins, take off my dress,' and he reluctantly did so. She then said: 'Hawkins, take off my tights;' which he did. 'And now,' said the heiress, 'take off my bra.' The butler did so. Lady Cynthia then said: 'Thank you; and if I catch you wearing them again, you're fired!'

1130

Able-Seaman Bert Wryken was shipwrecked on a lonely Pacific island. But Bert wasn't lonely because there were three young stewardesses and three young cruise hostesses living on the island; the victims of an earlier disaster off the reef. Then one day as the group lay on the golden sands under the palm trees drinking coconut milk and eating bananas, they saw a bedraggled man struggling through the sea and realised that another castaway was arriving. Bert got up, waded into the sea and helped the exhausted victim ashore. The stranger blew out a mouthful of plankton and breathed: 'Thanks, duckie! You've no idea how I've suffered in that nasty old ocean.' Thought Bert, morosely: 'There goes my day off.'

1131

A bearded explorer just back from a ten-months journey up the Amazon in a single-seater outrigged native *kakruk* was interviewed at Heathrow by a TV reporter. He said: 'By tonight I hope to be back with my loved ones. And at the weekend I hope to get home to my wife and kids.'

1132

On the outskirts of our town the publicans serve spirits so weak that anyone can drink two bottles of sub-bourbon without feeling any effect until the landlord asks for the money.

1133

George is such a nerveless, intrepid character. When he read somewhere that most accidents are caused on the road and in the home he went straight out and bought a motorised caravan.

1134

Speaking of accidents it is not widely known that most of them are caused by the young. Which is only fair considering that most of the young are caused by accident.

1135

God invented mothers-in-law. Which shows how farce-sighted He was.

1136

My neighbour has a great deal of personal drive. It takes him three minutes to reach his lock-up.

1137

When he is driving long distances alone he uses a road map. When his wife is with him he drives by ear.

1138

You could say that he is the world's most impatient driver. In any traffic jam he has a bigger snarl-up than any other motorist on the road.

1139

Then there's the cowardly bank robber: before he raided any bank he had to steel himself.

1140

We know a social worker who spends a great deal of his time talking to people behind bars. Especially Florrie and Pamela at the Duke of Wellington.

1141

A busy financier ambled into his local barbershop where the head cutter was famous for his voluble chatter. 'Shave or haircut?' inquired the barber as the tycoon seated himself. 'The shave, please,' replied the customer, 'today I don't have enough time to hear your haircut.'

1142

Our friend Jason went into a West End hairdressing saloon for a short back and sides. The operator gave him a style that was so short clipped Jason looked in the mirror, had a mild attack of apoplexy and snorted: 'What are you, a barber or a bloody Sioux Indian immigrant?'

Jokers
Wild

1143

A fat, bald-headed playboy, whose bulk rose above the bar, remarked to the glamorous blonde seated next to him: 'I'm not really as tall as this. I'm sitting on my wallet.'

1144

The solicitor objected to a lawyer calling the State's evidence 'tainted testimony'. His objection was sustained by the judge, before whom the case was tried. 'The testimony isn't tainted,' he declared.

' 'Tis,' replied the lawyer.

'Tain't,' shouted the judge.

1145

A man stopped at the vet's to collect the family puppy. When he reached home he told his wife, 'He can't have enjoyed the visit. He barked all the way home as if he was trying to tell me something.

'You're right,' she agreed. 'He was trying to tell you you brought the wrong dog home.'

1146

An evangelist was exhorting his hearers to flee the wrath to come. 'I warn you,' he thundered 'that there will be weeping and wailing and gnashing of teeth!'

At this point an old lady stood up.

'Sir,' she shouted, 'I have no teeth.'

'Madam,' roared the evangelist, 'teeth will be provided.'

1147

A man in Alaska was arrested for polygamy. He had a wife in Nome, another in Fairbanks and still another in Juneau. The judge looked at the culprit sternly, 'How could you do such a thing?'

Replied the man, 'Fast dog team.'

1148

The new play was a failure. After the first act, many left. At the end of the second, most of the others started out. A cynical critic as he rose from his aisle seat raised a restraining hand. 'Wait!' he commanded loudly. 'Women and children first!'

1149

Benny planned to take Stella surf-riding but he couldn't get the saddle on her.

1150

Some women who do not wish to have their ears pierced prefer to go to a political meeting and have them bored.

1151

A new patient consulted a wealthy Harley Street psychiatrist. The doctor said, 'Lie down on that couch and I'll ask you some questions.' The patient got on the couch. 'You'd better tell me your name, first,' said the psycho. The man said: 'I'm Harvey Strimbly-Carstairs, Lieutenant-Colonel, 23rd Infantry, Retired.' 'Oh,' said the psychiatrist, 'then get off the couch and lie on that groundsheet.'

1152

A survey taken last summer revealed that half the population of the United Kingdom were badly housed, undernourished and badgered by insufferable rules and regulations. Obviously it is time something was done about seaside boarding houses.

1153

We note that a certain Sunday newspaper complains that its circulation has dropped by 345,000. But so has the blood pressure of 345,000 former readers.

1154

His hair is so long it's fairly obvious that the last time he had a cut was when he was circumcised.

1155

A man who had trouble getting to sleep at night went to his doctor who handed him on to an expensive psychologist. The psychologist treated the patient for two months at five pounds a visit and finally came up with the solution. He told the man to stop his wife playing the trombone in bed.

1156

A national polling organisation has been finding out how much viewing the public does at night. They asked one citizen and he told them he viewed for about six hours. 'Which programmes?' inquired the interviewer. The man said: 'Oh, not TV. I'm a Peeping Tom.'

1157

A chap walked into Moss Brothers and asked if he could rent a pair of trousers. The salesman gave him a pair, the customer tore them apart down the middle, and walked out.

1158

She spent so much time crying on his shoulder that he ended up with rusted epaulettes.

1159

A country man raced anxiously to the village mission and asked the padre if he saved fallen women. The priest admitted that such was part of his duties, and the man said: 'Then hurry—my wife's tripped down the well.'

1160

Perkins urgently needed new clothes to smarten himself up for an unexpected interview so he went into a store and said to the manager 'Do you have any ready-mades ?' The manager called: 'Forward, Miss Allison.'

1161

One comedian had the audience in the palms of his hands: he had to get that stranglehold on him or else talk to himself.

1162

Anthropologists have been puzzled by the apparent shortage of village idiots in rural Britain. But how are they gonna get them back on the farm after they've been working in Whitehall all these years ?

1163

He was so stupid that when he joined a local razor gang he couldn't find anywhere to plug his in.

1164

Jones absconded with Smith's wife, but after a week he felt so guilty he sent Smith a £5 postal order as compensation. Smith sent him £4·75 change.

1165

A man went into the chemist's shop and asked for a strong bottle of tonic. Serving him, the assistant said: 'This'll put hair on your chest.' The customer grunted: 'Then give me a packet of razor blades as well. It's for the wife.'

1166

It wasn't much fun for Ken when he took Doris to see *Love Story* at the Essoldo Cinema. He spent most of the time holding her orange squashes and ice-creams while she wept.

1167

Said the vicar piously: 'Christmas is a time of great and enduring joy for all of God's two-legged creatures.'

An equally pious vegetarian, old Mrs. Talbot, stood up and remarked: 'Try telling that to a turkey.'

1168

On Christmas Eve, Bill told his wife with consummate cunning that he was just popping out to get a few more stocking fillers. Four hours later the police brought him home from an orgy.

1169

Dental surgeon Mr. Krazer had his patient leaning well back in the chair and was probing busily, examining molars and investigating canines. Suddenly he pulled the patients' mouth open wide and cried:

'Good heavens! Look at this! Tsk, tsk! I never saw anything like it. It must be the biggest cavity anyone ever had. Biggest cavity anyone ever had!'

The patient snapped: 'All right. All right. You don't have to repeat it.'

The dentist said: 'I didn't. That was the echo.'

1170

A wife caught her husband rooting through a large pile of vitaminized corn flakes which he had emptied out on to a large plate.

'What on earth!' she exploded. 'What did you want to do that for?'

He said: 'Look on the packet. It clearly says "this breakfast food provides absolutely everything you need for your daily requirements" —doesn't it?'

'So what?' she inquired.

'Well, I'm looking for some money.'

1171

It was a pretty dismal party and the husband badly wanted out. Suddenly, during a brief break in the intense conversation going on between several women he nudged his wife and whispered: 'Look, Annie, you've dropped one more name than any of them—how about quitting while you're ahead?'

1172

Dad was chastising his son and heir, a fourteen-year-old member of the contemporary super-race of the generation gap. 'All I can say is that I'm damn glad there were no teenagers when I was your age.'

1173

When she was putting her little six-year-old curly-headed angel to bed on Christmas Eve, Mrs. Hopkins noticed that the child had left a badly-wrapped cylindrical parcel hooked round the corner of the bed-board where she had hung her stocking. It was addressed to Santa.

'What's that, then?' inquired Mom, curiously.

The little girl said: 'Oh, it's just some anti-freeze. I don't want him to feel too cold and stiff to fill my stocking.'

1174

Someone has just invented a watch guaranteed to last a lifetime. When the mainspring disintegrates it slashes your wrist.

1175

When the geese were flying south for the winter one small-sized bird began to tire too quickly and panted to the goose ahead of him: 'Why do we always have to follow the same stupid leader?' Came the reply: 'He's the only one with navigational charts.'

1176

When the wife of a furniture manufacturer invited a friend over to have a look at the new range of garden furniture which was arrayed on the patio beside the swimming-pool, the other woman was so impressed with the design and exquisite quality of the new lines that she thought it sacrilege to leave the stuff outside in inclement weather. 'What on earth do you do if it rains?' she inquired. Her hostess said: 'Oh, we crawl under it.'

1177
Mr. Greene was pottering around in his front garden when his wife came ambling through the gate, a happy flush on her face and a large expensive-looking gift-wrapped package in her arms. She shouted: 'Hullo, love . . . I bet you thought you'd forgotten my birthday.'

1178
The wife of a best-selling author of white-hot passioned novels spends an hour every morning washing his typewriter out with carbolic soap.

1179
There's a millionaire living near Luton who won't have an alarm clock in his mansion. He hires a company to fly a super jet over the place at eight o'clock every morning at 1,200 m.p.h.

1180
A woman went into a bookstore and asked for a copy of *Childbirth Without Fear*. The salesgirl asked her: 'Have you had it recommended to you? I'm getting married myself next month and I wonder if it would help me.' The customer said: 'It's not for me, dear—it's for my husband.'

1181
Arnold thinks that convenience packaging is a crate for a lavatory basin.

1182
Labour relations get more and more complicated. Last week in Glamorganshire picketing miners employed unemployed machinists to do their picketing for them.

1183
A staggering line is the shortest distance between two joints?

1184
She's the sort of girl who doesn't mind what sort of a line you use on her as long as it's a supply line.

1185
A young blonde went with her kid sister to see the new young doctor in the village: when it was her turn to go in she warned the kid: 'Look, if I'm not out in ten minutes, break down the door.'

1186
A little boy came home from the Cubs and said to his mother: 'Ma,

what's a Lesbian?' His mother said: 'Don't ask me, darling, wait until your father comes home, and ask her.'

1187
Two's company, then three's accrued.

1188
True love is when billing and cooing becomes willing and doing.

1189
Martin's girl wears glasses, but she's so fashion conscious she has different glasses to match her clothes. When she wears a green summer dress, she puts on her green-framed specs; when she wears a red evening gown she puts on her red-framed glasses; when she's wearing a brown tweed costume she puts on her tortoise-shell glasses. Tonight—she says she'll wear her rimless bifocals.

1190
Horace was in a new musical called 'Pedro the Bullfighter' and one night while he was singing the part where the bull is waiting to be demolished, the animal suddenly rushed him and gored him in the middle of his aria . . . Now he's singing mezzo-soprano at the Valencia Opera House.

1191
I've been a musician for years now but only now have I started making big money . . . Last night I was arrested. I was making the money half-an-inch too big.

1192
As we danced I said to this girl: 'Do you come here often?' and she said: 'Not any more. You just dislocated my hip.'

1193
There's a meticulous atomic scientist working at the new research station in Pafadigbrodeen in Scotland, trying to perfect a parachute for radioactive fall-out.

Conversion Tables

1194
By mistake the following conversion table was printed in an official document relating to the Common Market:
100 French francs converted into £7·50.
208 Jews converted to Methodism.
213 Christians converted to alcoholism.
21 Atheists converted to nudism.

65 Roman Catholics converted back to paganism.

105 Protestants converted to Catholicism, but under protest.

4 Britons converted to existentialism.

1 Briton converted into a sabre-toothed salmon by a Congolese witch doctor.

319 Vegetarians converted to weight watchers (2 died).

28 Cannibals converted to vegetarianism (27 died. One cheated).

1195

A Cuban embassy official from London fled to Russia and asked for political asylum. The Russian authorities told him 'Our political asylum is full; you'll have to go to some other hospital.'

1196

My uncle in Wales has just been made the new Bard. He's been barred from every pub and club in Glamorgan.

1197

The last time Shortie Smith played guitar at the Folk Club all the girls screamed and screamed. There was a rat loose in the auditorium.

1198

Tom Jones, millionaire, ex-miner, vocalist, was driving home one night in one of his Rolls Royces when he ran into a thick mist. So he put his hand up to his helmet and switched on his headlamp.

1199

Ill never go to a Chinese restaurant again. I went to one yesterday run by a Jewish Chinaman named Isadore Moses Tu Ling. Before I was allowed to order my meal I had to name my next of kin.

1200

I wish I'd never taken that new flat in the new high-rise block they built in our town. One day last week I couldn't get up to my flat. It was so foggy the elevators were grounded.

Railways

1201

At the next station I got out and changed carriages and just as I sat down and the train began to move off I noticed a commotion had been going on in the door for several seconds. People were pulling and tugging at a fat old man who was jammed in the doorway. Finally they managed to drag him aboard and slam the door closed. Then the fat man yelled: 'You stupid lot of dumb fools . . . I was trying to get OFF.'

1202

I asked the porter if he could tell me the times of the return trains. I said: 'I'd prefer a late train if possible,' and he said: 'You pick one yourself, mister—all our trains are late.'

1203

I remember the time I was in a railway accident. The train was coming towards a tunnel and I'd noticed a lovely young blonde sitting opposite me, next to a stern old man who looked like her father. When the train went into the tunnel I leaned over and kissed the beautiful girl on her ruby lips . . . and that was how the accident happened . . . just before I leaned across, the girl had changed places with her old man.

1204

The porter told me that the train on Platform 4 was going to Chesterfield in five minutes. I waited for the slow train—I don't mind speed, but London to Chesterfield in 5 minutes . . .

1205

Woman to booking office clerk: One single.
Booking Clerk: You'll have to pay for that child, madam.
Woman: Nonsense. My baby is only 3 years old.
Clerk: He looks more like 13 to me.
Woman: Can I help it if he worries about the state of the world?
Clerk: Oh, well, I'll stand for it this time. One single to Birkenhead. Eight pounds fifty pence.
Woman: What? The fare should only be two pounds.
Clerk: Well it's like this lady; the station-master has been messing around with my wife, so I'm messing around with his railway, see?

1206

The train stopped at a station and a porter came along the platform to assure everyone that it was just an intermediate stop which would only be for a second or two. Unfortunately when he came to my carriage he sneezed long and loud and awakened a man who was asleep in the corner. The porter sneezed again, and the man jumped to his feet, grabbed his suitcase off the rack and dived off the train. The porter called him back and explained about the stop being unofficial. The man said: 'Blimey, I thought you shouted out Llanfairfechan twice.'

1207

She walked into the butchers shop and said to the man behind the counter: 'Do you keep dripping?' He said: 'No, not since I had it fixed.'

1208

She was considered so sexy, the birds and the bees used to tell their offspring about her.

1209

When she began to feel she was looking older she decided to have beauty treatment to prevent her looking like a little old woman. After the course she looked much different—she looked like a little old man.

1210

We recently traced the origin of the expression, 'Hurrah for our side!' back to the crowds lining the streets when Lady Godiva made her famous ride sidesaddle through the streets of Coventry.

1211

The couple stepped up to the desk clerk of one of the city's nicer hotels. 'I'd like a room and bath for my wife and myself,' said the gentleman. 'I'm terribly sorry, sir,' said the clerk, 'but the only room available doesn't have bathroom facilities.' 'Will that be all right with you, dear?' the gentleman asked the young lady at his side. 'Sure, mister,' she said.

1212

A man knocked on the door of an apartment, calling to see his girl friend. The door was answered by another tall, dark man, wearing nothing but a pair of briefs. 'I'm terribly, sorry,' stuttered the caller. 'I hope you won't get the wrong idea about me and your wife.' 'Idiot,' said the other man. 'The fool's still on that business trip.' And slammed the door with a smile.

1213

He only made the long trip out to the Australian bush because he'd been told it was virgin territory.

1214

A young recruit in the pits was sent down to the chief ganger. The overlord asked him: 'Now see here, son, I know you're fresh from school and have always been at home until now, but this is a dangerous job down here and you have to have your wits about you. First off, do you know the Gas Regulations?' Said the boy: 'Well, I know it's Mark 4 for toad-in-the-hole.'

1215

A young son of a very rich man was summoned for the offence of riding his bicycle without lights. The boy's father was digusted by all the press publicity, so he hired a very expensive lawyer who charged him £100. The solicitor briefed counsel, in sheer determination to get the boy's case dismissed; the barrister charged £250 and insisted on pre-payment. Because of the rich man's determination, the case was fought to the bitter end, running into several days. The boy was found guilty, so the rich man appealed. The appeal failed. The bill now ran close to £15,000. So the man made his solicitor go to the High Court. The High Court case ran for about a fortnight, and in his closing speech the defending counsel said: 'This unfortunate youth had suffered several disappointments on the day of the alleged offence; he had had an argument with his girl friend; he had broken his guitar; he had been told that he had failed his examinations; his mother had run off with his father's accountant; and to top it all, someone at the local coffee bar had stolen his month's pocket-money. I put it to you that there were mitigating circumstances, not the least of which is the fact that the poor boy was not concentrating on his actions. When the constable stopped him on the road, he was frightened out of his wits.' Despite this impassioned plea, the High Court upheld the earlier decision and the boy was found guilty and his fine increased to £15, plus costs, which now amounted to £25,000. After the case, the boy and his father were chatting to the defence counsel and the rich man said: 'Ah, well, we fought it to the bitter end. At least we didn't let the authorities off the hook too easily. I'm sure you did your best, Sir William.' Then the boy said: 'But, Dad, what I can't understand is why we didn't just tell the truth. That when the fuzz pulled me up on the lane, it was eleven o'clock, and broad daylight.'

1216

If they really wanted to stop smoking in the cinema they should stop screening 'X' movies.

1217

A Hell's Angel adherent out on a rampage attacked a man coming out of the cinema, just for kicks. The Angel was beaten almost to death by the victim. Rejoining the gang, and asked to explain away his bruises and weals, the Angel said: 'Well, I'd have done the old codger if he hadn't fought dirty.' The gang asked for more details. 'Well, I'd have put bofe boots in if 'e 'adn't hit me wiv his crutch.'

1218

A multi-millionaire was at a Charity Ball in Park Lane when his companions started boasting about the gifts they were buying their kids for Christmas. One said he was getting his beautiful young daughter a mink wrap as a surprise. Another claimed he was buying his eldest son an E-type Jaguar. A third topped this by boasting that he was going to give his step-daughter a winter cruise. So when they asked the multi-millionaire what he was going to get for his only son, Leopold, he answered: 'Oh, I'm getting him a chemistry outfit.' A woman smiled and said knowingly, 'I bet it'll be one of the biggest on the market.' The man said: 'Maybe. They don't come much bigger than I.C.I.'

1219

What walks across the wet sand at low tide and leaves yellow footprints: A lemon sole.

1220

Anxious Modern Mom: 'Willie, if you eat any more you'll explode like an atom bomb!' Willie: 'Shove that cake over here, and start the sirens.'

1221
Teacher: How many bones do you have in your body?
Basil: Oh, about three thousand and twenty-two.
Teacher: That's ridiculous. *I've* only got about a hundred.
Basil: Yes, but you didn't have two kippers for your breakfast.

1222
A man went to his bank manager and said that he had a wonderful new invention and needed a £5,000 loan to launch the venture. The manager was dubious until the customer said that he had found a way to mass produce good quality fat turkeys with eight legs, and that the business was cast-iron. He also promised to repay the loan within six months. The bank manager was duly impressed by the thought of eight-legged oven-ready Xmas turkeys and loaned the man the £5,000. About eight months later the banker became worried as no money was repaid. He visited the new turkey farm and sure enough the place was crammed with enormous plump turkeys all with great fat edible legs—eight each. He said to the customer: 'With all these turkeys ready for market —about seven thousand I reckon—you ought to be able to repay the loan easily.' The customer said: 'Well, there are actually nine thousand birds, but I can't repay the loan because of a slight snag . . . I can't catch the perishers!'

1223
In Belfast a little man walked into the local pub and ordered a pint of beer. He cried: 'When I drink—everybody drinks.' There was a stampede for the bar. Then the man put down the exact money for his pint. He shouted: 'When I pay—everybody pays,' and ran out.

1224
Two Americans were sitting in a café and saw an old man having tea. They argued whether or not he was the Archbishop of Canterbury. Eventually they decided to settle the matter with a bet. The first American went over to the old man's table to ask him. Seconds later he returned and sat down again. 'Well,' said the second American, 'What did he say?' Replied the first, 'He said I was an inquisitive slob and told me to go and drown myself.' 'What a pity,' said the second; 'Now we'll never know!'

1225
A prisoner in efforts to reduce monotony and retain his sanity, patiently trained a little ant to dance, sing and recite Longfellow. On his release he took his performing ant to a top theatrical agent to demonstrate his 10-year-old prodigy. Placing the insect on the table, he pointed to it and said 'What do you make of *that*?' The agent smashed his fist on the ant and said: 'Yeah, we get a lot of those little pests this time of year.'

1226
Two army officers were standing in a bar ordering three glasses of

scotch, drinking one each and putting the third on the floor only to bring it up seconds later empty. Unable to contain himself, the barman looked over and saw a third officer only $7\frac{1}{2}$ inches high. 'Good Lord,' said the barman, 'how on earth, did you get as small as that?' One of the officers looked down and said, 'Go on Cruthers tell him about that time in Nairobi when you called the witch-doctor a black-faced twit.'

1227

During a particularly severe winter the chief of an Eskimo village insisted that all the fishing was to be done by the man who happened to be the best fisherman. He didn't mind too much because the job had its perks. What bothered him was the extreme cold. He hit on an idea. He took a pile of twigs, placed it on the bottom of his canoe and lit it. This warmed him but also burned out the bottom of the canoe. It sank and he was drowned. The moral of the story is: 'You can't have your kyak and heat it'.

1228

The new immigrant family did not know the local drill about putting out the dustbins on Wednesday morning. So when the dustman called he knocked on the door. 'Where's yer bin,' asked the dustman. 'I's bin in the bath, man, where's yo bin?' asked Mrs. Sovocobo.

1229

'Let's go and buy a pub,' said one drunk to another. 'I don't know,' said the other, 'You have to put up with a lot from customers.' 'Who said anything about customers.'

1230

A large orchestra on a world tour visited a number of African states and the flute player, who suffered from insomnia, used to stroll through the jungle and admire the scenery by moonlight. One particular night a lion jumped in his path. Without quick action he would have been devoured. His mind worked overtime and he whipped out his flute and commenced to play. The lion stopped and sat and listened to the music. The airs and strains of beautiful music wafted through the jungle and pretty soon every type of bird, animal and insect were sitting in an enthralled circle around the flute player. Then a large jaguar walked into the circle, went straight up to the musician and with one blow killed him stone dead. The lion was enraged. 'What did you do *that* for?' he snarled. The jaguar put a paw to his ear and said; 'Eh? Wassat?'

1231

A ritzy restaurant famous for its massive menu promised that if anyone ordered a meal they could not provide they would pay the customer £20. There were many people trying to beat the restaurant but none was successful. 'A crocodile omelette,' one diner requested. He got it. 'I'll have an Algerian glacht salad,' said another. He got it. Then someone said: 'I'll have a round of elephant sandwiches.' There was turmoil in the kitchens, and the waiter came back, red in the face. 'I'm sorry,' he said, 'we can't do it. We've run out of bread.'

1232

A man was sitting in the middle of Oxford Street making all the actions of rowing a boat. A policeman went over to him and said: 'What do you think you're doing?' 'Rowing a boat,' was the reply. 'I don't see you with any boat,' said the policeman. The man stopped rowing, looked around and said 'Oh.' And started swimming.

1233

The new arrival was bragging that with his experience he could make any animal do anything he wanted. Said a tough docker: 'A fiver says you can't make *my* dog do anything.' The braggard accepted the wager, picked up the dog, walked across the pub and threw him on the fire. 'Get off,' he ordered, sharply.

1234

The new golf club recruit had astonished all the members by doing the course in fifty. Not only that, his choice of clubs was between a broom, a walking stick and an umbrella. When asked why, he replied: 'All my life I have been naturally good at sports so I prefer to do everything the hard way.' They bought him a whisky and he tossed the contents of the glass high into the air, did one back flip, two somersaults and landed on his back with his mouth open in time to catch the whisky. 'See what I mean,' he said. Then someone asked him if he was married. 'Yes,' he said. 'And in anticipation of your next question—on roller skates, standing up in a hammock.'

1235

An international gourmet thought he had tried everything, until he heard about 'poy'. Apparently, this could only be found in an Amazonian village. For months he travelled until he eventually found the village far up the Amazon. But unfortunately this dish 'poy', was only served on May 13th. He waited patiently until the great day arrived. Going to the nearest eating place, he expectantly ordered a large helping of 'poy'. 'Yes sir,' said the waiter, 'Which sort—apple poy, cherry poy, meat poy or blackcurrant poy . . . ?'

1236

A local dance hall ran a prize competition every Friday night. Eight completely nude girls assembled on the stage: Some were facing, and some had their backs to the audience. The object was to guess what music the tableau portrayed. It went on for weeks with the prize money mounting up and then at last, a little chap jumped up one night and shouted 'It's the William Tell Overture!' 'Correct,' said the M.C. 'How did you figure it out?' 'Well,' said the winner, 'I was sitting there with tunes running through my mind and it suddenly struck me . . . Tiddy-bum-tiddy-bum-tiddy-bum-bum-bum . . .'

1237

The learner driver stalled at the crossroads. The lights kept changing . . .
Red . . . Amber . . . Green . . . Amber . . . Red and so on. After several
minutes the driver behind called out: 'What's the matter, dear? Isn't
there a colour you like?'

1238

The vicar was well known for his fondness for alcohol but he did his
best to keep it a secret. A woman sent him a case of cherry brandy, on
condition that he announced it in church on Sunday morning. When
it came to the Notices, the Vicar quietly announced: 'I wish to thank
Mrs. Jones for her gift of fruit and the spirit in which it was given.'

1239

A bankrupt man tried to destroy himself. He went to a cliff which
overlooked a hundred feet drop, tied a rope to a tree and put the other
end around his neck. As he jumped he pointed a gun at his head and
drank a bottle of poison. Unfortunately, he had taken so long with his
preparations he had not noticed that the tide had come in. The shot
from the gun severed the rope. He dropped into the salt water which
broke his fall and made him sick. If he hadn't been a good swimmer—
he could have drowned.

1240

Three Irishmen walked into a pub and one went straight to the bar.
'Oi'm ordering three points of moild, two loight and bitters, four
brown ales, six lagers and a double whisky . . . What's you two having?'

1241

During the early part of the Arab-Israel War the one and only Israeli
submarine had penetrated the Suez Canal. 'Up periscope,' called the
captain, 'Egyptian cruiser—1,000 yards.' They continued sailing to
get a better position. 'Up periscope,' called the captain. 'Egyptian
cruiser—800 yards.' This is it thought the crew. 'Up periscope,' called
the captain. 'Egyptian cruiser—600 yards.' Once again the sub moved
on. 'Up periscope,' called the captain, 'Egyptian cruiser—300 yards.'
Ensign Cohen could stand it no longer. 'Please captain,' he pleaded,
'Fire a torpedo—*I'll* pay for it.'

1242

The twins had been told of the coming of a new baby. As it was due
near their birthday, mother, along with the facts of life, had also
built it up as her additional birthday present to them. The baby did
arrive on their birthday and was much loved. Came the next year, and
the mother asked the twins what they wanted for a present. They
didn't know, so she gave them time to think it over. They came back
and said: 'If it wouldn't be too much for you do you, think you could
manage a pony this year, instead?'

1243

A magician doing the celebrated trick of sawing a woman in half always used a lot of inane patter. The girl was extremely lovely and her shape was encased in a very clinging little swimsuit. As he began the trick the magician said to the audience: 'After the show, this young lady's brain will be presented to the medical world, and the rest of her will not be wasted, it will be thrown to the dogs.' Immediately every man in the front row started to bark.

1244

A man came to the surgery covered with blood and bruises. 'What's the matter?' said the doctor. 'It's my wife. Another of her nightmares!' 'Don't talk silly man! She might have kicked you, but not these injuries . . .' 'Listen, she had one of her nightmares, and shouted: "Get out quick, my husband's coming home" and me being only half awake, I jumped straight out of the window.'

1245

Thirty years after the war, two ex-Gestapo prisoners were released from jail, and the prison psychiatrist assured the parole board that the two men were completely tamed and fit to mix with normal people. The two ex-officers did indeed show signs of improvement because they bought a piece of land and began to breed pigs. But one day a party of do-gooders, keen to assist ex-jailbirds, decided to visit the pig farm to see how the two Germans were coping in their new career. They were shown around the farm by one of the Gestapo men and eventually came to one of the modern breeding pens. Inside they found the other Gestapo man with a whip in his hand; two spotlights aimed at three little pigs cowering in a corner. The man lashed out with the whip and with a maniacal leer on his face snarled: 'Ve haf vays of making you pork!'

1246

He was making good time with a very pretty creature he bumped into at a bar in Sunderland. Quite an intelligent girl, and not easy to shoot a line to. But she was such a good looker and had such a wonderful southern aspect that he wolfed on. After an hour or so, and ten gins, the girl said: 'You sure do work hard at it, mister! You don't fool me, though, I've been around more than a revolving door. The next thing you'll tell me is that your wife doesn't understand you?' He said: 'Let's be frank. My wife understands me alright. It's just that she's fat, ugly, unpleasant, old and frigid.'

1247

His wife installed a robot answering device to her telephone for when she went shopping. The recording starts off: 'This is Calthorpe 297, Mrs. Jones is out, and your message is being recorded. Start your rumour now . . .'

1248

Nuclear fission is the difference between what's right and what's left. A Martian landed on Earth after an arduous three-months' trip from outer space. Looking rather despondent and deprived he knocked on the door of a big house. A man answered the door, looked in astonishment at the Martian, recognised the situation and said: 'My God! Do you want me to take you to our Leader?' The Martian said: 'Yes. But first, take me to your sister.'

1249

Married British men are usually disillusioned with their lot when they visit Ireland and see all those gorgeous naturally lovely girls. They return home; greet the wife at the door with an aloof, 'Hullo, George.'

1250

At the local sports meeting yesterday in Brinstead, a young runner named Fred Tookes accidentally backed into the tip of a javelin and won the 5,000 metres in record time.

1251

Useless Information Department. A report in the *Sporting World Weekly* gives the result of a probe into the popularity of different soccer referees. One strange fact to emerge was that 80 per cent of them appear to have been born out of wedlock, according to football fans.

1252

A new Irish bricklayer happened to be late for work for the third morning running and the foreman was starting to get irritated, so he said to the chief surveyor: 'Murphy's late again. He should have been on the job an hour ago.' Said the other man: 'P'raps he's still on the job—back home.'

1253

A drunk was driving the wrong way along a one-way street late at night and complained to his colleague: 'Here, we must be very late—everyone's coming back already'.

1254

A friend of mine up north is one of those contemporary painters who uses the action-painting technique. He smothers nude girls with different coloured oils, and presses them against the canvas. Last night I wrote a letter telling him I wasn't interested in his artwork, but I offered him a good price for some of his old paintbrushes.

1255

Passing one of those florists' shops I noticed the sign 'Say It With Flowers' so I went in and ordered a cheap bunch of violets to be sent to my girl friend. The assistant said: 'You're a mean cuss, ain't you?' and I said: 'No, we only whisper sweet nothings to each other'.

1256

Me and the girl were having a heated argument, so I said to her: 'But put yourself in my place . . .' and half an hour later we were there.

1257

One of my associates was taking his darling fiancée window shopping prior to the wedding and as they stood admiring a well polished set of bedroom furniture she said: 'And to think they made all that out of lots and lots of crinkly little walnuts'.

1258

Last week I was wandering down The Lanes in Brighton where all the antique shops are and outside of one of them I noticed a sign: 'Step Inside and Buy What Your Grandmother Threw Out'. So I went inside and the first thing I saw was Grandad.

1259

Barbara's old man bought her a bubble car for her 21st birthday and she was so proud of it she washed it down every day with a watering can. One evening a man watched her as he passed by and inquired: 'How long does it take to grow them to full size?'

1260

Did you hear about the proud father, taking breakfast with his small daughter and trying to encourage her to eat? 'Nelly,' he said, 'eat up your damned cereal—do you want to grow into a lousy fashion model?'

1261

The Bishop decided to send personal letters to the county's more influential citizens in an appeal for help because nearly all his houses of worship were in need of rebuilding, re-roofing or repair. One of the letters was to the village doctor in Mushford, and read: '. . . so, I trust, dear doctor, that you might consider doing something to alleviate the distress that my derelict tabernacles are causing me'. Back came the taut reply: 'Dear Bishop, there is nothing I can do until I give you a personal examination, so please 'phone for an appointment'.

1262

Have you ever been to a barn dance? The night I went to my first barn dance, the caller yelled: 'Take your partners' and I was half way up the stairs with mine when they dragged us both back.

1263

I've had a very hard life. In fact I was left on a doorstep when I was frail and helpless . . . That was the first time I ever got blind drunk. Our family doctor suggested treatment, so I went to an alcoholic clinic where they fed you gallons and gallons of hard liquor until you got absolutely sick of the stuff. The cure wasn't much good, but, oh boy, the treatment!

1264

At the start of the cruise to the West Indies, a fluffy young blonde asked the purser: 'Who is responsible for all the berths on board?' The purser said, 'The captain, miss.' She said: 'Okay, put me in with him'.

1265

A nervous young man, intent on buying his girl friend something for her birthday went into a luxurious West End store and said to one assistant, a comely wench of ample proportions: 'Have you got anything new in bikinis?' The assistant said: 'No, just the same old thirty-eights and don't get so fresh'.

1266

Dad had been nursing the baby all night; pacing up and down while the poor infant cried in pain over his shoulder. At five a.m. Dad slapped his wife awake and complained. 'Oh,' she said, annoyed at being awakened, 'just go and get some soothing syrup.' So he pushed the kid into her arms and went downstairs and poured himself half a bottle of Scotch liqueur.

1267

Kleinman committed suicide after his factory went bankrupt. The coroner asked his wife if she could offer any evidence as to his state of mind. She said: 'Not really, but as he was always shouting that the business had gone to hell, maybe he just went after it.'

1268

He was so conceited and thought himself so smart he bought a set of *Encyclopaedia Britannica* just to go through and pick out all the mistakes.

1269

A disappointed man, stranded on a lonely road with a car which had developed about ninety serious defects after twenty miles went to a nearby house and asked permission to use the 'phone to call the car showroom. When he was connected he said to the salesman: 'Remember that car you sold to Mr. Dickson this morning—the new model?' 'Yes,' said the salesman, 'are you ringing to say how pleased you are with it?' 'No,' said Dickson, 'I'm ringing to tell you it's reverted to kit form, and I'm stuck out here twenty miles away without the diagram that shows which part goes where.'

1270

'What happened after you were thrown out of the side exit on your face?' 'I told the usher I belonged to a very important family.' 'So what?' 'He begged my pardon, asked me in again and threw me out of the front door.'

1271

A very valuable dachshund, owned by a wealthy woman, was run over.

The policeman detailed a man to tell the woman of her misfortune. 'But break the news gently,' he said, 'She thinks a lot of this dog.' The man rapped on the mansion door and, when the woman appeared, he said: 'Sorry, lady, but part of your dog has been run over.'

1272
Fred met his mother-in-law going down the street with a duck under her arm. 'Hey! Where are you going with that pig?' 'It's not a pig, it's a duck.' 'I'm talking to the duck.'

1273
Two cowboys out riding, came across an Indian with his ear to the ground. 'What's up Indian?' 'Half hour ago stage coach pass here, three white horses, one black, four passengers, driver and much luggage. It go at great speed.' 'That's fantastic! How did you know that?' 'It run over me.'

1274
'Does your mother drink?' 'Drink! When she makes Scotch broth she uses real Scotch.'

1275
A Jewish businessman was knocked down by a 'bus. An innocent bystander ran to the scene of the accident, removed his overcoat, placed it over the man and asked if he was comfortable. 'Of course I'm comfortable, I've got five betting shops.'

1276
'I say, waiter, the flowers on this table are artificial, aren't they?' Yes, sir. That's the worst of running a vegetarian restaurant—if we use real flowers, the customers eat them.'

1277
Teacher was telling her class little stories in natural history, and she asked if anyone could tell her what a ground-hog was. Up went a little hand, waving frantically. 'Well, Carl, you may tell us what a ground-hog is.' 'Please, ma'am, it's a pork sausage.'

1278
'Hello, Dr. Banyan? Yes? Come right away. My husband has another one of his terrible spells.' 'Why didn't you send for me sooner?' said the doctor half an hour later, 'You should not have waited till your husband was unconscious.' 'Well,' replied the wife, 'as long as he had his senses, he wouldn't let me send for you.'

1297
Phyllis lacked any professionalism but spent a lot of time writing novels. One submission was sent to a disgruntled publisher who wrote back with the rejected manuscript of some 80,000 words and com-

plained: 'Your handwriting is so illegible that I'm damned if I'm going to waste hours trying to decipher it, so I suggest that you rewrite the whole book in typescript and let us have another look at it in due course.' Phyllis angrily telephoned him and said: 'Do you think I'd waste *my* time writing books if I could type?'

1280
A well-known young author hired himself the most luscious young blonde secretary. One evening the author's wife was taking her hard-working husband a slurp of Scotch and soda, and she found the door to his den locked. She banged, and the secretary shouted through the door 'Go away. Your husband is creating.' The wife called back: 'Oh, is he—well stop it, the pair of you, and get back to the book.'

1281
A report in a theatrical newspaper stated: 'At the celebration party given by the producer of 'East Wind, West Wind' at the Criterion Arts Centre on Thursday, among the most sensual showgirls was Leonard Henry Parkin, who wrote the music.' How lucky can you get?

1282
Everyone knows the legend of Sir Walter Raleigh's courtesy, but few people know about the little incident which occurred behind the scenes on the occasion when the bold knight saved his Queen's feet from getting soaked by laying down his cloak across a muddy puddle. As soon as Queen Bess placed her dainty size sixes on the garment someone in the watching crowd fainted clean away. A bystander inquired: 'Was the poor old fellow overcome by the sheer chivalry of Walt's gesture?' 'No,' said the other man, 'it's the tailor who made the cloak, and Walt hasn't paid for it, yet.'

1283
A young wife known for her meanness lay in a maternity hospital in Glasgow, recovering from the birth of her first son. When her husband visited her, they decided to get the news to the girl's mother who lived in Bournemouth and was not on the telephone. To save an expensive telegram the girl wrote out a message for her husband to transmit. Two hours later, in Bournemouth, grandma studied the telegram and frowned at the simple words: 'Isaiah 9:6, love Mollie and Ted'. Which, interpreted, meant 'Unto us a child is given, unto us a son is born'. Grandma said to herself: 'Fancy that, I suppose Mollie means that she's had the baby and it weighs nine stone six ounces, but why the hell do they want to call him Isaiah!'

1284
Now that the Stock Exchange is accepting the idea of women members we can look forward to a very interesting development. While the men deal with the bulls and bears, the women can handle the stags and rams.

1285

I'll say there's inflation! The Chiltern Hundreds are now worth six-fifty.

1286

The Building Societies are so flush with investment money, one of their high-pressure salesmen now goes around the bingo halls and when anyone shouts 'House', he offers an immediate mortgage.

1287

This yarn will explain how legends are born and myths created. For years a marine explorer investigated a local story that there was a scarifying monster living in the ocean just off the Seychelles. Natives had told him, goggle-eyed, about the old legend of a big ship that had been wrecked off the island by this fantastically enormous beast, and the story had been embellished over the decades during which intrepid biologists had sought the monster of the deep. Then one day a very old English settler, an inveterate drinker, was chatting to the marine explorer in the island's only hotel, and the subject of the sea monster came up again. 'Corrr,' drooled the drunken man, 'S'terrible, I tell you. Makes me shudder to think of it, even now. Yessir! 'Orrible! Just imagine the sight, mister . . . rearin' up outa the sea in that force-12 gale . . . heavin' about . . . her great back shudderin' in the wind . . . God! Eight hundred feet . . . sixty-four hands . . .' The professor said: 'This monster has eight hundred feet? Sixty-four hands? You must be exaggerating?' 'Monster?' repeated the drunken ex-patriate, 'What monster? I'm talkin' about the *Santa Fernando*: You must've heard the story—went down off the island in 1720 . . . sank eight hundred feet with the loss of the captain an' sixty-four hands . . .'

1288

American advertising executives were stumped for a firm manufacturing chastity belts. One keen new executive came up with an idea, and got sacked. 'Nobody Loves a Fairy When She's Fortified.'

1289

They're very cruel at London Zoo. I was visiting there last week and heard an elephant trumpeting. Then some nosy old zoo-keeper came up to the elephant and took the trumpet off him and gave it back to the kid who'd lost it.

1290

I dropped in on Ken yesterday and he poured me a drink from a freshly-opened bottle and then downed the rest of the liquor in one swig. 'What's the hurry?' I asked him. 'I wanna make a reading lamp,' he said.

1291

While serving hot new potatoes from the vegetable platter to a young woman dining in the restaurant, the waiter accidentally dropped two of the small spuds down the unfortunate female's decolletage, which happened to be fairly expansive. Quick as a flash, the waiter picked up a spoon and spooned out the offending veg. while the poor girl shrieked with pain. The captain grabbed the waiter and rushed him to the office. 'Perkins,' he snapped, 'you have been with the hotel long enough to know better! *Next* time, warm the spoon before you use it.'

1292

Unexpectedly, her husband came home having missed the night train. His wife, looking very embarrassed, realised her husband was suspicious as soon as he entered the bedroom. She said with nervous coyness: 'Oh, a man came to see you, and I asked him to wait.' Hubby said: 'Oh. All right. Is he in the library?' She said, pointing. 'No, he's in the wardrobe.'

1293

While dancing at the club last week I happened to notice that one girl, who was a dark brunette, was wearing a blonde wig. I went over to her to have a bit of fun, and said: 'Julia, I'd know you anywhere. You really ought to go and put on some clothes.'

1294

Two Scots boys in kilts were walking down the road when they were overtaken by two monks wearing long habits. One Scot said to the other: 'Here, I wonder if they wear anything under them?' 'I doubt it,' replied the other—'black one's would be too sexy for the Order.'

1295

Woman went to the police to report her husband missing. The helpful policeman asked for a description. Said the forsaken wife: 'Well, he's about five-foot three, bald-headed, with a large paunch, close-set eyes, a drooping chin, sloppy ears, always got a cigarette end stuck on his lower lip, smells like a disused brewery, has large flat feet and . . . oh, forget it!'

1296

The Bishop was invited to dinner by a wealthy property shark in Westminster whose apartment was a spacious penthouse with art treasures all over the walls. Pinups cut from *Playboy*. Mine host said 'Now how about a good stiff whisky for a start, my Lord Bishop?' 'Dear me,' said the cleric, 'I'd sooner commit adultery than imbibe strong liquor.' Said mine host, 'Who the hell wouldn't.'

1297

In Africa last year I visited a village in the Congo called Mdumbo and one of the local chiefs was working quite a racket. All the stuff sent out by Britain as foreign aid was being filetted through this black pirate's organisation and sold to neighbouring tribes. One of the chief's huts was raided and the police found it stacked with porcelain lavatory basins. When apprehended the chief calmly shrugged and said: 'It only goes to prove that people in grass houses shouldn't stow thrones.'

1298

Freda was telling her best friend Veronica about her success. 'I've finally made Gerald propose. We're going to be married next month. Hey, that reminds me, as I'll be leaving the flat here there's one or two things I don't want any more that you might as well have.' Veronica said: 'Gee, thanks. I'd very much like the studio couch and the Waterford vase . . .' Freda said: 'No, silly, I mean my eyelashes, inflatable bra, blonde hairpiece, support stockings, reinforced girdle and my contact lenses.'

1299

A girl went to her solicitor to try and sue a man who had assaulted her on a bridle path. The solicitor asked her exactly where the incident took place and she said: 'Right in the middle of the bridle path through Ellsemere Wood to Bromingham.' 'That's a great pity,' said the solicitor, 'unfortunately that path happens to be a Public Right of Way.'

1300

A woman complained to the doctor that her husband was driving her mad by insisting on bigger and bigger eggs for breakfast. The doctor advised her to surprise him by getting the largest ostrich egg she could buy, and making him eat it all, as a cure. The woman did this and reported back to the doctor. Her husband refused to eat breakfast in the bathroom. 'Why did you make him eat *there*?' inquired the medicine-man. 'Because it's the only room we've got with a big enough egg cup,' she explained.

1301

We got lost in an African port one day, and ended up right out in the jungle where we were captured by cannibals. They'd already captured a pretty American girl, and the chief was busy with her, so we had to wait. The witch-doctor explained that the chief liked to play with his food.

1302

Like all sailors I've got a girl in every port. And whenever I'm in port I see that there's a port in every girl . . . that way they get more co-operative. And have you ever tasted co-operative port?

1303

We were shipwrecked on a desert island and the natives surrounded us. The captain yelled at the chief: 'We are hungry—kill us a fat pig'— so the chef served up his mother-in-law.

1304

The Egyptians don't send their clothes to a laundry; they just take the clothes down to the edge of the River Nile, soak them in the water, and bash them against rocks. The Egyptian women love doing it, especially if their husbands are still wearing the clothes.

1305
The crowd was perplexed by the dog that kept running around the pitch after the referee, all through the match. When it was over and the home team had suffered a defeat, a spectator asked his neighbour about the animal. 'Oh, that's the ref's seeing-eye dog,' said the home supporter.

1306
We went to the camp by road. What a job we had packing all the stuff into it. The tent, the bedding, the food, the cooking stove, the ground-sheets, our clothes—there were cases, boxes and parcels on the roof, in the trunk, on the back seat and even tucked down the side of the battery. At last we got started and drove forty miles with the springs protesting at the weight. Then my wife said: 'We've forgotten something.' I said: 'Impossible.' And she said: 'But where are the kids?'

1307
Mrs. Cox had recently acquired a dog and was proudly demonstrating his good points to a friend. 'I know he's not what you would call a pedigree dog,' she said, 'but no tramp can come near the house without him letting us know about it.' 'What does he do?' asked her friend. 'He crawls under the sofa.'

1308
She went to the clinic to be examined mentally. The two doctors worked a partnership; one did the mind and the other did the rest . . . She sat down in the mind-doctor's office and he said: 'All right. Take off your clothes.' She said: 'But I only want you to examine my *mind*, to see if I'm crazy.' The psychologist said: 'Sure, I know, but if you don't get undressed my partner will think *I'm* crazy.'

1309
Two men who had been at the same college as boys met for the first time after a long period of time. Each had in his own way made considerable progress. The first was wearing the uniform of an Admiral of the Fleet and the other man was in full Bishop's regalia. The Bishop recognised his old boyhood chum but didn't let on. After the conference he walked out and saw the Admiral standing just at the bottom of the steps. Going up to him he said: 'My good man, would you be good enough to cancel the taxi I ordered. It's such a nice day, I think I'll walk.' The Admiral recognising the Bishop looked him over and said: 'Do you think you should, madam, in your condition?'

1310
A mountain-climbing expedition consisting of six men and seven girls were stranded on a tall peak in the Scottish Highlands. The mountain-rescue team went out to help them. Fergus the Fly, renowned

147

mountaineer, did yeoman service during the operation and finally reached the isolated ridge where the prettiest of the female climbers was perched. The wind had torn the clothes off her back and she was shivering with fright and cold. Said Fergus as he reached for her. 'You're the fourth molested woman I've rescued today.' The girl said in surprise, 'I *haven't* been molested!' Fergus said: 'You haven't been rescued, yet, either.'

1311

A coloured gentleman walked into a bar and said to the bartender: 'Do you serve Africans here?' The barman said: 'We have to serve everyone. There are no exceptions under the Racial Discrimination Act.' The coloured man said: 'You are sure you are allowed to serve Africans?' The barman said testily: 'Yes!' 'All right,' said the customer, 'Give me a couple of pygmies, two slices of bread, and a glass of beer to wash it all down.'

1312

They stood in the soft glinting moonlight, holding hands while the water lapped at their feet. 'Darling,' he said, '—I wish your bloody landlord would get your roof mended.'

1313

The new bride was preparing herself for bed in the honeymoon suite when she muttered: 'Jack, know something?' 'What,' he inquired, breathlessly. 'Well,' she said, 'I think they've redecorated this room since I was last here.'

1314

An anxious-looking girl in the dentist's surgery stammered to the overworked surgeon: 'Mr. Hacket, I'm sure I don't know what's worse —to have two teeth filled or to have a baby.' He snapped back: 'Make up your mind fast, Madam—I've got a lot of other women waiting out there.'

1315

In a night-club one night a diner ordered chicken and when the waiter brought his meal, he looked at the plate and said: 'Look, you've given me a chicken with only one leg!' The waiter gesticulated and said: 'I thought you wanted to eat it, not dance with it.'

1316

Two Martian youngsters met at a discotheque, and the young male Martian was very attracted to the young female Martian. So, as was the custom, they went together. Afterwards the male one said: 'By the way, I'm BM 2331. What do they call you?' The female one said: 'I'm YDS 324.' 'That's strange,' said the male, 'You don't *look* Jewish.'

1317

A man saved all his spare money for a trip to America, longing to fly in the new Boeing super jumbo jet. But one day, in Soho, he got another urge, and went to a place where the girl gave French lessons and massage. She said her name was Pamela Anne. Having completed the course he reluctantly paid up, admitting to the girl about his lost trip. 'Never mind,' she said, 'Pam Anne also makes the going great.'

1318
Harold was fed up with the monotony of things, so one night he said: 'Come on, Nadia, let's try it a different way.' So they moved the bed away from the recess and put it opposite the fireplace.

1319
There was a young woman walking down the main street completely nude; nothing on except a smile, and a policeman walked up to her, tapped her on the shoulder and said: 'Excuse me, Miss, haven't you forgotten something?' She said: 'Oh, dear, yes! I'm late for the office! Have you got the time.' And he said: 'No. I'm on duty.'

1320
Cohen of the Secret Service was trapped the other day in Cairo. Someone passed him a secret message which ended . . . 'read this and memorise it, then chew it up and swallow it.' But Cohen hesitated, and the Egyptians pounced. If only he could have been *sure* the paper was kosher.

1321
Last night at the dog track, the equipment went wrong and the mechanics spent an hour trying to get the race started without success. So I went over to the workmen, pushed one of the electricians aside, and sprinkled the glide-rail with fluid. 'What's that?' they asked. I said: 'Hare restorer—that'll get him going.'

1322
The prisoner was being tried for attempted rape. The judge listened to all the evidence and said: 'For the offence you committed the sentence should be ten years in jail. But I'm going to be lenient with you. Fined five shillings.' Afterwards the clerk asked the judge why he had been so lenient considering the magnitude of the crime. The judge said: 'I always believe in giving a man a second chance.'

1323
He said to his girl friend: 'If you don't let me love you, I shall die.' 'Aw, well okay,' she said, 'after all, you can't take it with you.'

1324
A couple of days after I was run down by a car my wife visited me in hospital and she only stayed a few minutes. 'I've got to rush,' she said, 'I've got to meet mother—we're having a day out, spending the insurance money.'

1325

She applied for a job as personal secretary to a young director. He asked her name, age and address and then told her to strip off while he got a tape-measure. 'What do you want to measure me for?' she asked suspiciously. He said: 'Don't be silly, how do we know what size desk you take?'

1326

She attended the audition, a lovely young, shapely blonde with ambitions to attain the heights of stardom. The producer interviewed her in his private office and she passed the audition with honours. As she was leaving she said: 'Don't call me, *I'll* call YOU.'

1327

Alfred was a fairly good husband, but he did like staying out late at night and leaving his wife on her own. Every morning when he left for work he used to kiss her on the cheek and shout cheerfully: 'Goodbye, mother of three'—then go to the office, and return home around midnight after a long session with the boys at the local. One morning, his wife feeling even more despondent than usual, decided to settle matters. Her husband went through the usual morning routine, collected his gear and strode to the door. He kissed her on the cheek and said cheerfully: 'Goodbye, mother of three.' His wife kissed him on the other cheek and said: 'Goodbye, father of two.' All the way to the office, and all the day through, he pondered upon this anxiously . . . and that night he went straight home after work.

1328

After the family had increased to three, it was decided to employ a nursemaid. 'My husband is very particular about whom we engage,' said the mistress to a girl who applied for the job. 'Are you faithful? Have you a kind and loving disposition?' Said the girl 'Am I taking care of the baby or your husband?'

1329

'Did you get home all right from the party last night?' asked a man of his colleague. 'No trouble at all,' was the reply, 'except that just as I was turning into my street, some fool stepped on my fingers.'

1330

'I thought I wired you not to bring your mother home with you,' said the husband. 'Yes,' replied his wife, 'that's what she's come to see you about.'

1331

A man was fumbling for the keyhole in a door. 'Hey,' said his pal, 'you're holding a cigar butt.' The drunk looked at it with astonishment. 'Well, whaddaya know?' he said. 'I must have smoked my key!'

1332

An Irish Jew emigrated to the States and while he was in New York his son was born and he wished to have him circumcised. Being a stranger he asked a cab driver where to find the Jewish circumciser and was directed to an address on 44th Street. The immigrant walked there, found a long street of shops and houses and started looking for number 4522. After hours of searching he failed to find the right address so he stopped a policeman and told him he wanted the Jewish circumciser. The cop said: 'Shure and it's the second doorway from where we're after standing right this minute!' The Jew went back along the street and saw that the number 4522 was a shop with a window full of clocks—grandfather clocks, alarm clocks, cuckoo clocks, big clocks, wee clocks—hundreds of them. Then he realised that there was a door beside the shop, leading to a staircase up to the floor above. He went up and sure enough the circumciser Mr. Feinbaum, was up there. He made the arrangements and then said to Feinbaum 'Tell me, why do you mislead people by filling the shop window with *clocks*?'

The rabbi shrugged and said inquiringly: 'So vhat *vould* you expecting me put in mine vindow, Mr. O'Isaacs?'

1333

I got talking to a chap waiting at the doctor's and he was telling me about his rheumatics. I said to him: 'You don't look very old, I'm surprised you've got a complaint like that.' He said: 'Oh, it's not my age, it's an occupational disease, I'm an Income Tax Inspector.' I said: 'But you blokes work in nice warm offices.' He said: 'Yes, but we spend so much time crying over people's troubles that we get rheumatism from damp shirts.'

1334

A man I know has discovered a good racket—he sells cheap day-return air trips from Dublin to Sark and when the airliner is full he disguises himself as a terrorist and hi-jacks it, diverting it to the Bahamas; once there he charges the passengers £100 each for a week's holiday in a luxury hotel.

1335

In the Bahamas I found a Jewish gent on holiday, buying a cheap box of Christmas cards. I said: 'What on earth do you want with Christmas cards? What are you celebrating?' and he answered: 'Look, you'd celebrate Christmas yourself if you had a large factory in Whitechapel turning out four million Christmas puddings every year!' I said: 'But don't you get a lot left on your hands?' 'Are you crazy?' he said, 'I stir them with a spoon not my hands.'

1336

'Father,' said Jimmy, running into the lounge, 'there's a big black cat in the dining-room.' 'Never mind, Jimmy, said his father, drowsily; 'black cats are lucky.' 'Yes,' was the reply. 'This one is—he's had your dinner!'

1337

A patient was complaining to his doctor: 'After the first, doctor, I'm ever so tired. Then after the second I can hardly get my breath and my asthma gets worse. After the third I get terrible aches and pains in my back and I have to gasp and wheeze to keep alive . . .' The doctor said: 'I can't understand you—why don't you just stop after the first ?' 'How can I ?' the patient replied, 'my flat's on the fourth.'

1338

There's a wonderful new book just out written by a Welsh doctor who specialises in emotional disturbances. It's called *Schizophrenia for Beginners* and is written by Dr. David Jones and Dr. David Jones.

1339

The parents of a very precocious child asked her: 'What would you like for your birthday ?' She said: 'I want a watch.' And they said: 'Well you can't.'

1340

Then there's the dim gal who wrote to Linguaphone and asked them if they had a set of records that taught people how to speak Lesbian.

1341

On holiday the wife got into trouble while bathing in deep water. Her husband showed commendable bravery—he ran all over the beach gathering flotsam and jetsam to build a boat. Neither of the two men proved much of a shipbuilder. An hour later, fortunately, a handsome lifeguard saw the poor woman's predicament—he could hardly help it because she had struggled out of her bikini. The lifeguard dived into the water and struck out boldly—at the two other lifeguards who had the same idea. Swimming fast, he finally reached the place where the woman was drowning slowly in four feet of ocean. By the time he reached her he had finished the overarm and the butterfly and was working on the breast-stroke. For which he held two Olympic gongs. He grasped her scientifically and gave her the kiss of life. She panted: 'Wait a minute; wait a minute! I'm not unconscious yet.' So he knocked her unconscious and then rolled her over on to her back and back-stroked her to the shore. Her husband rushed up, obviously relieved and thankful. He pumped the lifeguard's hands as the lifeguard pumped the water out of the wife. 'Thanks. I'll never know how to repay you,' the husband yelled at him. 'That was wonderful, I'm so grateful! You don't know what that woman means to me!' Then he gave the lifeguard a sixpenny tip.

1342

They were having a spot of bother with grandma because she would insist on sliding down the bannisters to breakfast. So they thought of a fine idea—and laced the rail with barbed wire. The following morning Grandma didn't go down to breakfast until nine o'clock.

'What kept you?' asked the young wife. Grandma said: 'That barbed wire didn't half slow me down.'

1343
Two Red Indians happened upon a Nudist Colony near Texas and one of them pointed to a red-head in the distance and said: 'Her paleface.' The other one said: 'Her not only pale *face*.'

1344
Two Jewish citizens were boasting of the respective renown of their local rabbis. 'Everybody knows Rabbi Cohen of Lincoln,' said one. 'When he goes to London he is invited to stay at Buckingham Palace.' 'What's that?' deprecated the other, 'A few years ago our Rabbi Solomon of Croydon visited Rome, and took a walk with the Pope. You know what happened? Hundreds of Italians asked, "Who's that bald-headed little fellow with Rabbi Solomon?"'

1345
Jones was intrigued by an advertisement offering a canary that could sing every song in the world. What's more, the bird lived up to all his advance notices. On request, he warbled 'Melancholy Baby', 'Rule Britannia', and an aria by Bach. 'How much?' said Jones. 'Two hundred quid,' said the proprietor, 'and you'll have to buy this other bird with him.' 'The two hundred is enough,' complained Jones, 'Why must I buy this other bird as well.' 'The canary needs him,' said the proprietor, 'That's his arranger.'

1346
A Greek professor tore his suit and took it to a tailor who had been born in Athens. The tailor examined the suit and asked, 'Euripides?' 'Yes,' said the professor. 'Eumenides.'

1347
Joe dashed into a chemists and cried 'Quick! Give me ten pence worth of aspirin and some insect powder. I've got a lousy headache.'

1348
A cannibal chief's wife became interested in a number of worthy charities. Her husband finally refused to bring home any more guests for dinner. He explained, 'I'm tired of having my wife put the bite on them.'

1349
A Rolls-Royce stopped in front of a bookshop the other evening, and the chauffeur announced rather sheepishly. 'My lady wants a couple of new murder stories committed by nice people.'

1350
MacGregor and MacPherson decided to become teetotallers, but

MacGregor thought it would be best if they kept one bottle of whisky in the cupboard in case of illness. After three days MacPherson could bear it no longer and said: 'MacGregor, ah'm not verra well.' 'Too late, MacPherson. Ah was verra sick masel' all day yesterday.'

1351

Mr. Smith's wife was dead for a full year, and still the bereaved widower showed no signs of recovering his spirits. Alarmed friends persuaded him to consult an analyst. After a long talk, the analyst said, 'No wonder you're melancholy! A man of your age needs some female companionship.' Smith protested this would be unfaithful to the memory of his departed wife, but the analyst scoffed, 'Nonsense! The living cannot exist on memories. Get yourself a girl. I prescribe it as your doctor.' Half convinced Smith announced sheepishly that he didn't even know a girl. 'That's easily remedied,' said the analyst, reaching for a pad and pencil. 'Just take this slip to Mary Guire at 932 East Street, and she'll be glad to go out with you.'

Mr. Smith found Miss Guire's company satisfactory in every respect. As he was bidding her an affectionate adieu, she reminded him, 'Most of my boy friends leave a little gift. Shall we say twenty-five pounds?' Mr. Smith was rather taken aback, but rallied quickly. 'Okay,' he said, 'here's the twenty-five, but I'd like a written receipt if you don't mind. I belong to the Shield Health Plan, and they take care of all my medical expenses.'

1352

A Hollywood film star had had five wives, each of whom had promptly divorced him. He was now declaring his love for the prospective sixth. 'I've heard some queer stories about you,' said the girl. 'Don't worry about them,' said the star. 'They're only old wives' tales.'

1353

Three lads fell to boasting about the earning capacities of their respective fathers. Said the doctor's son, 'My dad operated on a movie producer last month and sent him a bill for a cool five thousand quid.' The lawyer's son spoke up: 'My old man was the mouthpiece for a big racketeer a week ago and got a fee of ten grand for one day's work—all paid in crisp new bills.' The minister's son said quietly, 'On Sunday, my father preached a sermon in church, and it took eight men to bring in the money.'

1354

'I haven't met your husband. What's he like?' asked Mrs. Home of her friend. 'Just the ordinary type,' was the reply. '42 around the waist, 42 around the chest, 92 around the golf course, and a nuisance around the house.'

1355

She was fat and over forty, but she was still kittenish. The young man she had cornered at the party was thinking hard for some excuse to escape. At last he murmured, 'Do you remember the youngster who used to tickle you under the chin at school?' 'Oh,' she said, gushingly, 'so that's who you are?' 'No,' he replied, 'that was my father.'

1356
A dear old lady presented a crossed cheque at a bank. 'I'm sorry,' said the clerk, 'but this is not payable over the counter.' 'That's all right,' said the old lady, 'I'll come round.'

1357
Two silver-haired old ladies wobbled down the main street in their moth-eaten coupé, made an illegal turn, and compounded their felony by ignoring the outraged traffic officer's endeavours to stop them. He finally caught up with them in front of Ye Olde Waffle Shoppe. 'Didn't you hear my whistle?' he demanded angrily. The perky octogenarian at the wheel looked at him coyly and admitted, 'Yes, I did, officer—but I never flirt when I'm driving.

1358
A woman walked into the office of the head of a private detective agency and demanded an interview. Before the startled head of the firm could say a word, the woman launched into a tirade against her husband. Finally, when she stopped to get her breath, the detective was able to get a word in. 'Just what do you want me to do, madam?' he asked. 'I want my husband and that woman followed,' snapped the visitor. 'I want them followed night and day, and then I want a complete report on what she sees in him.'

1359
A bridegroom after the wedding was over and the guests had departed, began to search anxiously among the wedding gifts. 'What are you looking for, darling?' asked the bride. 'That fifty-pound cheque of your father's,' he said. 'I don't see it anywhere.' 'Poor dad is so absent-minded,' said the bride. 'He lit his cigar with it.'

1360
A trapeze artist married the India-rubber man, and is now twisting him around her little finger. The lion tamer is angry at his lady friend because, he says, she kisses him and gives him a brush-off at the same time. Seems she's the bearded lady. The assistant manager has tried tonics of eleven different colours to cure his dandruff. He reports, 'I finally got rid of the dandruff, all right, but now my head is full of confetti.'

1361
The henpecked husband was seeing his wife off at the railway station. 'Don't come on to the platform, dear,' said the wife, 'It will cost you threepence for a platform ticket.' 'That's all right,' he replied. 'It's worth more than that to see you off.'

1362

Lander invited a friend to join a poker game one night. The friend said: 'Sorry I can't manage it, I promised my wife I'd be home to celebrate because it's our 21st anniversary. Twenty-one years! It seems like yesterday.' Then he paused and added: 'And you know what a lousy day it was yesterday.'

1363

A woman goes into a large store and a helpful floor-manager goes up to her and asks politely 'Good afternoon. What is Madam's pleasure?' The customer says: 'My main pleasure is men but I came in to buy a hat.' The manager beckons one of the supervisors over and says: 'Take this lady to the third floor and put something floppy on her.' The supervisor shrugs and says: 'If you mean George, he's still at lunch.'

1364

An oil-rig expert who was earning vast amounts of money on a scheme to research for oil and natural gas in the North Sea had to visit a dentist for a check up, owing to company regulations. The company dentist probed carefully around in the oil-man's mouth and said. 'You've got a fine set of good strong teeth. I don't see anything that might develop into trouble at the moment.' The patient said: 'Drill anyway. Today I feel lucky.'

1365

A Rabbi told his congregation, 'God is good—he takes care of everyone. A woman died in childbirth and her husband was too poor to buy milk for the baby. The baby's father prayed to God, "Don't let my baby die of starvation." God grew breasts on the man, and filled them with milk.' A member of the congregation stood up and asked, 'Rabbi, wouldn't it have been simpler for God to have given this man money to buy milk?' 'You see,' replied the Rabbi, 'even for God Almighty it's easier to perform a miracle than to raise money.'

1366

The 'upper crust' consists of a few crumbs held together by a load of dough.

1367

Here is the latest list of some of the most inconsequential men in the world.

Lord Godiva	Mr. Beatrice Potter
Lord Hamilton	Father Superior
Whistler's Father	Grandpa Moses
King Bodicea	Count Borgia.

1368

A woman visited a psychiatrist and was asked: 'What's your problem?'

'It's not *me* it's my husband Napoleon. He keeps thinking he's Mr. Robinson.'

1369
An Irish farmer crossed two strains of cattle—a Holstein bull with a Jersey cow. Now he's got a beast that says 'Noo?' instead of 'Moo'.

1370
A newly-rich woman had treated herself to a luxury round-the-world cruise and was eager to know the details of the trip because she wanted to visit as many places as possible. Going through the itinerary she asked a Cockney steward: 'Can you tell what comes after Haiti?' 'Yes ma'am—Heighty-one.'

1371
A young woman on a world cruise kept a comprehensive diary for posterity. Her note in the book on the first night afloat was: 'Today I met the captain. Charming.' The second note: 'Had dinner at the captain's table. Cocktails!' The third note: 'Captain is showing very great interest in me. Gosh!' On the fourth page she wrote: 'Had tea in the captain's cabin. He kissed me and said if I didn't surrender he would run the ship on to a reef and destroy it.' The next entry proclaimed: 'Last night I personally saved the lives of eight hundred people.'

1372
Jolsen the Swede placed an advertisement in a Stockholm newspaper's agony column to announce: 'I will not be responsible for my wife's debts after today since she has now left my bed and smorgasbord.'

1373
Two drunks were sitting morosely in a saloon when a bug dropped on to the floor from the bar counter. Said one: 'Look! Bug.' The other one said: 'S'ladybug.' The first one said: 'You got damn good eyesight.'

1374
Billy optimistically telephoned a former girl friend after a long absence. 'Hullo Josey—doing anything tonight?' Josie said: 'No.' 'Oh,' said Bill, 'okay. Some other time, huh?' and rang off.

1375
A vicar's son had to give up a girl friend after several months because she kept using four-letter words. Like 'stop', 'don't', etc.

1376
Phillips received out of the blue a communication from an old working acquaintance: 'If you don't stop messing around with my wife I'll damn well shoot you.' Phillips wrote back: 'Dear Sid, thank you for your duplicated letter of the 5th . . .'

1377

A man went to the managing director of a large and progressive firm and told him: 'I've got a great idea which could save the company thousands of pounds a year!' The director said: 'Good God, Jenkins, how did you *know* we were thinking of firing you?'

1378

Vivian goes to see his old doctor. The doc sticks a stethoscope against his chest and says absent-mindedly: 'Cough.' The patient coughs. Doc says: 'Ai, ai—how long you had that cough?'

1379

A man was standing at the front door of his neighbour's house, chatting, when he saw another man coming through the garden gate struggling with a couch over his shoulder. 'Hey, been buying some new furniture?' he asked his friend. 'Hell, no!' came the reply, 'That's just our psychiatrist calling to see my wife.'

1380

An Irishman, an Englishman and a Jew were telling of their strange experiences and how they were mistaken for great men. 'Would you baylave it,' the Irishman said, 'I was once mistaken for President Kennedy?'

The Englishman turned to his fellow countrymen. 'That's nothing.' he said, 'I was once mistaken for President Nixon.'

'Huh!' the Jew said, 'I was standing on the street corner the other day and a cop come along and said to me, 'Holy Moses, are you here again?'

1381

Little Ike came up to his father with a very solemn face. 'Is it true, Father,' he asked, 'that marriage is a failure?' His father surveyed him for a moment. 'Well Ike,' he finally replied, 'If you get a rich wife, it's almost as good as a failure.'

1382

'Ah!' remarked his friend to the Jewish actor who had had his nose straightened by a surgeon, 'a thing of beauty and a goy forever!'

1383

The young dolly came to the hospital for a check-up.

'Have you been X-rayed?' asked the doctor.

'Nope,' she said, 'but I've been ultraviolated.'

1384

One of the members of the smart open-air club asked the lifeguard how he might teach a lady of his acquaintance to swim.

'It takes considerable time and technique,' the lifeguard said. 'First you must take her into the water. Then place one arm about her waist, hold her tightly, then take her right arm and raise it slowly . . .' 'That will be helpful,' said the member, 'and I know my mother-in-law will appreciate it.' 'Your mother-in-law?' said the lifeguard. 'In that case, just push her off the end of the pier.'

1385

A middle-aged woman stood watching a little boy on the curb smoking a cigarette and drinking from a bottle of beer. Unable to bear it any longer she stalked up to the lad and demanded, 'Why aren't you in school at this time of day?'

'Hell, lady,' said the boy, 'I'm only four years old.'

1386

Rosen was ill, and wished to consult a physician who was known to his friend, Moe Levin. He went to Moe and said: 'Moe, I'm a sick man. I ought to see a doctor.'

'Well, why don't you go and see my friend, Isaacson?'

'Yes, but ain't he awful expensive?'

'Well, he ain't so cheap, Rosen. He charges £15 for the first visit, but after that it's only £3.'

The next day Rosen went to see the doctor. As soon as the door was opened and the doctor came out, he said: 'Well doc, here I am again!'

1387

A newly-wed girl had lived for several weeks on a new estate where the thin-walled homes had been built to a very confined plan and where there was hardly any open space. She had joined the new church on the hill, and one day she invited the vicar to tea. All the time he was there a riot appeared to be going on next door, and the vicar became increasingly alarmed. The young wife said: 'I suppose you're wondering why I asked you to drop in, vicar?' Then she thumbed in the direction of the adjoining house and said: 'How'd you like to love *them* neighbours?'

1388

Adolescence brings with it tremendous changes. Between the ages of 12 and 18 most parents age by thirty years.

1389

A pig breeder and his neighbour, a small holder, met at the agricultural fair and later had a snack lunch at a cafe in the county town. As they were going out of the door, later, the pig breeder said to his companion: 'According to what I just paid for those ham rolls, every one of my pigs must be worth £2,000.'

1390

A horticulturist famed for his hybrids produced a really remarkable specimen one season and decided to send it to a young newcomer to the game who had recently been competing with him. He sent the bloom with one of his assistants, a handsome, buxom country wench. Later he telephoned the other man and asked: 'Well what did you think of that rose?' The man replied: 'First rate, Roger. An excellent bedding variety.'

1391

'Darling,' she whispered, 'will you still love me after we are married?' He considered this for a moment and then replied, 'I think so. I've always been especially fond of married women.'

1392

A vintner who experimented with new wines produced one which he considered particularly excellent, so he sent it to a well-known specialist taster, in sample form, asking him to comment. In reply the specialist wrote: 'I must say I thought that champagne very interesting. It reminded me of Charlemagne's sword.'

Checking the reference, the grower discovered that the sword had a reputation as being 'long, flat and deadly.'

1393

A parson with a sense of humour had put up a sign in his church: 'No mistakes rectified after leaving the altar.'

1394

Two men, Smith and Jones, were discussing their respective wives. 'You know,' said Smith, 'my wife tells me that almost every night she dreams she is married to a millionaire.'

'You're darn lucky,' replied Jones, 'Mine thinks that in the daytime.'

1395

An Englishman on a visit to the West decided to go horseback riding. The cowboy who was to attend him asked: 'Do you prefer an English saddle or a Western?'

'What's the difference?' he asked.

'The Western saddle has a horn,' replied the cowboy.

'I don't think I'll need the horn,' said the Englishman, 'I don't intend to ride in heavy traffic.'

1396

Tourist, having looked over the stately home: 'We've made a stupid mistake. I tipped his lordship instead of you.'

Butler: 'That's awkward. I'll never get it now.'

1397

Two Jews were walking through the park on a real cold day with their hands in their pockets. Levi said to Cohen: 'Why don't you say something?'. Cohen: 'Freeze your *own* hands!'

1398

A professor was one day nearing the close of a history lecture and was indulging in one of those rhetorical climaxes in which he delighted when the hour struck. The students immediately began to leave.

The professor, annoyed at the interruption of his flow of eloquence, held up his hand: 'Wait, just one minute. I still have a few more pearls to cast.'

1399
The Irish lad and the Yiddish boy were engaged in verbal combat. Finally the subject came down to their respective churches.

'I guess that Father O'Donovon knows more than your Rabbi,' the little Irish boy insisted.

'Sure, he does,' replied the Jewish boy, 'You tell him everything.'

1400
The stranger walked up to a casino dice table and laid down a £100 bet. He shook the dice, but as he threw them a third dice fell from his sleeve. The house operator was unruffled. He handed back two of the dice and pocketed the third, saying, 'O.K., roll again. Your point is 15.'

1401
Isadore was not being strictly kosher in ordering bacon, but the temptation was irresistible. Just one little order of bacon for breakfast might be overlooked by the universal powers. But when Isadore was about to leave the restaurant, he stopped at the door in dismay. The sky was heavy with black clouds, lightning rent the air, the ground shook with the rumble of thunder.

'Can you imagine!' he exclaimed. 'All that fuss over a little piece of bacon!'

1402
An elderly clergyman who was utterly hopeless at the game was frequently invited to join a group of local bigwigs who liked playing golf on Sunday and thought that if they got the churchman interested it would minimise his objections to their Sabbath-breaking.

One Wednesday afternoon another game was in progress and the clergyman was exasperating his colleagues with the most awful shots. At the sixth, the clergyman teed off and the ball swept high against the wind, was slewed towards a tree where it rebounded back to hit the hard turf and began to roll erratically. It zigzagged across the apron, along the front of the green, bounced a few times and skidded on towards the flag. Then it suddenly settled down to a slow roll, making unerringly for the hole, where it teetered for a breathtaking couple of seconds before dropping neatly in.

The clergyman stared somewhat angrily at the holed-in-one ball and raised his head towards the sky muttering sternly: 'Please Father— if you don't *mind* I'd rather do it *myself*.'

1403
Many long-married people are not so much a retired couple as a retired gentleman and his wife.

1404

Returning from the circus the father who had not accompanied his family asked young Frankie how he had enjoyed the show. 'It was great, Dad, but I was sorry for the man who taught the tigers because he was so tired he took a chair with him into the ring, but the tigers were so naughty he had to keep hitting them with his whip and so never got a chance to sit down.'

1405

Doris still thinks that a two-way switch is wife-swapping.

1406

Women don't have much of a life for the simple reason that life begins at forty, and most women don't reach that age until they are too far gone to enjoy life.

1407

When he told his girl friend that she had an ephemeral lustre that evening, she asked him to give her the chap's phone number.

1408

Little Harry came home from School at term-end looking somewhat abashed. He handed his report-card to his mother and said: 'I was going to bed early, anyway, and I'm getting sick of television.'

1409

A visiting party of Irish-Americans arrived in Ireland in time to be asked to join in a civic parade. The question then arose as to whether they would march under the nationalist flag or the Union Jack. After considerable debate and argument one of the Americans declared: 'Look, let's not have any bigotry. We march under the Irish flag or not at all, at all.'

1410

At a literary party, the main speaker treated the gathering to one of the most interminably boring personal anecdotes ever to waste lip-time and for a full twenty-seven minutes he paused only once to gulp some water. Then he began again but suddenly he paused and remarked. 'I'm sorry, I seem to be getting ahead of myself.' The woman sitting next to him grasped his wrist anxiously and implored: 'Never mind— for goodness' sake don't turn back now!'

1411

A builder took a prospect to see some inexpensive houses he had just erected. The prospect stood in one room, the builder in the next one, and the latter asked: 'Can you hear me?' in a very low voice.

'Very faintly!' answered the buyer.

'Can you see me?'

'No.'

'*Them*'s walls for you, ain't they!' cried the builder.

1412

While waiting for the speaker at a public meeting a little man of obvious Semitic extraction in the audience seemed very nervous. He glanced over his shoulder from time to time and shifted about in his seat. At last he arose and demanded: 'Is there a Christian Scientist in the audience?'

A dignified woman at the other side of the hall rose to her feet and said: 'I am a Christian Scientist.'

'Well lady,' requested the little Hebrew, 'would you mind changing seats with me? I'm sitting in a draught?'

1413

An Irishman and a Jew were holding a debate as to the respective merits of their religion. The debate waxed fast and furious, then the Irishman delivered a crusher to the Jew: 'Answer me this, Abe: could one of your boys be Pope?'

The Jew considered thoughtfully, 'I've a question for you, Pat. Could one of your boys be God?'

'Of course not.'

'Well,' the Jew shrugged, 'one of our boys made it.'

1414

Mrs. Toplin purchased a large old grandfather clock at an auction and then sent her unhappy husband to pay for it and carry the thing home. The husband had been to a formal dinner earlier in the evening and was still wearing his full-dress suit. He was having some difficulty with the unwieldy mechanism even before he met the drunk staggering in the opposite direction. They collided and the husband fell backward to the sidewalk, the clock on top of him.' Why in blazes don't you watch where you're going,' the angry husband demanded. The drunk shook his head, looked at the man in the full-dress suit and at the grandfather clock that lay across him.

'Why don't *you* wear a wristwatch like everybody elsh,' he enquired.

1415

The vicar of an impoverished rural parish kept writing to his bishop for aid until the bishop demanded an end to such appeals. For a time there was no correspondence, then one day the bishop received a letter saying: 'This is a report, not an appeal. I have no trousers.'

1416

For many years he was a confirmed bachelor, and his friends never believed he would marry. But eventually he did—and about three months afterwards was complaining vehemently about married life.

'What's the trouble?' a friend asked.

'She's always getting in my way when I try to cook the dinner,' the ex-bachelor moaned.

1417

On the first night of his new play the producer knew he had a hit on his hands. But it was only a flesh wound, and the gunman was arrested.

1418

'Uncensored,' to a publisher, means 'we have left all the dirty bits in.' 'Abridged' means 'we have taken all the dull bits out'.

1419

What's old and Roman and can shin up a wall? IV.

1420

'Are you positive,' demanded counsel, 'that the prisoner is the man who stole your car?'

'Well,' answered the witness, 'I was, until you cross-examined me. Now I'm not sure whether I ever had a car *at all.*'

1421

A woman who had just returned from a trip to Mexico called the police to report that a rattlesnake was loose in her overnight bag which the woman had thrown out of a window on to the pavement. Cautiously, they scattered the contents of the bag—only to find an electric tooth-brush, accidentally turned on.

1422

A teenage student named Bernard Watts phoned his father.

'Dad, can I have twenty-two pounds?'

His father said: 'Now look here, Bernie. You've had your allowance for this month and it's no good me encouraging your extravagant ways. I don't think I can let you have any more pocket money until the end of the month.'

Bernie said: 'I don't want it for pocket money. I want it for bail.'

'Oh, my God!' cried his father, 'What have you been arrested for, you young fool?'

Bernard said: 'It's not for *me*, Dad. It's Mom.'

1423

'Have you anything to say before I pass sentence?'

'Yes, m'lud. It's a bit thick bein' identified by a woman wot kept 'er head under the bedclothes all the time.'

1424

A church was raising funds for a new roof and the minister was calling on members for subscriptions. One of the pillars of the church rose, and said: 'I subscribe five pounds.' Just at that instant a piece of plaster fell on his head. Half stunned, he mumbled: 'F-f-five hundred' and the minister prayed, 'Oh, Lord, hit him just one more time.'

1425

A man was charged with shooting a number of pigeons, the property of a farmer. Counsel for the defence tried to confuse the farmer. 'Now,' he remarked, 'are you prepared to swear that this man shot your pigeons ?'

'I didn't say he shot 'em,' was the reply. 'I said I suspected him of doing so.'

'Ah! Now we're coming to it! What made you suspect the man ?'

'Well, first, I caught him on my land with a gun. Secondly, I heard a gun go off and saw some pigeons fall. Thirdly, I found four of my pigeons in his pocket. But it may be the birds flew there and committed suicide.'

1426

The judge was a very keen golfer. He was trying the case of a man who was summoned for cruelty to his wife.

'My client,' said the defending counsel, 'is a much maligned man. His wife is constantly nagging him and, in the end, driven to desperation, he beat her into silence with a golf club.'

At last the judge leaned forward with a sudden show of interest. 'A mashie ?' he asked.

'No,' said the lawyer, 'a No. 4 iron.'

'Case dismissed,' said the judge. Turning to the accused man, he added, 'And I'd like to see you in my chambers before you leave.'

1427

'Whom did the ancients believe supported the world on his shoulders ?' the teacher asked.

'Atlas,' one little girl promptly answered.

'Correct. Now if Atlas supported the world on his shoulders, who supported Atlas ?' the teacher quizzed.

Many small brows were puckered over this. 'Maybe his wife took in washing,' suggested Tommy Carter.

1428

The wife of a Cuban terrorist employed in a perambulator factory tried to induce him to steal a pushchair for their baby. He refused to do this, but agreed to purloin sufficient parts to make a complete machine. The great day arrived for the assembly of the parts. After five hours the wife went out to their backyard and found her husband in a state of exhaustion.

'It's no good,' he said, 'It always comes out a machine gun.'

1429

A Spaniard, an American, and a Scotsman were discussing what they would do if they awoke one morning to discover that they were millionaires.

Pedro said he would build a bull ring.

The Scot said he would go to Paris to have a rave-up. The Yank said he would go to sleep again to see if he could make another million.

1430

'You have a pretty tough looking lot of customers to deal with this morning, haven't you?' remarked a friend of the magistrate who had dropped in at the police court. 'You are looking at the wrong bunch. Those are the lawyers,' said the magistrate.

1431

A woman was testifying on behalf of her son, 'that he had worked on her farm ever since he was born.' The lawyer, who cross examined her, said:

'You assert that your son worked on your farm ever since he was born?'

'I do.'

'What did he do the first year?'

'The milking.'

1432

A gentleman called at a Chinese laundry for his clothes. On receiving the package he noticed some Chinese characters marked upon it. He asked, pointing to the lettering

'That's my name, I suppose?'

'No; 'scliption,' was the Chinaman's bland reply, 'Lil ol' man, closs-eyed, no tooths.'

1433

Mr. and Mrs. Strong were at the christening service of their ninth child, and the entire family accompanied them. Throughout the inaugural preparations several of the children were misbehaving, and the three-year-old Basil was playing up uncontrollably. Dad got so annoyed he grasped the infant by the arm, shook him and said: 'If you don't behave yourself, we won't bring *you* next year!'

1434

His wife was sitting knitting while he scanned the Sunday papers; silence reigned all morning, and well into the afternoon. Suddenly his wife looked up and said: 'Sid . . .'

'Yes,' he muttered.

'Pretend I'm a barmaid,' she implored, 'and talk to me.'

1435

Once upon a time, on the outskirts of West Bromwich lived a young and handsome collier who fell in love with an actress from the local repertory company and married her. They went to live on a new estate in Bloxwich and were comparatively happy except for small problems. One was that the young man didn't like the way his young new wife spent hours on her personal appearance because he was jealous of her many admirers. The other was that she chided him over his little idiosyncrasy of being scared of creepy-crawly things like spiders and cockroaches and centipedes.

One fatal day young Herbert was taking a bath in their glistening new bathroom when through the steamy atmosphere he spotted a nasty, multi-legged black insect which dropped off the window ledge on to the hand-basin.

Herbert struggled up in the bath, eyes full of soap, and in a panic-stricken agony of fearful horror bashed and massacred the interloping crawler with the long stem of the back-scrubber until it was a mass of crushed legs and sticky soapsuds. He hastily wrapped himself in a towel and went to the bedroom to get dressed.

Ten minutes later, Veronica, his wife, stomped into the room and and shouted 'What the hell have you been doing to my new eyelashes?'

1436
They say that Henry the Eighth was such a shy gentleman that when he wanted to get married it took him all his time to axe anyone.

1437
Nobody can understand why Singleton was born in Dublin.

1438
Then there's the Irish labourer who visited a chiropodist in London and told him frankly, 'Me fate is in your hands.'

1439
One year, Sven Olafsonn was made secretary of the United Nations Organisation. Before taking up his official role as head of UNO he spent some time on leave in Stockholm where he lived with his wife and eight children. It was a weekend of harassment, argument, altercation, dispute, recrimination, intimidation and chaotic mealtimes. He finally flew off to New York for his inauguration, feeling completely exhausted and defeated. Rising to deliver his primary oration he shook his head sadly and announced: 'Gentlemen—frankly I fail to see exactly why it is that we *want* to live together as one great international family!'

1440
A new executive with a large conglomerate had been in the saddle for several days when he developed a great depression and complained to a colleague on the seventeenth floor: 'What a lousy firm this is! I've been here for almost a fortnight and I haven't yet seen one solitary young, attractive, interesting girl to liven up the place.'

The following day he was checking some computer print-outs when an indescribably gorgeous young female walked into his office. In her twenties, slim, well-endowed, luxurious strawberry-blonde hair, wiggling walk; the lot. Giving the exec. a sunny smile with her immaculate teeth, she dropped an important-looking document on to the desk-top. It was addressed personally to him and marked, 'Urgent Attention'. He watched her in a trance as she turned neatly and swaggered sensually out of the room.

Shattered by the experience he absent-mindedly tore open the package. It contained a pair of racing binoculars and a note which read: 'How about me and you getting together at noon, in my room?' It was signed: 'Fiona Windlesham'. In some excitement he rang his colleague on an extension and asked who Miss Windlesham was. His colleague said: 'Oh, you mean Fiona? She's the firm's optician'.

1441

A primary school-teacher took a party of tiny infants to the local zoo. On their return to classes she asked them all to write a short account of their experiences with the animals. One little girl wrote, in painful capitals: 'The beast I liked best at the zoo was the Key Pout. Every time we went near him he spat at Lenerd Smif, and I hate *him*.'

1442

There's a chap working at Middlemore Hospital who is a wizard at unconscious humour. He's the chief anaesthetist.

1443

A small town zoo invested in a couple of lions specially imported from Africa. On their first day in adjoining cages a short-sighted attendant came around at lunch time and pushed two enormous sides of beef into the older lion's cage, and a bunch of bananas and a bag of peanuts into the younger lion's cage.

The same thing happened at tea time. The following morning when the keeper delivered breakfast the menu was the same: chunks of meat for the old lion, nuts and bananas for the other one. The young lion got annoyed and managed to grab the keeper's arm with his teeth. 'Hey,' he roared, 'what's the big idea. You trying to make a monkey outa me?'

1444

The secretary of a trades union was told to send a goodwill message to a colleague who was hospitalised. He sent a wire the following day. 'The General Committee has voted 24 to 18 to send best wishes for your speedy recovery.'

1445

An after-dinner speaker is a man who develops indigestion over a meal while worrying about having to get up and tell a lot of stories he can't remember to a bunch of strangers who have probably heard them all before.

1446

One speaker began his remarks with: 'Before I start my talk there is something I want to say to you . . .' It wasn't because he felt nervous, it was because he was reading from the script his wife had prepared.

1447

Her husband was lounging lazily on the studio divan, saying, 'Alice, I'll think about the leak in the washing machine in a minute—right now, I'm thinking about planning a new rockery.'

1448

Two girls were waiting for a 'bus on a damp morning when a regal Rolls-Royce coupé passed them, driven by a smart-looking executive-type young businessman. A very meaningful wolf whistle warmed the air, then the Rolls was gone. 'Eeeh!' exclaimed one of the girls to the other, 'just fancy that! Seven thousand quid's worth of motor whistling at a two quid C & A mini skirt and a blonde wonder-wig.'

1449

The motoring family, out for a Sunday jaunt, were looking for a suitable place to turn off and picnic. 'Keep your eyes open,' said Dad, the driver, to the four kids in the rear. 'What we want is an unspoiled bit of country-side near a stream or something.' About ten minutes later one of the youngsters excitedly hit his father on the shoulder and cried: 'There's a place!' Dad said: 'Where?' The kid replied: 'Over there' and pointed. 'That must be the place. See, it's all littered with bottles and plastic cups and paper.'

1450

Maids were hard to get, so wealthy Mrs. Frombrush had to make do with an unmarried mother who needed accommodation. Friends arrived one evening, and the girl was told to bring in coffee. She brought in a tray and laid out five cups of coffee on a side table, with straws stuck in them. The hostess reprimanded her, saying. 'You musn't use straws, girl.' The girl said: 'Well, all the spoons looked dirty, Missus, and anyway the coffee ain't hot, so it won't hurt the straws.' Mrs. Frombush snapped: 'And why are there no saucers?' The girl said in astonish-ment: 'Blimey, lady, don't you know folks don't drink from saucers any more!'

1451

A marital revolution was in full swing. The young husband, father of two, decided he had had enough. He left home and went to stay with a friend. Then he placed an ad. in the local newspaper deliberately to embarrass his wife: 'To whom it may concern, I will no longer be responsible for the debts of Mrs. Annie Falmer. Intending tradesmen take care because she is both extravagant and bad tempered. Signed, John Falmer.' A couple of days later the wife retaliated with an announcement of her own, in the same local paper: 'Dear John, please come home. The arm you broke is now a lot better since I had it in plaster. The children need you, the lawn needs mowing and the garden needs a worm like you. P.S. I have paid your gambling account. Signed. Anne Falmer.'

At this point the editor intervened and in the following issue he printed an ad. himself. 'Anne and John Falmer: This correspondence is now closed.' But the story has a happy ending: helpful readers of the newspaper clubbed together to pay for a divorce.

1452

An ambitious young graduate, weary of seeking a suitable job considered that he might do better if he spread his net wider. Feeling confident of both his physical strength and his academic abilities he advertised in the local paper: 'Can do anything that your husband can't.' The response was phenomenal—he got offers from thirty-nine spinsters.

1453
A pessimist is a woman who is scared she won't be able to drive her new 84-inch wide car between the 72-inch gateposts of the driveway. An optimist is the husband who believes she won't try it.

1454
The octogenarian during the middle of an operation for rejuvenation became very impatient.

'Don't be so restless,' growled the doctor.

The poor man went on moaning and sobbing.

'Don't worry—the pain will soon vanish.'

'I'm not crying because of pain,' explained the old man, 'But if you don't get a move on I'll be late for school.'

1455
Woman in garden to neighbour: 'First I dug the ground, turning under the compost. Then I added nitrogen fertilizer and raked a smooth seed bed. Then I carefully planted them one foot apart and one and a half inches deep, and that's the last I ever saw of the darned things!'

1456
The fire officer had spoken at a Rotary lunch. During the question period afterwards one man got up and said, 'I understand why firemen have to hurry to get to a fire, but I've never been able to understand why great speed is necessary on the return trip.' 'They have to hurry back,' replied the fire officer, 'before they forget which suit is trumps.'

1457
A young medical student received a very expensive microscope from his parents for Christmas. The card was signed: 'Mamma and Pauper.'

1458
A statistician working on a population census wrote: 'It will be about seven months before we see any significant bulge in the marriage figures.'

1459
A caravan company issued a brochure for its new van showing a picture of the bathroom with a caption: 'The shower door can be removed, for your viewing pleasure.'

1460
Two Irishmen driving through the country noticed that many of the barns had weather-vanes in the shape of huge roosters.

'Pat,' said one man to the other, 'can you tell me why they always have a rooster and niver a hin on the top of thim barns?'

'Shure,' replied Mike, 'an' it must be because av the difficulty they'd have in collecting the eggs.'

1461
A man suffered from a bronchial attack, and as a result of it he was

unable to speak above a whisper. The illness was slight, but painful, and he decided to call at the residence of the doctor who had just moved to town.

The patient appeared one evening at the doctor's front door, rang the bell, and after a short wait stood facing the doctor's young and pretty maid.

'Is the doctor home?' he asked in his bronchial whisper.

'No!' the maid whispered in reply, 'Come on in.'

1462

An Irishman got a job at an observatory. During his first night's duty he paused to watch the astronomer peering through a large telescope. Just then a star fell.

'Man alive!' exclaimed the astonished Irishman, 'Did you ever see such a foine shot!'

1463

The priest was writing the certificate at a christening, and paused in an endeavour to recall the date. He appealed to the mother.

'Let me see, this is the nineteenth, isn't it?'

'The nineteenth! Yer riv-rence must be losin' yer mind. This is only the elivinth I've had.'

1464

Jones was scared to ask his girl's father for permission to wed her because he sensed that he was not paternally favoured. He induced Sally to break the news to him first. While Sally went to her Dad's office to chat him up Jones listened outside the door. He heard a mumble of conversation as the old man vented a fusilade of violent criticism. Then Salley joined him in the hall. 'What did Daddy say?' asked Jones, apprehensively.

'He didn't half let me have it!' she said grimly, 'He thinks you must need your head examining to want to marry a woman like me.'

1465

When Mrs. Weston added several inches to her chunky frame, Mr. Weston used to hide his embarrassment at parties by telling everyone: 'I couldn't afford a new wife so I had the old one re-upholstered.'

1466

A bachelor is a male who can't be changed once he's out of diapers

1467

An irascible grandmother, referring to her daughter: 'She was single for eight years because she couldn't say "Yes", and now she's married and got four children because she can't say "No".'

1468

The ups and downs of life are kids. They get you down all day and keep you up all night.

1469

'Strewth' is for something stranger than fiction.

1470

A Norwegian fisherman won the International Gluttony competition by a clear 27 hot pies. He just ate like a Norse.

1471

Two promoters were discussing the forthcoming heavyweight fight. Said Abe: 'It's a foregone conclusion. Our boy doesn't stand a chance.'

Joe said: 'For goodness' sake, Abe! Have a bit of faith! Stop reminis cing.'

1472

Two hours after meeting a girl at a luncheon party, the man rang her up and said: 'Hello Janet. It's me, again, Ernie. I just rang you to say I'm ever so sorry and I hope you won't be mad at me. The truth is I just couldn't help myself.'

She said curiously: 'What are you talking about? Our date isn't until eight o'clock tonight.'

'True,' he admitted, 'But I know what's going to happen and you don't.'

1473

Harold paid a substantial fee to a marriage bureau and they matched him with a girl. After two weeks of marital incompatibility he went back to the bureau and asked: 'Excuse me, but does your firm do part exchanges ?'

1474

Having lived a long useful, life, a pious and wise man died and went to his reward. Years later, his most trusted follower departed this life, and, upon arriving on the other side, went searching for his old teacher. He found him sitting on a large cloud with a gorgeous blonde on his lap. 'How marvellous!' he exclaimed, 'I am delighted to see that you have been given your just reward.'

'Hell!' said the old man, 'She's not my reward—I'm her punishment.'

1475

When they left their friend's house after an unexciting social evening the husband said: 'Considering how dull it was, you seem to be very cheerful.' The wife said: 'I had a marvellous time! Sybil looked so dowdy; the food was awful; and the whole place needs doing over.'

1476

A bikini halter is like the government of a South American republic— everybody wonders if it will retain its stability and many are praying for it to fall.

1477

Mrs. Lila Scott is a woman of great charm and sensibility, a gentle and kind person with considerable glamour and a sparkling personality. And if you don't believe it ask her yourself.

1478
Business tycoon Phil Dowers was discussing his new secretary with his partner. 'Her shorthand is awful, her typing is atrocious and she's never punctual . . I shall have to find her some other job.' His partner said: 'But Phil, she's so cute! So pretty and such a good sport! And what about that figure of hers! Heck!' Said Phil: 'Exactly. I'm glad you approve of her because she's our new partner.'

1479
Laura went alone on a holiday to Italy but she couldn't have had much of a rest because she looked very pinched, but happy, when she arrived home.

1480
A young man narrowly escaped drowning. There chanced to be a nurse on the beach and she gave him the kiss of life until the ambulance arrived, and then went with him to hospital because he was still unconscious. In the ambulance he revived suddenly. The nurse asked solicitously: 'How do you feel?'
So he showed her.

1481
Some poor fellow had fallen forty feet on to concrete outside a seaside hotel. He lay bruised, battered and semi-conscious. A waiter rushed out and, raising his reeling head, held a glass of sherry to his lips. Reviving a little the victim gasped: 'Got any brandy?'
The waiter said: 'We only serve brandy to people who fall from the penthouse restaurant.'

1482
There's a handsome young actor in Chelsea who's so much in love with himself he never takes a very hot bath in case the mirror gets steamed up.

1483
The Marine sergeant bawled: 'Now you'll make for Westheath Junction which is a march of another fifty miles, with full packload and I don't want no flagging.'
One new recruit muttered: 'Flagging! I couldn't even wave you goodbye.'

1484
If Goldilocks had been for *real* she would have had forbears.

1485
A mission has arrived in Britain from darkest Africa to study infertility rites among our society of pillers.

1486

A boy of about thirteen went to the library assistant and asked: 'Have you got any books on family planning?'

The embarrassed girl said: 'You're a bit young to get married aren't you?' He said: 'I'm not getting married! Last night Mom told Dad that he ought to plan a holiday for the whole family this year and he asked me to pick up some litreature after school.'

1487

The Sundowner Film Company was making an exciting comedy feature about espionage and sex. The script called for a large mock-up of a control radar station. This balsa wood edifice was erected on location beside a convenient lake, and suitably camouflaged. A week after its completion the shooting was finished and two studio chippies were sent to burn the dummy buildings and clear away the debris.

Just as they were setting fuses to blow the place up, a large Moskovitch car, bearing C.D. plates, screamed up to the lakeside and two men rushed out and took a series of photographs of the installation. Then they got back into the car which accelerated away in a cloud of dust. When the chippies reported the incident to the studio about six hours later, the producer said: 'They must have been watching while you blew up the set. We had a phone call inviting both of you to the Embassy to receive the Order of Lenin!'

1488

A do-it-yourself enthusiast was doing some home repairs on his bathroom shower and he sent his wife to the local hardware store to buy a three-quarter-inch pipe plug.

The ironmonger asked her: 'Do you want a male plug or a female plug, or both?'

She said: 'George didn't say, but I think he just wants to plug up a leak, not breed them.'

1489

An agonised customer slouched into a chemist's shop and asked: 'Do you have a bottle of aspirins that doesn't have a squeaky screw-cap?'

1490

Many couples get married at an early urge.

1491

One removal man to his colleague as they transfer exhibits from the old Blackstone Museum into the new one.

'Idiots, they are! They spend two million on a new building and still keep these old ornaments.'

1492

'Come along,' he said, 'it's bedtime.'

She said: 'Oh, I don't feel at all sleepy.'

He said: 'If you did, there wouldn't be much point, would there?'

174

1493

Two friends had spent the whole day fishing and they went back to Benny's place for supper, empty-handed. But when his wife asked Benny if he'd caught anything he answered in evasive embarrassment: 'Oh! Just a couple of soles and a large bass.'

'Did he really?' the wife asked his friend, when Benny went to get some drinks, 'or is he lying?'

The friend admitted: 'Well, actually it was two old boots and a beer can.'

1494

They were arguing about their faith.

'I come from one of the oldest Christian families in the world. One of my ancestors was thrown to the lions,' said one man.

'Maybe,' said another one, 'but one of my forebears rowed the boat that took St. Paul to Cyprus.'

A third one said grandly: 'I can beat that by years! One of my ancestors was head of the gang which stole the Ten Commandments from the Jews.'

1495

A wealthy industrialist had his house architecturally designed and built by his son-in-law, Sidney, after subtle persuasion from his lovely daughter. The completed edifice was a complete mess. Subsiding foundations, leaking roofs, ill-fitting windows, flaking ceilings, insecure chimneys and cracking walls.

At dinner one evening the industrialist went over the repairs schedule with another builder and was annoyed to find that they would cost almost as much as the original building. His daughter came in with an Italian brochure to show her father where she and Sidney were going on tour. Looking at the pictures of Pisa, her father said, bitterly: 'I see Sidney has built an hotel out there.'

1496

Asked why he had given a large solitaire diamond to a girl known to be something of a dim-wit despite her very pulchritudinous aspect, he said: 'What else? It's the carat dangled in front of the ass.'

1497

The man said to this very attractive girl: 'Tell me your hopes, your wishes, your inhibitions . . .'

1498

He said bitterly 'My love life is just like any old American movie plot: "Man gets girl, man loses gold mine, man loses girl, man takes *mine*".'

1499

On a new estate down south social life was limited to church-going and pubs until an ex-actor started a dramatic society. Nearly every family down one avenue had a member in the acting club. They were casting a new production on the life of the disciple Judas, from the New Testament, and the producer had completed his list except for one principal character. This was a problem needing careful consideration.

One man, named Jenkins, was fairly confident that his audition had convinced the producer of his suitability but he was impatient to know if he was in fact getting the part.

The night of the final reading before proper rehearsals began Jenkins waylaid the producer in the local bar and asked him bluntly. 'Look Martin, have you made your mind up about who's to play the part of Jesus?'

Martin said: 'It was a hard decision to make because the part of Jesus calls for a great deal of genuine sincerity. But now I think we've selected the right chap.'

Jenkins said, 'You mean I'm getting it?'

The producer said: 'Oh, no. It's gone to that neighbour of yours, Lattimer.'

Jenkins slammed his beer mug down and snorted enviously: 'That silly ass! Lattimer? I hate the swine!'

The producer said: 'There you are! See?'

1500

I got home from the office completely exhausted, fell into an armchair and complained to my wife: 'I feel half dead.' Straight away she picked up the telephone. I said: 'There's no need to call the doctor,' and she said, 'I'm not calling a doctor, I'm calling the insurance company. I may as well collect half the money.'

1501

At a co-ed school a 15-year-old girl and a 16-year-old boy were waiting in a queue to see the headmistress. The girl said shyly: 'Just think—if it hadn't been for your hair hanging down your back and my hemline up by my waist, we would never have met.'

1502

The salesman was fed up after showing the pop star a wide variety of psychedelic kipper-ties, all of which had been rejected. Finally he pulled out a box, extracted the most flamboyant necktie in the shop and said. 'How about this one? It's not only colourful, it has a built-in volume control and echo-chamber.'

1503

They were on the set for the penultimate scene in a torchy movie, and the director was going over the action with his sexy superstar.

'Now, Brianca,' he said, 'This next shot is going to be a tremendous challenge to you—you'll be wearing clothes and so won't have any help from your natural artistic talents.'

1504

The family lawyer was about to read the rich man's will to the highly attractive but fluffily dumb young widow, sitting in his office.

'On the whole,' he said, 'you may find the stipulations very adequate. He's left all his money to the London School of Medicine, and his brain to you.'

1505
At the desk of the employment bureau the manager was arguing with a persistent old tramp.
'I keep telling you there's no vacancy available there. They already *have* a chairman for the Bank of England.'

1506
The salesman in the shoe shop had tried seventy pairs on the short-sighted lady without finding a suitable size. He went away to get another type of shoe and returned to find the customer peering down at her right foot; trying to wriggle her toes.
'This style doesn't seem *quite* so tight,' she said to him.
'No, madam,' he admitted, 'but that's the box.'

1507
All people throughout the civilized world are intrigued about the sources and derivations of joke stories. Some think that hard-working scribes burn midnight oil at both ends, forging funnies out of thin air. Of course the truth is that joke stories emanate solely from truth and fact. For example, the following excerpt from a recent newspaper will illustrate exactly how joke stories issue directly from normal everyday happenings; proving that scenes from the world of human comedy are sufficiently amusing to negate the need for writers to fictionalise:
'Housewife Evelyn Gale found a note written in Polish inside a jar of gherkins imported from Poland. Mrs. Gale, of Preston Lane, Banstead, Surrey, had it translated—and found it was a message from one Polish mother to another working in the factory warning her that someone called Richard was making eyes at her daughter in the pickling shed.'
This cameo has not only provided the basis for half a dozen gags and jokes in Warsaw, but it has also been dramatised into a ribald three-act play, and there are rumours that a celebrated American porn author is currently turning it into a thrilling sex novel. We would point out that, in Poland, making eyes at daughters in *pickling* sheds during office hours is a daring snub against authority as it is inclined to prime too many spicy stories.

1508
When the vicar opened up the box to see how much had been contributed to his 'Urgent Church Roof Repairs Fund' he found two 10p pieces, half a dozen old halfpennies and a second-hand copy of *Do-It-Yourself*.

1509
In a remote coastal town up north a lighthouse keeper has just been

compelled to divorce the bride he married only last month. He found out she couldn't sleep with the light on.

1510

So many footballers are being booked at both mid-week and weekend matches that referees in the north are demanding secretaries who can take dictation on the field.

1511

When George went to the barber's, the operator observed that his moustache had changed into several sprouting wiry whiskers, his head was covered with ginger fur and his ears had developed pointed apexes.

'Excuse me sir,' he said to the customer, 'Don't you think you should ask your wife what sort of tinned food she is feeding you on?'

1512

In Nottingham there's a foolish husband who allowed his wife to join a nudist sun club because he thought he'd save money on her clothes, only to find she was spending thirty times as much on French skin food.

1513

A pop-singer is someone who chants unmusical folk-songs about the troubles of the world as though they were all born at the same time he was, and just for *his* benefit.

1514

A smuggler is someone who reverses popular maritime hobbies by putting bottles into ships.

1515

The shy young man approached the rich company chairman and asked: 'Sir, may I have permission to marry your lovely daughter.'

'You had me fooled,' the tycoon replied. 'I must admit you don't *look* like a parson.'

1516

Five years old Dicky was annoying his mother by being naughty as usual. In a fit of desperation she yelled at him: 'Just wait till your father comes home!' Said Dicky: 'Don't be daft, Mom, he's still got another sixteen months to do.'

1517

There was trouble in the home of a newly-wed teenage couple when the young husband came home late one night from one of his beat-band gigs.

Tearful Joyce cried as she hung up the leather reefer he had tossed on the sofa: 'All right, Bernard! Whose is this long blonde hair on your shoulder?'

Glancing up from the comic paper he was looking at, he said: 'Don't be stupid, Joyce—it's mine.'

1518

Ex-Sergeant Phil Masters was recently awarded the medal of merit for bravery on the field. He has been a football referee for two years since retiring from the Army.

1519

What do they call an Eskimo who pads the walls of his ice-house with foam rubber? An igloonatic.

1520

On Macdonald's birthday, Jack Stuart went into the main Glasgow post office and sent him a greetings telegram, C.O.D.

1521

A scientist in the Scottish Highlands recently made a tremendous breakthrough by inventing instant whisky. His only problem now is how to keep it for seven years until it matures.

1522

A businessman went to a signwriter to urgently order a dozen large posters and showcards worded: 'Monster Sale', 'Everything Reduced', 'Over 50% Discount', 'Bargains Galore', and 'All Prices Slashed', etc.

The signwriter said: 'Ready in five days Mr. Rogers, and the whole twelve will only cost you £40.'

Mr. Rogers was annoyed: 'Last month you did twelve similar signs for only £15!' he complained.

'Yes. But you've come at a fortunate time. This week is *my* annual sale and I'm selling everything at extremely advantageous prices,' explained the sign expert.

'Damn it!—You're charging nearly three times the price. How can that be advantageous?' snapped Rogers.

'It is to me,' said the signwriter.

1523

By the roadside, well out in the country, on a cold, dark winter night, a car and caravan were parked with all the lights blazing. The anxious driver was standing in the middle of the road with a torch waiting for the AA patrol man after getting a passing motorist to telephone from the nearest phone box and alert the organisation. The AA man, soaked to the skin, arrived at last fresh from another breakdown.

'You took your time!' said the motorist. 'Have you brought the tyre lever and the hot water?'

The AA man said: 'Yes—and this is a fine night to have your engine freeze up *and* a puncture.'

The driver said: 'What freeze up? What puncture? You fool—my wife's in the van, having a baby.'

1524

'Mr. Jones always takes his wife a cup of tea first thing in the morning,' complained a wife. 'Does he?' replied her husband, 'Perhaps if I had a word with him he'd bring you one too.'

1525

A man named Thorpe had a very unfortunate psychological problem, finding it impossible to pursue an adequate social life because he was so shy and retiring. He couldn't even pass a lingerie shop without blushing. So his doctor sent him to a psychiatrist for treatment. The psychiatrist worked on the patient for two months and was very proud of the progress being made until one afternoon when he got back to his consulting room fifteen minutes later than the arranged appointment only to find that Mr. Thorpe had started without him and was already on the couch. With the psychiatrist's wife.

1526

A Northern business man on a trip to London for the first time was lucky enough to find a girl friend who invited him back to her flat for a drink. The hospitality became even more generous and they were on the sofa having fun when the door was suddenly pushed open and a man rushed in; a camera in his hand, taking pictures from different angles.

The Northerner jumped to his feet in alarm and slowly realised that he'd been duped. 'What a fool I am!' he cried. 'I've read about girls like you, playing the badger game! Now I suppose you're going to blackmail me!'

The girl said: 'Oh! for Pete's sake sit down! Don't take any notice of my husband. He's camera crazy—just loves taking unusual pictures.'

1527

Then there's the Swiss mountain rescue expert who was very frustrated on holiday at Happy Valley because he couldn't find any mountains to rescue.

1528

Admiring the handsome brooch worn by an old school friend, a lady asked, 'Anniversary?'

'No,' was the reply. 'Quarrel.'

1529

'Your little boy gets more like his father every day,' observed a neighbour, over the fence.

'Oh, hell! What's he been up to now?' the other woman asked.

1530

In 1815, the French diarist, Yves St. Pepys of Paris 16e wrote the following entries in his journal concerning Napoleon Bonaparte's departure from Elba:

March 9. 'The cursed animal has escaped from his den'.
March 10. 'The Corsican ogre has landed at Cape Juan.'
March 11. 'The villanous swine has arrived at Gap.'
March 12. 'The monster has passed the night at Grenoble.'
March 13. 'The Tyrant has crossed Lyons.'
March 14. 'The Usurper is directing his course towards Dijon, but the brave and loyal Burgundians have risen in a body and they surround him on all sides.'
March 18. 'Bonaparte is sixty leagues from the Capital; he has had skill enough to escape from the hands of his pursuers.'
March 19. 'Bonaparte advances rapidly, but he will never vanquish the brave defenders.'
March 20. 'Tomorrow Napoleon will be under our ramparts.'
March 21. 'The Emperor is at Fontainebleau.'
March 22. 'His Imperial and Royal Majesty last evening made his entrance into his Palace of the Tuileries amidst the joyous acclamations of an adoring and faithful people.'

1531
Two battery glow-worms were courting on the branch of a sycamore tree at midnight when they had a tiff. 'All right!', said the female, 'you glow your way and I'll glow mine.'

1532
Hungarians tell the story about two friends who met in a Budapest street just after the Russians' latest success in space. 'Have you heard?' asked one. 'The Russians have invented a device to take them to Venus!'
'What!' exclaimed the other enthusiastically, 'All of them?'

1533
In Leeds lived a fireman who was horribly mean both to his wife and his lodger. One night he brought home a splendid pork pie and ate half of it for his supper. His wife and the lodger had to make do with dry bread and cheese. He carefully put the rest of the pie away, and they all went to their beds.
In the middle of the night the fire bells rang, and off the fireman had to run. The wife entered the lodger's room, shook him awake and said: 'He's gone out. Now's your chance.'
'Are you sure it's all right?' enquired the lodger.
'Of course! Hurry up.'
So the lodger went downstairs and finished the pork pie.

1534
The big-game hunter had taken his wife on her first safari. He had bagged a few minor trophies, but the principal prize was the huge lion killed by his wife.
'Did she hit it with that ·303 Magnum rifle you bought her?' asked an admiring friend.
'No,' answered her husband. 'With the second-hand station-wagon we hired.'

1535

A negro boy came home painted white, and said: 'The kids at school painted me white all over,' so his mother beat him for getting messed up. Father came home, and said: 'What's going on?' so Mother told him: 'The kids at school painted our Sid white.' So father gave him another thrashing for not standing up for himself. Shortly afterwards a small voice was heard crying: 'I've only been a white boy for two hours but already I hate you black pigs.'

1536

Every good journalist has a good novel in him—which is an excellent place to leave it.

1537

Ricardo's wife is a busy little cook. She's always experimenting with new meals, and Ricardo always knows what's for afters. Chronic dyspepsia!

1538

The Colonel was passing through the parade ground when he came across two rookies having a fierce argument and slugging each other with some fervour. He angrily called them to attention and snarled: 'Get this straight, you two hooligans. If there's one thing I won't tolerate in this regiment it's fighting!'

1539

Cultural boarding-house beds in the North are famous for their Gothic itches and Ironic pillows.

1540

Her mother told little Sybil to pray for better weather so that her grandfather's rheumatism would ease up. She knelt down and said her usual prayers, ending with: 'And please, Lord, make it hot for Grandpa.'

1541

'Look Mummy! There's a cow tossing Daddy in the air, over in that field!'

'Veronica, don't be stupid! That's a bull.'

1542

A fiery Diplomat was the survivor of a dozen duels of honour. For one of them he had to journey to a country town some distance from Paris. He and his adversary arrived at the railway station simultaneously. The adversary bought a return ticket; the diplomat asked only for a single ticket.

'You haven't much confidence in yourself,' said the adversary with a sneer.

'On the contrary,' replied the diplomat. 'I always use my opponent's return ticket after a duel.'

1543

A newspaper was running a competition to discover the most high-principled, sober, well behaved local inhabitant. Among the entries came one which read: 'I don't smoke, touch intoxicants or gamble. I am faithful to my wife and I never look at another woman. I am hard working, quiet and obedient. I never go to the cinema or the theatre, and I go to bed early every night and rise with the dawn. I attend chapel regularly every Sunday without fail. I've been like this for the past three years. But just wait until next spring, when they let me out of here!'

1544

A wealthy art collector was asked if his ancestors were genuine Reynolds or Gainsboroughs. The tycoon replied, 'They're not even genuine ancestors.'

1545

A certain prominent business man lost his wife, and the funeral became a public occasion. All the dignitaries of the town attended, and almost all were known to the bereaved. There was, however, a stranger, and he seemed more upset than anyone. Before the funeral was over he broke down completely. The widower-husband asked who was this weeping stranger . . .

'Ooh!' whispered someone, 'didn't you know? He was your late wife's lover!'

The bereaved moved across to the sobbing man, patted him on the back, and said:

'Cheer up old boy, cheer up, I shall probably be getting married again shortly.'

1546

A woman telephoned her doctor late one evening and said, 'I know what's wrong with me. I've got hyperinsulism.' 'I know,' said the doctor. 'I just saw the same TV programme.'

1547

A camouflage battalion was training in Sussex, and Mike and Tim were doing very nicely as the front and rear, respectively, of a gentle-eyed cow. Suddenly Jim gave Mike a vigorous kick and muttered, 'Run like hell'. 'What's the matter?' said Mike. 'Matter?' echoed Jim. 'Here comes the general's wife with a milk pail.'

1548

A city motorist asked a farmer 'How far would you say it was to Flemington?' 'Wal,' calculated the farmer, 'it's 24,992 miles the direction you're headin'; you passed it about five miles back.'

1549

The first time Nussbaum and Shapiro went to Shanghai, a pixie guide steered them into an opium den and persuaded them to take a few puffs. 'It had no effect on me whatever,' boasted Nussbaum. 'Me neither,' echoed Shapiro. A few minutes later Nussbaum beat his breast soundly and declared, 'My mind is made up. I'm buying control of ICI.' 'Sorry,' said Shapiro, 'but I won't sell.'

1550
Did you hear about the poor chap who lost his circus job as a collector on one of the rides? He don't get around much any more.

1551
'Now Willie,' coaxed Mama, 'be a good boy and say "Ah-h-h," so the nasty doctor can get his finger out of your mouth.'

1552
This is the sad story of the publican who had just unlocked his premises for the day's business when a pink elephant and a purple rhinoceros mooched up to the bar. 'I'm sorry, boys,' said the bartender. 'He hasn't come in yet.'

1553
Two Russian scientists were discovered by St. Peter lurking just outside the pearly gates. 'You fellows can't come in here,' said St. Peter sternly. 'You're atheists.' 'We don't want to come in,' answered one of the Russians. 'We just want to get our ball.'

1554
'Is your husband a go-getter?' one girl asked another at a party. 'Hardly,' replied the second girl, flatly. 'I bought him a self-winding watch for his birthday last Monday and it's already run down.'

1555
Lips—the skin you touch to love.

1556
A large firm of corsetry makers has just patented a new padded bra under the trade-name 'Shamnesia'. It's for small-built women who haven't passed the Mensa mammary test.

1557
There's a new puff-pastry on the market which states on the wrapper: 'Sufficient for four persons or ten little tarts.'

1558
A masochist is someone who's starved of affliction.

1559
Alimony—an ex-husband a girl can still bank on.

1560
Mrs. Thorpe was told by the police that her missing husband had been

184

found trapped in his car on the bottom of a deep lake with a young blonde barmaid after he had run off the road in the fog. 'The swine,' she said. 'I never thought he'd sink so low.'

1561

After the village cricket match, the home team captain looked at his beer and found it flat, discoloured and short-measured so he went over to the bar and punched the landlord on the nose.

A friend told the other customers 'He's appealing against the light.'

1562

Before the children's party Mom told her birthday boy: 'And remember —when Daddy takes his third tranquillizer, the party's over.'

1563

The editor of the poultry journal received a letter from a reader. It read: 'How long should a hen remain on the eggs?' The editor replied: 'Three weeks for chickens and four weeks for ducks.'

Three weeks passed, and the editor again received a letter from the reader. 'Thank you very much for your kind advice,' it read. 'The hen remained on the eggs for three weeks, and there were no chickens hatched, and, as I do not care for ducks, I took her off the nest and sold the eggs.'

1564

In the highlands of Scotland an Englishman and his wife bought a farm because they wanted solitude and peaceful remoteness from civilisation. Driving home one day the husband was enjoying the empty vastness of the countryside when he suddenly saw a caravan being parked in a field and preparations being made by a family to set up residence. He accelerated the rest of the seventy miles to his farm and said to his wife 'Mary, you're not going to like this—we've got some new neighbours.'

1565

A husband returned home one night unexpectedly and went up to the bedroom to find his wife standing in front of the pier glass in a smart new negligée. He also noticed the toes of a pair of shoes peeping from under the long drapes covering the windows to the balcony. Swivelling round in a pretence of surprise and modelling the new night-wear she said to her husband: 'How do I look?'

Pacing to the window he said grimly: 'Guilty!'

1566

A burlesque is an airstrip where they take off on a short runway.

1567

A bright but unsuccessful English actress went to Hollywood, lived happily and got married forever after.

1568

Said the intending borrower to his unobliging banker: 'But it says in your advertisements in all the daily newspapers and weekly colour supplements that your bank is eagerly waiting to advance money to your customers.'

The manager said: 'I know. That's the worst of having an advertising manager who used to sell nylon stockings from a tray in Oxford Street.'

1569

Husband: What's for dinner?

Wife: All I could get was a can of meat loaf.

Husband: Oh hell! Let's eat out at some restaurant tonight!

Wife: April Fool! As a matter of fact I've made you one of my specials—fish soup, casseroled rissoles with curry and vegetables and Yorkshire pudding with rhubarb fritters to follow.

Husband: Oh hell! Let's eat out at a restaurant tonight.

1570

Three very clever and devious students in the drop-out category thumbed a ride in a shiny new limousine on a main trunk road. The driver, an amiable Northerner, asked one of them as they sped along: 'And what do you do for a living?'

The boy answered airily: 'Who me? Oh, I'm with digital computers.'

The other two lads laughed. The driver said to another one. 'And what's your line?' He answered: 'Oh, I'm on an open Rhodes scholarship.' Again the others laughed.

The driver asked the third one if he had a job, and the third one declared: 'I happen to be a motoring correspondent. I write letters home, sitting in cars.'

At that moment the driver happened to glance into the driving mirror. Pushing down the accelerator he said: 'You can start writing another one, lad. I pinched this lim from a car park fifty miles back, and there's a patrol squad right behind us.'

1571

The other day Mollie went into a cut-price store and saw a special offer of toilet requisites, so she bought them and took them home and decided to have a bath and freshen herself up. The shampoo she used on her hair was so stinging she was blinded, so she groped out of the bath, dried off, then reached for the talcum powder off the shelf and smothered herself with it. When her eyes cleared she found she'd used a scourer by mistake, and it took her two hours to get it out of the cracks.

1572

We've moved into such a small flat that my wife has had to train our dog to wag his tail up and down.

1573

She was so angry she could hardly contain herself . . . and that goes for the dress she was wearing too.

1574

Forty ducks were gathered in conference. The leader spoke: 'The farmer is planning a new feather bed and we're expected to supply the down, and winter is coming on. So—I vote that we have a whip round to buy the old boy a spring-interior mattress.'

1575

My girl has just bought something for her bottom drawer. It's a cure for dry rot.

1576

I came home and found my little lad on the telephone. He said to me: 'I won't be a minute, Dad, I'm talking to your bank manager about a loan.' I said: 'You're what? You don't need a loan.' And he said: 'I know I don't, but *he* does.'

1577

Atkinson's wife's just bought a new Living Bra—and now she doesn't know whether to breast-feed it or put it on the bottle. It doesn't really matter because it leads such an empty life, anyway.

1578

A three-time loser stood glumly on the corner of the street jingling his last few coins in his pocket. A well-nourished man in a smartly cut suit rolled past in his super-de-luxe Mercedes coupé, smoking a cigar. Muttered the pedestrian: 'There, but for me, go I.'

1579

Two men gatecrashed a society party in Mayfair. They went directly to the buffet where one of them indicated the punch bowl and asked his companion: 'Care for a drink?' His friend nodded, picked up the punch bowl and drank half of it; then he wiped his mouth with the back of his hand and said to the other man: 'Where's yours?'

1580

Ace news correspondent Walter Thurleigh of the *Daily Calamity* went out to the Middle East on a special assignment for his editor. It was a dangerous expedition in which he encountered death several times, starved for days, got wounded on two occasions and was kidnapped by militant Arab leftists and tortured on a griddle for five hours. His chief was so delighted he organised a little celebration on pay day, and then handed the reporter his salary cheque. 'Walt,' said the editor, 'I'm real proud of you, and to show my appreciation, here's a little something extra.' He then stood up and shouted: 'Hip, hip, hooray!' three times.

1581

An international magazine company organised a research programme to discover how many influential tycoons and aristocrats were readers of their old-established world-news commentaries. High-powered young go-getters were specially hired to interview the famous and the mighty all over the U.K. about which publications they favoured. One enterprising quizzer gained an appointment with Lord Chippendale-Frythe, chairman of eighteen corporations, who had a reputation for being involved in successive affairs with numerous society beauties, even at the ripe old age of seventy-one. In his lordship's teak-lined revolving office on the 34th floor of Chippendale Towers the interviewer sipped a vintage sherry and cautiously made his initial approach: 'May I ask you a question, my lord? Do you take *Time*?' The old rake paused to consider and then replied amiably: 'Young man, at my age, I have to.'

1582

An anxious man burst into the operating theatre of a hospital, grimacing with pain and lay down shouting: 'I'm in pain, I'm in pain!' A passing waitress from the hospital canteen heard his cries and went in. 'Nurse,' he pleaded, mistaking her identity, 'I'm in awful pain. Can't you do something?' She said: 'I'm sorry this isn't my table.'

1583

Patrick was passing the cathedral when one of the stone cherubs broke loose from the spire balustrade and dropped 200 feet to the ground, smashed in pieces. Patrick went into the cathedral, caught hold of a priest and cried: 'I have to report a fallen angel.'

1584

When an Englishman goes out for the evening he asks a neighbour to baby-sit. An American asks a passing stranger. A Frenchman asks his wife.

1585

There are so many mail-order firms now selling ex-government material that there must be hundreds of factories deliberately forced into manufacturing army surplus goods.

1586

The National Health Service is an organisation fully equipped to deal with emergencies strictly by appointment.

1587

What annoys Mr. Holdhurst, a master at Petersfield School, is the fact that the most rowdy and unruly lad in his form has an excellent attendance record and has never been late.

1588

Her husband arrived home one evening to find the house in a shambles of unmade beds, unwashed crockery and littered hallways. His wife was sitting on the sofa looking wan and harassed. 'I'm worn out,' she sighed, 'It's taken me since lunch time to tidy up my handbag.'

1589
Because Bobby had reached the ripe old age of thirteen, his father thought it was time to give his son some good advice so he sat him down in the den after supper and laboriously told him about the birds and the bees and sober habits and good citizenship. After this tirade, the confused youngster asked: 'Are those what are called the Facts of Life?'
'Yes,' said Dad.
Bobby thought for a minute and said, 'I wish I was dead.'

1590
Prayer brings a family closer together but if you prefer being agnostic you can always buy a bubble car for a similar effect.

1591
Sonny came home from school angrily waving his notebook which was smothered with red crosses and harsh notes scribbled in the margins by teacher. Going directly to the head of the household he pushed the book at him and said 'Call yourself a father! Look at the awful marks you got for maths!'

1592
Said the outraged young English actress when she got home after an evening out with an accomplished young French diplomat who owned an enormous estate in Lorraine: 'My god, he's got a lot of Gaul!'

1593
When anyone soft-soaps you, remember it's made of 90% lye.

1594
Computer Expert No. 1: Do you know that Miss Edwards in Accounts gets three thousand a year?
Computer Expert No. 2: Pounds or dollars?
No. 1: Propositions.

1595
Necessity primed the invention of mothers.

1596
Kuko the reindeer-trainer had an unblemished record except for one lapse. He once shot another trainer—he found his Lapp lass sitting on this other Lapp's lap. It wasn't her fault—she was a natural born Laplander.

1597
Husband studying bank statement: 'Well—at last we're out of the wood Dora—and up the creek.'

1598
Cliff Richard has just spent a small fortune having his spectacles reglazed with stained-glass.

1599

Movie producer: 'Right, Miss Welch—now in this next scene you get into the elevator and unexpectedly come face to face with your husband's secretary, played by Miss Loren . . .'

'Hold it, hold it!' said Raquel. 'It's impossible.'

1600

If an Englishman cannot make a go of his marriage he goes off to his club. An Irishman goes to his priest. An American goes to his attorney. A German goes to his bierkeller. A Frenchman goes to his mistress.

1601

An Englishman doesn't talk to strangers. A Frenchman only talks to female strangers. An American only speaks briefly as he rushes by. A Russian only speaks to himself—and then in a whisper.

1602

The Biggin-Fosters are so wealthy they even take their own branded ants with them on picnics.

1603

Phillip was having trouble getting through to his wife by phone. After a heated argument the operator asked coldly: 'Look—are you in a box?'

'No,' he snapped, 'Do I *sound* like a blasted cigar?'

The operator said: 'If you were I'd bite your damn end off!'

1604

Six-year-old Frankie came home early from his school friend John Stanmore's birthday party. His mother said: 'You didn't stay long! Didn't you enjoy yourself?' Her lad said: 'Oh it was quite all right—until I pinned the tail on Mrs. Stanmore.'

1605

The widespread miners' strike had caused the Central Generating Board to warn people about not wasting electricity. One nervous woman rang her local electricity office for some advice and was switched to a workman who was doing overtime in the stores. The young wife said: 'It's about the power cuts. Will it be safe for me to sleep on an electric blanket tonight with my husband?'

The electrician said: 'Don't ask me. You know him better than I do.'

1606

Two young lads were briskly scrubbing the walls of a country cottage down a lane when the vicar ambled by. Said he: 'It's wonderful to see you youngsters being so kind and helpful to a poor old lady like Miss Forde by helping her like this. It proves that *all* you youngsters are not the vicious, uncaring layabouts that the newspapers keep criticising. Are you cleaning the walls for nothing?'

One lad said bitterly: 'No we ain't! She got mad at us for throwing

paint over the cottage and she's got her shotgun trained on us through
the kitchen window.'

1607

Joan bought some seductive perfume called 'Conquest' which was so
powerful a strange man took her back there an hour later and bought
the store for her.

1608

A citizen who prided himself on being something of a Samaritan was
passing an apartment house in the small hours of a foggy morning
when he noticed a man leaning against the doorway.

'What's the matter,' he asked, 'Drunk?'

'Yup.'

'Do you live in this house?'

'Yup.'

'Do you want me to help you upstairs?'

'Yup.'

With much difficulty he half dragged the drooping figure up the
stairway.

'What floor do you live on?' he asked, 'Is this it?'

'Yup.'

Rather than face an irate wife who might, perhaps, take him for a
companion more at fault than her spouse, he opened the first door he
came to and pushed the limp figure inside.

The Samaritan groped his way downstairs again. As he was passing
through the vestibule he was able to make out the dim outlines of
another man in a worse condition than the first one.

'What's the matter?' he asked, 'Are you drunk, too?'

'Yep,' was the feeble reply.

'Do you live in this house, too?'

'Yep.'

The Samaritan pulled and carried him to the second floor, where he
said he lived. He opened the same door and pushed him in. As he
reached the front door he discerned the shadow of a third man,
evidently worse off than either of the other two. He was about to
approach him when the object of his solicitude lurched out into the
street and threw himself into the arms of a passing policeman. 'Fer
Heav'n sake,' he gasped, 'protect me from that maniac. He's done
nothin' all night long but carry me upstairs and throw me down the
lift shaft.'

1609

As the boat was sinking, the captain lifted his voice to ask: 'Does
anybody know how to pray?'

One man spoke confidently in answer, because he was a priest: 'Yes
captain, I do.'

'Good,' said the skipper. 'Go ahead and pray while the rest of us put
on lifejackets—we're one short.'

1610

'Halt,' yelled the sergeant to a new squad of recruits. But one of them marched on.

'Here, Jones, what were you doing before you joined the Army?' yelled the sergeant.

'National Hunt jockey,' replied Jones.

When the squad was marching again the sergeant cried: 'Squad halt! Jones, whoa.'

1611

His friend was worrying. 'Tell me all about it. Get it off your chest.'

'I wish I could,' groaned the sailor, 'I've got the name Maude tattooed there, and I'm engaged to a girl named Caroline.'

1612

The housewife gave the tramp a large piece of pie on condition that he would saw some wood. The tramp retired to the woodshed but presently he reappeared at the back door of the house with the piece of pie still intact save for one morsel bitten from the end.

'Madam,' he said respectfully to the woman, 'if it's all the same to you, I'll eat the wood, and saw the pie.'

1613

'Jiminy, Seth,' screamed a hillbilly bride to her bone-idle husband, 'Yer beard is caught fire.'

'I know it, I know it,' he answered angrily, 'Cain't you see me prayin' fer rain?'

1614

In a tight-fisted village congregation, the hat was passed round one Sunday and returned empty. The pastor cast his eyes heavenward and said reverently, 'I thank Thee, oh Lord, that I got my hat back; whoever took the band is welcome to it.'

1615

'Fifty pounds for this beautiful vehicle?' demanded an outraged motorist of a second-hand dealer. 'Do you realise I've owned this car eight years and never had a wreck?'

'What you mean,' corrected the dealer, 'is that you've owned this wreck eight years and never had a car.'

1616

Two Irishmen had been on holiday in Miami for about a week when one felt the urge to do a little gambling. His friend explained that reformers had clamped the lid down tight but that one backroom was running surreptitiously in an obscure night-club. Just before they entered, the friend warned, 'You realise, of course, that this place is crooked. The wheel is fixed, and I think the dice are loaded.'

'Not so loud,' pleaded the other, 'They might hear us and not let us in.'

1617

Traffic wardens are finding their work harder. Yesterday alone eight men were fined for illegally parking on yellow lines and were indignant because it wasn't their fault there was such a queue at the social security office when they went to collect their subsistence allowances.

1618

I love Hawaii. It's about the only place on earth where people put flowers on you while you're still alive.

1619

Then there's the golfer who had five or six swipes at the ball and still didn't quite connect. He turned to the caddy and said 'Well, I think it'll be cool enough, now. Let's tee off.'

1620

Cosmetic chemical combines make a lot of money these days because teenagers are plentiful, and their goods dye the young.

1621

An irate housewife called her husband, who was in the midst of an important business conference, and babbled, 'John, that nasty butcher just told me to go to hell! What do you advise?' The husband said: 'Well, don't take your mink coat, you'll look too conspicuous.' And rang off.

1622

Mrs. Flynn came home from an afternoon of shopping and discovered her husband packing a suitcase. 'Where do you think you're going?' she asked.

'London,' he said defiantly. 'I just read in the paper that men are so scarce there that women are paying them £2 to take them home and be nice to them.'

Mrs. Flynn nodded her head a few times without saying anything. A few minutes later Mr. Flynn found that his wife also was throwing her belongings into a case. 'Where are you bound for?' he asked.

'I am going to London too,' said Mrs. Flynn. 'I just want to see how you are going to manage to live on £4 a month.'

1623

A helpful little old lady contributed a pair of pyjamas to the Red Cross. 'I made them myself,' she said proudly. They were perfect in every detail except that there was no opening in the front of the trousers. When the inspector explained the error, the old lady's face fell. Suddenly she brightened. 'Couldn't you give them to a bachelor?' she suggested.

1624

Little Sydney had been absent the previous day when Miss Jones, had been teaching the rest of the class some nursery rhymes. She was asking them questions about the book they had read together, and she forgot that Sydney had been absent. After quizzing several other infants, she said to Sidney: 'Now, what was it Humpty Dumpty sat on, Sydney?'

Sydney looked embarrassed and confused. 'Come along, Sydney,' she repeated, 'Look at the picture.' She showed him the picture but it still meant nothing to Sydney who couldn't read the words under it. 'Well? What is he sitting on?' Miss Jones persisted. Sydney muttered: 'His bum, I suppose, but an egg don't *have* a bum.'

1625

It's such a fine day,' said the store chief to his assistant, 'that I think I'll go down to the club for a round of golf.' 'I wish I was rich,' the assistant said later to his secretary, 'I wouldn't mind getting out into this sunshine once in a while myself.' The secretary told him: 'How will the boss know, if you call for your wife and sneak off to the beach for the afternoon?' The assistant thought this was an excellent suggestion. At his home, however, he had considerable difficulty getting the front door open; when he did force his way in he saw his boss making love to his wife. The assistant stole silently out of the house, and ran back to the office. 'What happened?' asked his secretary. 'Didn't you go to the beach?'

'What happened,' echoed the assistant. 'You and your fancy ideas! On account of you I darn near got fired!'

1626

A social visitor sat by the bedside of a patient who was in hospital with a wound in his arm. 'I'm sure your dear little wife must miss you terribly,' she said conversationally.

'She didn't this time,' he said.

1627

Farmer Thomas bought a sow and it wasn't long before he thought it would be nice to have a litter of little pigs to go with it. A pigbreeder who lived three miles away offered him the use of his boar for £2. Thomas put his sow into a wheelbarrow and pushed it the necessary three miles.

The next morning he came down expecting to find a lot of little pigs gambolling about, but found the sow in solitary grandeur.

'No wonder,' said a colleague when he heard about this experience. 'What do you expect for £2? I've got a prize-winning boar at my place fifteen miles from yours that I will let you use for £10.'

The next day Thomas put his sow in the wheelbarrow and pushed it for fifteen miles. 'This time I am sure to have some little pigs,' he told himself, but the next morning he was disappointed again. A few weeks later he read in the paper that Spriggins, who lived thirty miles away, owned a national champion boar, and offered the use of same for £50.

The persistent Thomas loaded his sow into the wheelbarrow again and trudged home. The next morning he woke up early. 'I'll bet there'll be twenty little pigs around this time,' he told his wife, and rushed down to the sty. He was wrong again. There wasn't a little pig in sight, but the sow was sitting in the wheelbarrow.

1628

A woman complained to the police that she had been slightly molested on her way home one night. The police caught a suspect and organised an identification parade with eight other men. The woman was asked to pick out the culprit. She went along the line and pointed to the man in the middle of the group. 'Him!' she said positively. 'Is this the man who accosted you?' asked the superintendent. The woman said: 'Oh no, but I *prefer* this one, if I can have him.'

1629

A deaf woman stood beside an American tourist on the packed underground train from Piccadilly. She was so polite that when the Yank started talking to her she went three stations beyond her destination to avoid the embarrassment of telling the stranger about her impediment. When the tourist finally got off the train the deaf woman was so relieved she turned to a Cockney nearby and said, 'I've got to go back three stops now just because I couldn't hear what that American gentleman was saying to me.'

The Cockney said: 'Who? him? Cor, love you ducks, he wasn't talking, he was just chewing gum.'

1630

Escort Service—a firm which deals in negotiable blondes.

1631

The man who was suitably bribed by one girl to ensure that she won the beauty contest obviously wanted him to judge for herself.

1632

Chinese voyeur—a Pekin Tom.

1633

Rest home for exhausted bassoons—An umpah-dump.

1634

One schoolboy to another: 'I found a pornographic dageurrotype in my father's secretaire yesterday.'

The second boy said: 'What's a secretaire?'

1635

Gerald lives in a village which boasts over fifteen banks for 270 inhabitants and yet he can't borrow a penny. He says he's in a very tight spot.

1636

A young girl rambler called at the remote farm feeling very thirsty. She asked the farmer if she could have a cold milk shake. The farmer took her along to the cowshed, opened the door and said to the cow, 'Mabel, jump up and down for the lady.'

1637
On the nudist club campus they installed a coin-slot weighing machine which also gave character readings. The nude sunlovers could thus keep a check on their adipose tissue. Miss Harris tried the machine, which threw out a card stating that her weight was 'eight stone, four pounds,' and she 'had a very shy and retiring nature'.

1638
It was raining, so two hard-case hooligans dashed into a museum of art for sanctuary. They huddled near a very bizarre modern abstract mural. One of them snatched the arm of his friend and said in panic— 'Quick, let's get out of here before they say *we* did it.'

1639
The father of a fifteen-month-old male baby reckons he gets insufficient sleep because there's only about two hours between sunset and son-up.

1640
A pretty girl gets dated frequently but a friendly one gets inundated regularly.

1641
Two men were nattering at the bar. One said that his girl friend was a bit too shy and he felt frustrated. His friend said, 'It's probably just embarrassment. Give her a bit more rope.' A week later they were in the bar again and the wise one asked. 'Did you give Marian a bit more rope?' 'Yes,' said his colleague, 'but now she wants to tie the knot.'

1642
A successful photographer is a trendy young artist who turns on more models than film.

1643
You can tell what a remarkable movie star he is. He was personally responsible for a chain of fifty cinemas being converted to bingo.

1644
At a society *soirée* one wealthy woman couldn't help admiring the magnificent pendant diamond lying upon the creamy bosom of another guest. The proud owner said: 'Ah yes! This is the famous Bolstrover Diamond—almost as notorious as the Hope Diamond.' Asked the inquisitive one: 'Does a curse go with it?' 'Yes, *Mr.* Bolstrover.'

1645
For ten years, a staunch trade unionist night worker named Fred Carlton kidded his wife that his shop steward would not allow him to do repairs and other chores around the house. And for the same period

she kidded *him* that she'd been doing them herself. Then he discovered that all along an odd-job man named Bill Swift had been doing all his homework for him while he'd been on nights.

1646

A motorist was taking his wife and her mother for their weekend country trip, and as usual he was constantly instructed about the route, the speed, the oncoming traffic, his braking, his steering and his cornering. It had gone on for six years and he suddenly felt the urge to assert himself. He braked abruptly, and ran the car on to a grass verge. His wife shouted angrily: 'That was no way to drive off the highway, Cyril!' He swivelled round to glare at her and snapped: 'Look, who's driving this car, you or your mother?'

1647

Two drunken men were passing the door of the Honeymoon Suite at the Bedford Hotel when they paused to listen. Inside the room the man was saying to his bride: 'Avril, you are so deliciously lovely, your fabulous beauty ought to be captured for posterity by the best artist in the world.' The two drunks banged on the door immediately, and the husband shouted: 'Yes, who is it?' The men answered: 'It's Reubens and Rembrandt.'

1648

The following conversation was overheard between a police car patrol man and the driver of the car flagged down.

'Going fairly fast, weren't you?'

'Well, you know how it is: these cars are still doing fifty when they're standing in a car park.'

'All right, what's your name?'

'Bradhall.'

'Where are you going?'

'Walsall.'

'Where did you come from?'

'Siddall.'

'What make of car are you driving?'

'A Vauxhall.'

'And what have you got in the boot?'

'Nothing!'

1649

Funny incident on beach last summer. A woman goes swimming in the sea while her husband is taking a nap. An hour later he wakes up. No wife. He searches the beach anxiously and comes to a sand dune behind which he sees the lifeguard busy doing what comes naturally with a girl. 'Please,' cries the husband, trying to pull him away from the girl who is half hidden in the sand. 'I've lost my wife! She's out there in the sea, somewhere, drowning! You must save her!' The lifeguard says: 'Aw, don't get so darned hysterical.' The husband cries: 'But she's drowning! You're a lifeguard! Save her! Save her!' Suddenly the girl drags herself out of the sand dune and says to the man: 'Herbert, don't be so silly. I'm not drowning at all.' With relief in his anguished voice the husband says: 'Stella! You're there! Thank God you're safe!'

1650

A salesman for heating appliances primed potential customers by making free-shot telephone calls from local directories. He had some success on the telephone with one woman subscriber and arranged to call at the house with plans, specifications and illustrations. 'I'll come tomorrow morning at ten o'clock,' he said, 'if that will be convenient.' The woman said: 'Oh dear. Thursday is one of my busiest days. I'm afraid you'll find me in a bit of a tizzy.' The salesman said eagerly: 'Don't worry about that. I've called at many a house where the woman was only in a bit of a kimono.'

Suburban Wife's Monologue

1651

'Before we were married you cracked on you were a professional writer. You didn't tell me all you wrote was begging letters. I wouldn't have minded, but when I won thirty pounds on the pools I got one from you myself.

'You claimed to be a 'do-it-yourself' enthusiast but once we got married, every time I asked you to do a job for me you said 'Do it yourself'.

'You used to say that cheap fur coats wouldn't be good enough for your wife and you intended to get some natural skins made up to measure. Now it begins to look as though the only natural skin coat I'm likely to get is a banana cape trimmed with orange.

'I remember the time when you reckoned you could set the world on fire for a girl like me. Now you won't even get up in the morning to light the stove.'

1652

An old man lay on his death-bed surrounded by his family consisting of three useless sons and their wives. The oldest man of the three sons was the first to suffer the dying father's spleen as he growled: 'Percy, you never was no good—all you ever think about is your allotment and your kitchen garden. You even married a woman named Lily.' To the second son the old man grunted: 'And as for you, Albert, you're nothing but a sponging parasite—all you ever think about is money—why you even married a woman named Penny.' The remaining son was getting a little angry. He suddenly turned to his own wife and snapped 'Damn it all, the old man's off his rocker. Come on Fanny, before we get insulted.'

1653

Two Black Friars were invited to a cocktail party at which the hostess wore a very low-cut revealing dinner gown. She was fat and the gown fitted her like a credit squeeze, and two thirds of her was bulging so provocatively it embarrassed one of the Friars who turned to her and whispered, 'Madam, thy cups runneth over.'

1654

The young man parked the car on a lonely lane after make the original comment that he had run out of petrol. The girl said: 'It's nice and peaceful here in the moonlight. Just listen to those crickets chattering.' The man said: 'Those aren't crickets—they're zippers.'

1655

The elegant male secretary knocked on the door of his boss's private sanctum and said to him: 'Mr. Jarvis, there is a woman salesman outside asking to see you.' The boss said: 'If he's selling blondes I'll take half a dozen, size 36.'

1656

Two Black Friars were walking along the main road when they came across a dowdy old woman crying her eyes out. One of the friars asked her what ailed her. 'I've been sacked from me job,' she wailed. 'Where were you working?' inquired the second friar. 'I 'ad a good job as an attendant in the Ladies' the old woman answered. So the first friar inquired: 'But why did they give you the sack?' The old lady sobbed: 'I couldn't remember the prices.'

1657

Overheard at Westminster: one M.P. saying: 'You know, I can't make up my mind what to do about that Abortion Bill.' The other M.P. said: 'Pay it, before someone finds out.'

1658

'The trouble with Harold,' one pretty blonde said to another, 'is that he never knows where to stop.' The other one said: 'I was out with him last night, and he found quite a good place.'

1659

Fed up with her husband she divorced him. The case was heard by a very deaf old judge who confused three other trials—so the husband got custody of the daily woman and she got four months in Holloway and a paternity order against her.

1660

She married a self-made man and then gave him a refresher course.

1661

'My wife's been up to something,' Jim confided suspiciously to his best friend. 'How do you know?' his friend inquired. 'Well,' said Jim,

'When I left home on this business trip she asked me to bring her back a mink coat, and she just telephoned to say not to bother about a mink coat—a plastic mack will do.'

1662

Then there's the amateur photographer who cheated at a session where his fellow club members were photographing gorgeous dancing girls. He put film in his camera.

1663

They met and married very quickly and about three weeks after the quick honeymoon she said to him: 'Don't keep calling me darling all the time, John. My name's Rita.'

1664

He parked the car and said to the girl: 'Get in the back,' and she said: 'No.' 'Please get in the back,' he persisted. 'It's warmer there." No,' she repeated. 'Oh, go on,' he said. 'No,' she persisted, 'I want to stay here in front with you.'

1665

Why is it that the people who shout loudest for free speech are invariably the illiterates?

1666

Then there's the stingy man who was annoyed by a woman collecting for charity on a street corner, just because she thrust her can at him.

1667

A fashionable woman went to the local psychiatrist and found him playing with his food—juggling with two poached eggs and balancing a mashie on the end of his nose. She was currently writing an article for *Vogue* on Ascot Millinery. She told the psychiatrist that she kept having a horrible dream, in which she found herself walking stark naked, stripped to the buff, along Piccadilly in London, wearing only a hat. The psychiatrist stood on his head and said: 'That's very serious. I suppose it makes you feel self-conscious, embarrassed and shocked if you have that sort of dream every night.' The lady said, 'Of course I do, you fool. It's always last year's hat.'

1668

A shapely young girl visited her doctor complaining of pains in the stomach and chest. He said he'd have to examine her and asked her to get undressed. She said: 'I know it's silly but I'm very shy and I just couldn't take off my clothes for *anyone*, doctor.' The doc said: 'I quite understand, but I spend half my life examining ladies, my dear. I'll tell you what; I'll turn out all the lights and then you can get undressed in the dark. That shouldn't embarrass you.' So the girl agreed, and the doctor switched out all the lights and pulled down the blinds so that the consulting room was pitch black. A couple of minutes later the girl said: 'I'm sorry to be such a nuisance, doctor, but now I can't see where to put my clothes.' He said: 'I know, I'm having the same problem myself.'

1669
The physical culture expert was admonishing his class and roared: 'Take it from me, boys; always keep yourself in trim. I always start the day with a quick dive out of bed, five minutes of furious exercise near the window, several yoga positions, a twenty-second ice-cold shower and a slick rub down with a rough towel. Then I feel rosy all over.' One of the boys shouted out: 'Never mind about the routine, sir, tell us more about Rosy.'

1670
Her mother scolded her fiercely and said: 'And if you're not in bed by half-past-eleven, I'm going to lock you out.' The daughter said: 'Aw don't worry Ma. If I'm not in bed by half-past-ten, I'm coming home.'

1671
A man called at an apartment in a New York block and looked for the name Miss Angela Cruebrook. He found the place, rang the bell, introduced himself and went in. He had some drinks, made her happy, then gave her fifty pounds and left. That evening he called again, found her looking extremely lovely and eager; made love to her and gave her fifty pounds and left. The following morning he called again. He made beautiful music with her, gave her fifty pounds and left. That evening he rang her bell again: she pulled him inside and let nature and him take their courses. He gave her fifty pounds and then said: 'We shall not be meeting again, my dear. I'm taking the night plane back to England. By this time tomorrow I shall be back working in the little parish of Maplehurst in Sussex.' The girl said in surprise: 'You come from England? That's wonderful. I have a sister living there, in Sussex.' The man said: 'I know. Who do you think sent you that two hundred quid?'

1672
The doctor said to the male patient: 'You're in a very bad state. The best thing you can do is give up females, frothy beer and football.' The man said: 'Well, what's second best?'

1673
One drunk said to the other as they walked home after celebrating their club's two-nil win at soccer. ' 'Ere, Albert, how about a deal? You can have my season-ticket if you'll let me spend the night with your missus.' The other one said: 'You rotten swine, you cheap, dirty skunk, making a suggestion like that.' His friend said 'But Albert, you know how much you like the game, and you were lucky to get into the ground today.' 'I know all about that,' said the other man, 'but the ruddy season's half over!'

1674

One drunk said to the other: 'Here, how's about havin' just one more for the road, an' then get out and rustle up a couple of girls?' His mate said: 'Aw, no. Not for me. I've got more sex than I can handle at home already.' The other one said: 'S'all right then; one more for the road, an' then back to your place.'

1675

The sportsmaster and the French teacher stayed back at school one afternoon and had fun. Then she said: 'I don't know what to do, Frank. How can I ever face my class of innocent schoolgirls knowing that I've sinned twice in one afternoon.' He said: 'Twice? It wasn't twice.' She said: 'Oh, Frank, you're not leaving already are you?'

1676

A chap bought his girl a necklace for her birthday, and she said he could fit it around her neck. She stood with her back towards him and he fixed the necklace, but as he did so the clasp broke and slipped down the back of her dress. The girl told him to find it, so he put his hand down her back and felt for the clasp but couldn't locate it. 'Try further down,' the girl advised, impatiently and angrily. The man pushed his hand down further, blushing frantically and finally said: 'I can't find it, and I do feel an ass.' The girl snapped: 'Never mind—find the clasp.'

1677

The husband marched unexpectedly into the bedroom having missed his train, and found his wife entertaining a visitor. 'Here. What's the game!' The fellow said 'I don't know what it's called, but boy, will it catch on!'

1678

In Somerset there was a farmer who searched all over his haystack to find the needle in order to stop his bone idle son from sowing his wild oats. All he found was one of the milkmaids doing a little fancy work.

1679

Two glow-worms met on a mulberry bush at midnight and one said to the other: 'Are you a girl glow-worm or a boy glow-worm?' The other one said: 'Why?' The first glow-worm said: 'Well, I need a push—my battery's gone flat.'

1680

Bill went on a blind date with a girl who was pretty but had no figure whatsoever. In the pictures he put his arm around her and began to make a few passes. The girl froze on him and snapped: 'Here. Here!' Bill whispered urgently in her ear 'Where, where?'

1681

Two young gents were nervously pacing up and down in the waiting room of the local maternity hospital. 'Your first?' one asked. 'Yes,' nodded the other. 'Mine, too,' said the first man, 'And it's rotten luck— we were on our holidays.' The other chap said: 'What are you moaning about. We were on our honeymoon.'

1682
Teacher was trying unsuccessfully to explain about the Vikings' helmets but one small boy was somewhat ignorant about horns. Finally she said: 'Look, Tony, what does a bull have two of?' So Tony told her.

1683
Mr. and Mrs. Sawyer were enjoying their honeymoon at a small hotel on the coast. On the first day they made excellent friends with the hotel manager and had a few drinks with him at the little bar before making an early retirement. At midnight a telephone call came through from Birmingham for Mr. Sawyer. The hotel manager raced up the stairs, tapped on the couple's door and shouted: 'Sawyer! Sawyer!' Mr. Sawyer opened the door, adjusting his pyjama jacket and said angrily: 'You can keep your beady eyes from the keyhole then; we are married, you know!'

1684
A neighbour was reprimanding his teenage daughter for her bad conduct and her past failings. He said: 'Look at that time you joined that Society at work where you pay two shillings a week and then get a five pound plum pudding at Christmas. You came home and without a word of proper explanation calmly announced that you were in the pudding club . . . It must have taken five years off your mother's life. And it took five years off *mine* when I asked you who was involved and you said you weren't sure but at a guess it could be half the factory!'

1685
She used to go out with a dark handsome man, but he not only lied about his beautiful yacht in Cannes harbour, he even made her row it.

1686
The pianist's clothes had seen better days. It was obvious to the whole bar that the seams of his trousers had come apart. One kindly old woman felt he should know about it. She went across and whispered to him. 'Excuse me. Do you know your seat's showing through your trousers.' 'No Madam,' he said, 'but if you sing the first eight bars, I'll soon pick you up.'

1687
St. Peter was checking in the new arrivals.
   'Cause of death?' he asked the first.
   'Well, I got home early today and caught a man with my wife. He jumped out of the window and down the fire-escape so I went into the kitchen and chucked the fridge out of the window. I suppose the exertion brought on a heart attack.'

'Cause of death?' St. Peter inquired of the second.
'Killed by fall,' was the reply.
'Cause of death?' St. Peter asked of the third.
'I don't know,' was the reply. 'I was sitting in this fridge . . .'

1688

A British trade union official was being shown over a Moscow factory. 'Here Comrade,' said his guide, 'we start at seven in the morning and we work through until 1 p.m. We have a ten-minute lunch break. We then work until 5 p.m. when we have five minutes for tea, and then work until 8 p.m. It is then time to go to cultural evening classes. Is it the same in England, Comrade?' The official shook his head. 'No. You'd never get our lot to do that. They're all good communists.'

1689

The vicar started off the service: 'Dearly beloved brethren . . .' One wavy-haired lad in the front pew turned to his friend and said: 'Did you hear that Cecil, he's one of us.'

1690

The glamorous young blonde visited a strange doctor in a new town complaining of pains in her back and shoulders, which she attributed to the damp weather. The doctor examined her and found that she had very bad rheumatism. He said: 'There is a definite sign of acute sciatic inflammation. I'm surprised you haven't been laid low for years.' The girl said: 'You must be joking.'

1691

The wife who drives from the back seat isn't any worse than the husband who cooks from the dining-room table.

1692

My girl Eileen has become a policewoman. One of those tough young girls who march around looking for young offenders. To my mind it's silly for girls to do that kind of work, but I suppose it's better than walking the streets.

1693

The police were suspicious just because Alf bought a wreath for his wife a few seconds *before* she died. Then he explained what really happened . . . . He went home with a bouquet of roses for his wife; she gave one look at them and the shock gave her a heart attack.

1694

A fellow came out of the saloon, staggered up the road and stumbled. Some coins fell out of his pocket. Three hours later a policeman discovered him searching around the street. The drunk explained that he had lost some money, so the policeman helped him look for it. Then the policeman said: 'Where did you lose this money?' and the drunk said: 'About two hundred yards up the road.' The policeman said:

'Then why are you searching for it here ?' and the drunk said: 'Hic—the light's better here.'

1695

A drunk climbed into a taxi and told the driver: 'Hey—drive me around the square twenty times.' The driver shrugged and set off. On the fifth circuit of the square the drunk leaned forward and tapped the driver on the back and shouted: 'Hi! Step on the gas, bud. I'm in a hurry.'

1696

There was once a man working in the circus whose stunt was to be fired from a cannon four times a day, and he was known far and wide as the Cannonball Man. Then one day he got fed up and gave in his notice. The circus owner was annoyed. 'Where else,' he demanded, 'am I going to find a man of your calibre ?'

1697

A honeymoon couple called a cab and asked the driver to take them to Southbeach, a small out-of-the-way coastal village eighteen miles from town. It was a dark night and for the first six or seven miles the cabbie kept getting lost. 'Never mind,' said the groom from the back,' keep driving and I'll give you directions.' They pressed on. Then there was a lot of shouting and howling from the back of the cab. The cabbie turned his head and said to the groom 'Which way ?' The groom said: 'I don't know. Can't you see I'm busy!' The cabbie drove on. Again there was some commotion in the rear. Then the bride tapped the cabbie on the shoulder and said: 'Look, why don't you give *him* some directions ?'

1698

A woman went to the doctor with a strange complaint. She told him that every time she sneezed she had a yearning to be loved. The doctor wrote out a prescription for her. 'Is it anti-histamine ?' she inquired inquisitively. 'No,' said the doctor, 'cayenne pepper.'

1699

The doctor told him that in view of the condition of his heart he should not kiss any women other than his wife, to avoid getting over-excited.

1700

The rural lady had been coming into the city hospital regularly to give birth to her annual child. When she was packing up to go home after her tenth visit the nurse said, 'Well, I suppose we'll be seeing you again next year, as usual ?' 'No,' said Mrs. Slocum. 'My husband and I just found out what's been causin' it.'

1701

Eight weeks after a husband returned from a fishing trip to Scotland his wife accosted him at breakfast: 'Sam,' she said, 'remember that trip up to Inverness a couple of months back, when you caught those two whacking great salmon?' 'Sure, I remember it well,' he agreed, 'Why?' His wife said: 'Oh nothing, only one of them telephoned while you were at the office and said you're going to be a father.'

1702

On board the new liner a passenger said to the captain: 'It's a fine boat. Goes very well. I suppose that's because of the twin screws.' The captain looked at the other man dubiously because the ship only had one nuclear-engined-propeller. 'Which twin screws?' he asked. The passenger frowned and said: 'I don't know!'

1703

'Don't worry about me being away for a few days,' said the young virile husband to his wife. 'I'll be back before you know it.' 'Oh,' she said, 'I'd prefer it if you 'phoned or sent a wire.'

1704

The new Dial-A-Prayer telephone service has been such a raging success that an association of atheists is jealously planning to steal the idea. The only difference is, when you call them, nobody answers.

1705

Fred says that his woman is just about the most perfect female the world has ever known, in fact there's only one thing he holds against her.

1706

The boy took the girl to the new *discotheque* where they watched with fascination as one athletic young girl gyrated and wriggled in ecstasy. The young man said to his partner: 'Have you ever done anything like that?' She said: 'Not standing up.'

1707

The sweet young thing was telling her mother about the great time she had at the mountain resort: 'I met a man in the recreation hall and we played Ping-Pong all afternoon. What fun, Mother!' 'Why dear,' remarked the mother, 'I never knew you enjoyed table tennis.' 'I do now,' the daughter said. 'I'd hit the ball the wrong way and we'd both go after it under the table. Then he'd hit the ball the wrong way and we'd both go after it under the table. We played all afternoon. It was wonderful.' 'But I don't understand,' said the mother. 'Where does the fun come in?' 'Under the table!'

1708

'I notice your daughter didn't get home until three o'clock this morning,' said Mrs. Taylor to Mrs. Foster across the backyard fence. 'My daughter was in the house before midnight.' 'I know,' answered Mrs. Foster coolly. 'But, you see, my daughter *walked* home.'

1709

Two monks went to work mucking-out the stables. One of them got back to the monastery so dirty that he had to take a bath. He kept his shorts on because he couldn't bear to look down on the unemployed.

1710

There was a strange medical case in Sweden last month. A man was examined by his doctor and found to be pregnant. The patient was extremely upset and said to the medico: 'Och, what will the neighbours say, I'm not even married.'

1711

In the tailor's shop where I went to order a new suit there was a lovely young new salesgirl and when I asked where the tailor was she told me he had gone for lunch, and that *she* could measure me. So I let her measure me four or five times, because I was anxious for her not to make a mistake. I'm particular about the trouser-leg length. When she'd got the measurements she said: 'And shall I measure you for the waistcoat and the jacket?' I said: 'To hell with the waistcoat and the jacket—let's have another two pairs of trousers.'

1712

Two spinsters were sitting quietly at home, one reading a news report about a film actress who had just had her fifth husband cremated. 'Ursula,' said the spinster, 'isn't that just like life! Some of us can't get a man at all while other girls have husbands to burn.'

1713

When they were courting they had to sneak out secretly for their assignations and steal kisses behind the summer house. After thirty-seven years of active marriage, Fred is still saying the same thing, but now he says it in bed with far less vigour: 'Alice, we can't go on meeting like this.'

1714

She visited her solicitor to find out how things were concerning her husband's reluctance to return home to her. The solicitor greeted her with the words: 'I have to tell you that your husband has filed his petition.' She said: 'And about time, too.'

1715

They were out in Sid's broken-down old pre-war Austin and it was two o'clock in the morning, very dark, on a lonely country hill miles from anywhere. The engine gave a couple of snorts and packed up. Freda said: 'We've stopped, Sid.' Sid said: 'I know. Shall we get out and try a push?' Freda said: 'If you like, Sid, but we can't leave the car parked in the middle of the road, can we?'

1716

While being shaved at the barber shop, a young chap asked what he could do about his thinning hair. The barber said: 'Don't worry about it. Baldness is a sign of virility and passion.' Ever since, that young man has been scouring the neighbourhood looking for baldheaded redheads.

1717

A gay old dog visiting Japan went to a famous tourist centre where the polite old hostess offered him the company of a girl named Passion Flower. About three hours later he staggered downstairs and said to his samaritan: 'Madame, do you have one called Patience?'

1718

With all these transplants going on in medical spheres the ordinary human being has to be on the lookout. Last night at the club I sang 'I Left My Heart In San Francisco,' and a doctor jumped out of his seat and offered me a hundred dollars for it, plus postage . . . My wife went to the butcher to get some giblets for the soup and came home with enough stuff to build a woman. I know a chap who went in to hospital to have one of his parts replanted and now he doesn't know whether he's coming or going. We're no longer people, we're just so much walking offal. One of these days you might limp into a National Health supermarket and see your big left toe in the deep freeze cabinet marked '3p off.'

1719

The Financial Times declares that there is only one infallible method of keeping up with the rising cost of living. Drop dead.

1720

Maria is looking for one of those new machines that does the work of ten men.

1721

The beautiful Countess of Swanage visited the hospital where her chauffeur was being treated after a car accident. 'He's a very sick fellow,' said the matron to the Countess. 'Are you his wife?' The Countess said haughtily 'Certainly not! I'm his mistress.'

1722

A newly ordained priest went out to meet his flock. His first call was at O'Reilley's place, a devout family with twelve offspring. 'Good day to ye, O'Reilley,' said Father O'Toole, 'you're a credit to auld Oireland, with the bonniest family in the parish.' From there he went up the road to another house at the top of the hill where he saw a man in the garden reading the latest banned book and keeping an eye on seventeen children playing cops-and-robbers.'Good morning,' said Father O'Toole, breathlessly,' 'tis a foine soight to see you the happy father of such a wonderful quiver of kiddies. You're a patriotic Catholic and a credit to the country . . .' 'Sorry, Father,' said the man, 'but I'm not a Catholic, I'm a Christian Scientist.' 'The hell you are,' said the priest, 'you dirty, rotten good-for-nothing sex maniac.'

1723

Harold is a staunch trade-unionist, a shop-steward and convenor. Last night I had to pop in there to give him a message and he said 'Wait a minute, I'm just telling the kids a good-night bedtime story . . .' and then I heard him begin the story of Cinderella . . . 'Once upon a time-and-a-half Cinderella was staging a sit-down strike in front of the fire in the Capitalist-Swine Baron's castle . . .'

1724

The doctor was examining a woman selected for a space-shot to Venus. The doctor asked her 'How many children and how old are they?' She said: 'Five children aged five, four, three, two, one . . .' The doctor said: 'Why the hell didn't you press the abort button?'

1725

If your wife cannot stand the prospect of you undressing it is probably because of whom you are undressing.

1726

When we were in Africa we sat at dinner next to a cannibal who had just popped over for the day from the jungle. He was looking through the menu and beckoned the waiter over and pointed to one of the listed dishes. The waiter said: 'You can't have Guiseppi Travatorolli. That's the manager.' The cannibal said: 'Whassamarrer? Is he off?' The waiter said, 'Yes sir. Your wife was here for lunch.'

1727

The young people were snogging mildly on the sofa and suddenly the lovely young lass said to him: 'Here, how about playing Mummies and Daddies?' The young man jumped up excitedly and said: 'Eeh, that's a marvellous idea . . . but what can we row *about*?'

1728

The conductor of a philharmonic orchestra fell under the spell of his pretty young viola player, and one night they practised at her flat. I looked through the keyhole and there he was with his baton in his hand shouting: 'Okay, let's have that second movement again, from the top.'

1729

The couple settled into the honeymoon suite of the hotel and the page-boy looked around to make sure everything was okay. Then he said to the eager young man busily kissing his partner on the bed, 'Will there be anything more, sir?' The man looked up, thought, and said: 'I don't think so.' The page said: 'Anything for your wife?' The man thought again, shrugged, and said: 'Yes, maybe you'd get me a picture-postcard? She's in Italy and I haven't written all week.'

1730

The Judge during a brawling case, was re-questioning the defendant, a rather stocky, uneducated, aggressive character. 'Tell me again,' said the Judge, 'exactly what happened when you took this—er—female companion into the cabin of the cargo boat.' The man said: 'Like I told yer, we went into the - - - -ing cabin, turned on the - - - -ing light, had a couple of - - - -ing whiskies, and then she got kind of - - - -ing awkward and - - - - me if she didn't start chucking - - - -ing things around, so I grabbed her to knock some - - - -ing sense into her and, well, somehow we fell on the floor, and before I knew it, if you'll pardon the expression, your Honour—we indulged in intercourse.'

1731
A sickly man went to his doctor for advice. The doctor said: 'All you need is a course of injections—I'll give you one now.' The doctor forthwith went to his equipment cupboard and began preparing ingredients which he transferred to a very large syringe. Somewhat worried by all this impressive preparation, the patient inquired anxiously: 'What's that in the syringe?' The doctor said: 'Two of sand and one of cement.'

1732
The Judge was having difficulty with one of the witnesses who refused to be specific. The prisoner was accused, at one stage, of having used a four-letter word and the witness refused to repeat the word in court. Said the Judge: 'I have every consideration for your feelings, but this is a public court, and we hear a lot of things here which are distasteful. But the course of justice must be served, and I must insist that you give your evidence precisely and accurately. There are many, many four-letter words, and the court has to know which one the defendant employed.' The parson hesitated and then said: 'Well, your Honour, it was "work".'

1733
The au pair girl had an accident in the kitchen while she was washing up. She broke twenty pieces of pottery, when she accidentally knocked over the kitchen cabinet. She cried to the husband of the house because she thought she might be sent home. The husband said: 'Look, you be nice to me and I'll slip out and buy another tea service, and my wife will never know anything about it.' Half an hour later as he was going to get the new tea-set he was just opening the back door and said: 'I'm glad you were sensible about it, and remember—my wife won't know anything about it.' The au pair girl said: 'I wouldn't be too sure about that. She's under the cabinet.'

1734
Two labourers were taking time off for a smoke around the back of the shed and one said: 'My missus didn't half paste our young lad Tommy yesterday, just because he said a five-letter word.' The other labourer said: 'You mean a four-letter word, dontcha?' 'Nah. Tommy thinks you spell it like philosophy.'

1735
An effeminate recruit was on parade on the forecourt. He was so stupid

the sergeant was close to an apoplectic fit. The poor little recruit could do nothing right, and was constantly crying like a schoolgirl. In desperation the sergeant screamed: 'Look son, you'd better pull up your socks and learn something about taking care of yourself. In a month's time you're going to be posted to the Far East to fight for Joan Bull.'

1736
She bought me a pair of cuff links for my birthday and I explained to her that I never wore long-sleeve shirts. So she said nastily: 'Look, those cuff links cost me 22p and I'm not wasting money! Get your wrists pierced.'

1737
The very fat man went courting an equally obese woman. As he left he said: 'Thanks for the service.' 'Not at all,' she sneered, 'thanks for the tip.'

1738
The prospective buyer of a country cottage was being shown round by the owner. As they looked at the country style privy at the bottom of the garden, the buyer said: 'Hullo, the lock's broken on the door, I should have to get a new one.' The owner said: 'I shouldn't bother, it's been like that for years and we haven't had a bucket stolen yet.'

1739
A wealthy financier who spent a lot of his time abroad on business came home one night unexpectedly when his plane was cancelled owing to a strike. He reached the house and stormed in angrily intending to relieve his feelings on his wife. However, she was in bed, so he had a nightcap and hoofed upstairs. Entering the bedroom he was surprised to notice that the room reeked of cigar smoke. Suspiciously he nosed around; the ash-trays were empty, but stubbed in the cactus pot he noticed the best part of a discarded cigar. 'Where,' he boomed indignantly at his wife who cowered down in the bed, 'did this butt come from?' Silence reigned. Again he shouted: 'Mary, where did this cigar come from?' Then a masculine voice from the wardrobe called back, 'Boothmans of Pall Mall.'

1740
The Judge asked the young woman in the witness box: 'You claim that the defendant raped you on the night in question?' 'Yes' she answered, 'and it was the same *every* time he took me out.'

1741
A rabbi and a Catholic priest were neighbours. They irked one another. The priest bought a Bentley; the rabbi went out and bought a Rolls Phantom. The priest had a new driveway built; the rabbi had his house remodelled. The priest was out early one morning, pouring water over his Bentley's bonnet. The rabbi called down to him: 'What a stupid way to fill the radiator.' The priest said: 'I'm not topping the radiator,

211

I'm christening the car with holy water. And you can't do that.' An hour later the priest was on his way to service when he saw the rabbi lying down under the rear of the Rolls Royce with a hacksaw and a file in his hand, sawing off the end inch of the exhaust pipe . . .

1742

His pal told him: 'Hey, you want to be more careful. I was passing your house last night and the blinds were up and I saw both you and your wife giving a performance.' 'The joke's on you' said the man, 'it so happens I spent all last night at my club.'

1743

He went to the doctor and complained that he was having trouble. The doctor gave him a thorough examination and finally said: 'I'm sorry, I don't treat worms.'

1744

She went to the doctor and he examined her for symptoms and finally told her: 'You've got acute angina.' She said: 'Never mind admiring my assets, just tell me what's wrong.'

1745

When they were undressing for the steam bath one man said to his friend: 'Hell, how long have you been wearing that girdle?' His friend said: 'Ever since my wife discovered it in the glove-compartment of my car.'

1746

After the honeymoon night at the hotel the groom rang 'room service' and ordered breakfast of grapefruit, ham, eggs, sausages and toast for his *own* breakfast, and two small lettuce leaves for his bride. The desk-clerk said: 'Is that all the breakfast madam is having?' Said the groom: 'Yes—I want to see if she eats like a rabbit, as well.'

1747

A man returned home unexpectedly to find his wife entertaining a gentleman friend in their bedroom. The man rushed to the tallboy drawer where he kept his automatic pistol, grabbed it and aimed it at the interloper who had by that time got as far as the window. 'Stop!' said the husband. 'Have you one last request before I shoot?' 'Well, said the cuckolder, 'I wouldn't mind reading the Encyclopedia Britannica again.'

1748

He said: 'I just don't know how I'll ever get over a girl like you.' She said: 'We could always put the 'phone in the middle.'

1749

The daughter of the house was despondently sitting by the window, reluctantly knitting little garments in white wool. Her father looked over and said: 'I'm glad to see you taking an interest at last in something besides running after men.'

1750

A producer thought he would go one better than the ordinary showman specialising in frontal-nudity productions by actually showing the act itself on stage, and so he hired an athlete to perform with twenty successive women, on stage, to the music of Wagner. On the first night the athlete actor had to retire from the stage after the fifth demonstration. His producer was angry. The actor said: 'I just can't understand it. I was all right at rehearsal this afternoon.'

1751

A young priest from the monastery was despatched to the nearby nunnery when the Mother Superior requested help in repairing an outhouse which had suffered gale damage. The priest spent several weeks on the job. Some time later he was sent for by the Abbot. 'Brother Jasper, I am astonished. It appears that since your visit to St. Agnes's last month, twenty-eight of the novices there have become pregnant. How do you account for that ?' The young priest thought and then said: 'You forgot, Father, last month was February.'

1752

She said to him: 'How about half an hour on the rug, Bert?'

Bert said: 'No, I don't feel like it just now.'

She said: 'Oh, come on, it'll help relax you. Just half-an-hour on the rug.'

'I told you . . . No,' he insisted.

'Please, Bert!'

'No. No.'

'Look, Bert, if we don't get on with it, we'll never get it finished and bound for the week-end.'

1753

A man had eight children and the cost of living kept rising. He told his wife that if she had any more kids, he'd go out of his mind with worry. Two months later she admitted to him that she was pregnant again. He opened the sideboard drawer, pulled out his old service revolver, held it to his right temple and prepared to pull the trigger. 'Stop, stop,' shouted his wife, 'You're killing an innocent man!'

1754

An armed man broke into the home of a young actress and she caught him searching all the furniture for valuables. 'Stop that!' she said irately, 'I can assure you that you won't find anything of interest in my drawers.'

1755

Did you hear about Big Mike. He nearly committed suicide over a woman. His lawyer got him off.

213

1756

A famous British actor told his friend 'I'm going to Hollywood to make love under southern stars.' His friend asked: 'Have you anyone special in mind?'

1757

Two women were waiting at the bus stop for over half-an-hour. Unable to hold back her anger any more one of them said to the other: 'When's it due?' 'March,' replied the other woman. 'Hells bells, the damned service gets worse and worse,' said the impatient one.

1758

Waiting for the Brighton Belle in London two men got chatting. One said: 'Are you a commuter?' The other one said 'Yes. I've got no option—we have separate beds.'

1759

Two urchins were playing in a dingy backstreet, littered with garbage, demolished brickwork and sludge. A large Rolls Royce pulled up outside a tumbledown tenement house and a gorgeous girl got out wearing furs and jewels. She came over to one lad, handed him a bag and said: 'There's a hundred quid for Mom, a fiver for you. Take it up to Mom straight away.' Then she got back into the limousine and the chauffeur drove off fast. The lad said to his friend: 'That's my big sister wot Mom says got herself ruined.'

1760

Diner: I'd like Iris Tew.
Waiter: Sorry, it's her night off.
Diner: Then I'll have French Patti.
Waiter: She left early.
Diner: Then bring me soft roes.
Waiter: It's Rose's week off.
Diner: Minny Stroney?
Waiter: Look, why don't you eat first and we'll find a girl for you later.'

1761

A man went into the advertising dept. of a local newspaper to arrange an announcement in celebration of the birth of his first child, after years of failure. Delighted with the situation he talked to the desk clerk happily. The clerk gave him a form to complete, helping him with the wording to be used in the births column of the classifieds. The customer wrote it out and gave it to the clerk who read it. Then the clerk said: 'How many insertions?' and the man said: 'God knows; we stopped counting.'

1762

A disgruntled husband moaned to his wife concerning her frigidity. 'I'll be glad when I'm dead and in Heaven' he said, 'I bet there'll be lots and lots of girls up there, just waiting for a chap like me.' She turned her head and said: 'Idiot, you know the rules. You can't take it with you.'

1763
The professor was taking a class of teenagers for sex instruction at college. He told them 'It has been scientifically proved that over-indulgence in hedonic sexual activity can seriously affect the hearing'. At the end of the front row a pretty girl stood up, raising her hand. 'Please, sir,' she said, 'could you please speak up a little ?'

1764
A girl stopped to talk to the vicar on her way out of church. 'Vicar, is it really bad if people have intercourse before a wedding ceremony ?' 'Yes,' said the vicar, it is. 'For one thing it is immoral, and secondly, it blocks the aisle.'

1765
Having a drink in a strange bar, a newcomer asked the landlord: 'Tell me, is there any historical reason why this hotel is called 'The Two Gay Highwaymen ?' The landlord said: 'That's odd, I never got asked that before, and I don't really know. But if you hang on a sec, I'll ask my wife.' The landlord then went to the foot of the stairs and called up: 'Cyril, have you got a minute ?'

1766
The little boy was inquisitive about his mother's shape and asked what it was. 'Daddy has given me a little baby,' she explained diplomatically. The boy went away and she later found him throwing a full bag of jelly-babies into the fire. 'Don't you like them,' she asked him. 'Yes,' he said, 'but they ain't half fattening!'

1767
When he arrived at the hotel and went to his room he found the maid in there still finishing the clean-up. 'If you don't make the bed properly,' he said, 'you and I are going to fall out.'

1768
'Take me,' pleaded Dora, 'Take me, take me!' He said: 'No.' 'Please take me,' she insisted. 'No, no,' he said, 'I've seen that stupid old film four times already.'

1769
'What big hands you have,' commented this girl. Sid said: 'They're not hands, my dear, they're booby traps.'

1770
'Doctor, is it all right for me to take the Pill ?' The doctor said: 'Well, yes, provided of course that you only take it when under strict medical supervision.' She said: 'That's why I came to see you. I want you to

supervise everything.' 'Okay,' he said, picking up his pencil and prescription pad, 'Your place or mine?'

1771

A ravishing young Texan landlady spent each Saturday visiting all the apartments to collect the rent. And although she was very familiar with the geography of the large house she owned, she rarely got further than the Mexican boarder.

1772

Henrietta said to Josey: 'Did you hear that Katie is getting married?' And Josey said: 'No. I didn't even know she was pregnant.'

1773

Said Mrs. Latimer to her old schoolchum: 'Now take my husband, for a start. He's very reliable. For instance he never has anything to do with married women. In fact he hardly ever comes near me.'

1774

When the new vicar heard about the activities of Miss Lydia Friendly he thought he must do something to turn her from the path of iniquity, so he visited her one afternoon. She called out: 'Come in, it's open' when he knocked on her door. He walked in to find her stretched out on the bed, starkers. 'Young lady,' he remonstrated, 'I've heard all about you. You ought to be down on your knees.' 'Oh,' she said, 'well, if it's kinky, it's extra.'

1775

A sailor came home from the sea after an absence of four years to find his wife nursing a set of six-months-old quads. 'Who's responsible for this?' he cried angrily. 'Was it my friend Jim Smith?' 'No' muttered the wife. 'Was it my friend Bill Bates?' 'No, it wasn't.' The sailor said, 'Then was it my best friend, George Watson?' 'No,' said his wife. 'Could it have been my friend Jack Stevens?' His wife said angrily, 'Your friends, *your* friends: I'm sick of hearing about *your* friends. Don't you think I've got any friends of my own?'

1776

A young police recruit was being instructed by a female police examiner on the subject of highway robbery. He asked her 'What's the difference between a "stick-up" and a "hold-up"?' She said 'Age.'

1777

It was just around the end of March when he walked into the bedroom, looked at her and said eagerly: 'Guess what you're having for Christmas!'

1778

After indulging himself with the suspect girl in the Soho flat, the young officer revealed his true identity. 'I happen to be a member of the Regional Vice Squad.' She shrugged as she put away the currency note and said: 'I'm sorry, kid, I don't want to join—I've got my own private connection.'

1779

I did a silly thing yesterday. I couldn't find anywhere to park my car, and I had to leave it on an empty lot. But what I *thought* was an empty lot was a car-breaking dump. Before I could rescue it, a dirty great thousand-ton machine had grabbed the car, swung it into the air, whisked it into a trench where a two-thousand-ton press transformed it into a large cube of crushed metal the size of a sea-chest. I said to the foreman. 'What the hell am I going to do?—that was a month-old de-luxe American Pontiac with every conceivable extra.' The foreman shrugged and said: 'By law it's now our property, but you can buy the cube for fifty pence, the scrap value.' 'Fifty pence!' I shouted. 'You've wrecked my new car and you want me to pay *you* fifty pence?' 'I know, I'm sorry. It's too damn bad' the foreman said. 'But what's worrying me is that it might cost you even *more* to get it repaired.'

1780

Dad had the problem of trying to tell his six-year old son that his wife was expecting another child. He sat Tommy on his knee and said awkwardly, 'Look Tommy, in a few days time, a big beautiful stork is going to come flying right over our house, flapping his mighty wings, and he'll make a three-point landing on our roof, and drop a big package of joy straight down our chimney—a special gift from Heaven.' Tommy pulled a face and said: 'I hope the stupid bird doesn't frighten the daylights out of Mom, didn't *you* know she was pregnant again?'

1781

They were sitting on the sofa and suddenly the gold-digging blonde said to him: 'Here—let's play Mummies and Daddies, eh?' The young man said eagerly: 'I'll drink to that!' 'Good,' said blondie, 'then go on—take off your trousers.' He took off his trousers and threw them over a chair—whereupon the girl got up, and ransacked his pockets looking for his wallet and loose change.

1782

Bill was ill, so he called down to his wife from the bedroom. After an interval of an hour she struggled up the stairs, hair in curlers, body in corsets, stockings sagging, and looking very annoyed that Bill was not at work for once in his thirty years of toil at the docks. 'Well, whadaya want?' she demanded, fag drooping from corner of mouth. Bill said: 'I ain't well. Fetch the vet.' Said his wife, astonished: 'Vet? You mean the doctor.' 'No,' croaked Bill, painfully, 'I work like a horse, I eat like a pig, I'm treated like a dog and I live with a cow. The vet'll do.'

1783

She was applying to the court for a divorce. 'What were your relationships with your husband like?' asked the judge. 'Diabolical,' she said. 'Was he a friendly man?' asked the judge. 'Look, she said, 'in the four

217

years of our marriage he only ever spoke to me three times.' The judge went back over the evidence in front of him, then shrugged and said: 'Divorce granted. And I give you the custody of the three children.'

1784
Two hippy beatniks were getting married and the ceremony proceeded fairly well even though the priest was nervous because of the couples' long hair, flowery attire, unisexual appearance and evident lack of respect for the occasion. Impatiently, when the priest paused towards the end of the proceedings, the bridegroom snapped: 'Look, ain't you gonna pronounce us man and wife?' The priest said: 'Well, all right—but you'll have to sort it out among yourselves.'

1785
A witness was in court telling the judge how the defendant had bust into his home to rob the safe, and had viciously attacked and beaten up his wife. The judge said: 'But you were there—why didn't you help?' The husband said 'No need—he was doing all right on his own.'

1786
A marriage bureau introduced a wealthy stockbroker to one of their clients; a young, beautiful, educated, intelligent girl. The stockbroker liked her on sight, and the marriage was duly organised. A fortnight later the stockbroker returned to the marriage bureau and told the manageress angrily 'You're a rotten, swindling witch! What sort of a dirty trick is this? When we were on honeymoon I bumped into a colleague of mine and he tells me my wife has a most deplorable reputation! Do you know she's slept with half the men in Salford! The manageress said: 'I'm surprised at you making such a puerile complaint. After all, how big *is* Salford?'

1787
Two women welfare-office trainees were visiting a hospital as part of their course, and they came to the intensive-care unit of the maternity department in which rows of premature babies were lying in incubators. Phyllis stared with interest and said to her colleague: 'Look, Mavis! What's all this?' Mavis said: 'It must be that new method I read all about in "Readers' Digest"—where they make babies by electricity.' 'Oh,' said Phyll, 'I prefer the old way.'

1788
A young lovely was emerging starkers from the bathroom when someone rang the front-door bell. She shouted down: 'I can't let you in; I'm not dressed.' A voice called back: 'That's all right, lady. I'm a blind salesman.' She shouted 'Well that's all right, then,' and went down to open the door. The man pushed inside, looked at her and said: 'Thanks, miss. Where shall I put the blinds?'

1789
The weedy husband was being examined by the doctor. He asked him

'How long is it since you had intercourse?' The patient thought, then said, 'It must have been around 1915.' The doctor said: 'That's an awful long time to go denying yourself a perfectly normal practice.' The patient said: 'I don't know, doc, according to your clock it's only 19-25 now.'

1790
When I first got engaged I gave Brenda a lovely hundred-carat diamond ring and she said: 'Ta, awfully. I'll treasure it always, no matter who I marry.'

1791
My friend Frank had tough luck all his life. His marriage didn't turn out too good either. Decided to consult a marriage guidance clinic. Got there, went in, and who's managing the place but his mother-in-law.

1792
When I was in Greenland, travelling in ladies' underwear (and that's a chilly prospect out there) I got lost in the hills one night and knocked on the door of an igloo. An Eskimo came out and offered to put me up for the night. They have a good scheme, those Eskimos. They're so hospitable, they not only share their food and fire with you, they also insist on you sharing the wife. So this chap offered me his. 'Only one thing,' he told me, 'before she can get ready for bed you have to thaw her out.' 'Oh,' I said. 'And,' he added, 'when you've thawed her out, you have to scrub all the candle-fat off her.' So I said: 'Look, if you don't mind, I'll just kip down on the floor. Can you lend me a sleeping-bag?' He said: 'I already did that, and you turned her down.'

I could see I'd made a mistake because he was sulking. Apparently it's a terrible insult to refuse hospitality. So I thought, if I spend a lot of time thawing her out and scrubbing the candle-fat off her, it would take me most of the night, and I'd be able to avoid the worst. So I started thawing her out and scrubbing the tallow off. About eight hours later I said to him: 'This is taking a long time, I don't think I'll go to bed. What time does the dawn come up in these parts?' He looked at the calender and said: 'In about four months and three hours—the nights last six months in these parts.' That was such a shock, I said: 'Look, she's still unthawed. You'd better do it yourself. You're more used to her.' He said: 'To hell with that, I ain't sleeping with *her*—I never could stand frigid women.'

1793
Crime is everything nowadays. Anyone who hasn't organised a bank robbery is considered antisocial. Just yesterday I was in the street and I saw a man hurrying along when he was accosted by another chap, wearing a nylon stocking—in his breast pocket—who shoved a gun in the other feller's stomach and said: 'This is a stick-up. Hand over your money.' The victim shouted: 'You'll have to wait until I'm on the way back—I'm just going to hold up a train.'

1794

Three men, close buddies, were drinking at the 'Rose and Crown', their local pub. John was married to the town's recent Beauty Contest Winner. He bought a round of drinks and said nonchalantly: 'Incidentally, chaps, Sybil is going to have a baby in September.' Fred raised his glass high and said: 'That's wonderful. Congratulations, Stan.'

1795

The Labour member of the council was protesting about the Planning Committee's intention to build a gentlemen's convenience opposite the Town Hall. He shouted 'If the local inhabitants of Scudbank stand for this they will stand for anything.'

1796

A patient visited his psychiatrist in a very sick condition. He kept muttering one number after another. 456, 865, 432, 334 . . . After two hours the psychiatrist asked him what the matter was because this man was known to be very very wealthy and the doctor was interested in his case. Especially his note-case. He said: 'What's wrong with you?' The patient said: 'I've got amnesia.' The doctor said: 'I can cure you, but it will cost you a thousand pounds.' The wealthy patient said: 'In that case we're both in trouble. All my money is locked away in a secret numbered account in a Swiss Bank in Zurich—and I've forgotten the bleeding number.'

1797

'Why are you eating with your knife, Bobby?' asked mother. 'Cos my fork leaks.'

1798

A beautiful woman was cuckolding her husband. One night the husband returned unexpectedly and caught her in a compromising position, with his best friend Mr. Lessing. He shrieked: 'How dare you entertain Mr. Lessing while I'm away! I'll kill the swine. I'll murder the old buzzard.' He really was very angry. The wife pleaded: 'Don't kill him, Stanley. Be reasonable. Where do you think our apartment came from? And the Rolls Royce. And the yacht. And my sable coat . . .' The husband paused and said: 'The car? The flat? Your pretty clothes?' His wife nodded miserably. The husband shrugged, put his gun away and said to his wife: 'Annie, don't let him stand around there with nothing on—get him my dressing gown, he'll freeze to death.'

1799

The psychiatrist said: 'Well, I'm pleased to tell you that I think you are now fully recovered and there is no need for any further consultations, Mrs. Edgnicott.' The patient was delighted and said: 'Gosh, doctor, I feel so happy I could kiss you.' He said: 'No, no. There's no need. Actually we shouldn't even be on this couch together.'

1800

A Scotsman lay seriously ill in the general ward of a Men's hospital. The doctor asked him if he had any last request and the Scotsman said he would like his friend Mac to come and play the bagpipes. Mac came and played the bagpipes all day long that Friday. The Scotsman recovered but all the other patients died in agony.

1801

A girl was telling her friend about a night out with a sailor: 'So I said to him, "You might be a deck-hand but that isn't a deck you've got your hand on now, and I'm not planning on promoting you to first mate." '

1802

I think a low neckline suits her, it goes with her character and upbringing.

1803

A young cadet at the O.T.C. passed out with flying colours at a tender age and was posted to a regiment in Germany. The C.O. of the regiment took an immediate liking to Lieutenant Carstairs. After the brief interview and an exchange of credentials, the C.O. said: 'By the way, Carstairs, this is a very happy mob what we have 'ere. We sort of live it up. Now on Wednesday night we're having a bit of a do in the Mess. Loads of booze; even a few dozen bottles of Champers and some of that filthy Bavarian Liebfraustlich—you know, women's alcoholic milk. Like you to come along, Carstairs, and get to know the other chaps, what?'

Carstairs pinked a little and said: 'Sorry, Colonel, sir, but I'm not one of the drinking types. Just half a Horlicks, and I'm asleep in ten minutes. I'd like to give Wednesday a miss.'

The C.O. beamed and said: 'Quite understand, me boy, never mind. Look: on Thursday we're celebrating my birthday. It's going to be a hell of a night, me boy. Some chicks from the village; not to mention a few WRAF officers; pretty nurses from the rehabilitation centre, and the withdrawal unit . . . You'll be available on Thursday, won't you, Carstairs?'

Carstairs looked awkward and said: 'I'm terribly sorry, but I had a very strict upbringing. In fact I never even looked at a girl until I was at the training camp and we had a woman M.O. It hurts me still, every time I cough. Not girls, sir. I'd rather be A.W.O.L. on Thursday, sir.' The Colonel shrugged and said: 'Very well, me boy, I quite understand.' The lieutenant saluted and went to the door.

The Colonel said: 'Just one more minute, Carstairs?' 'Yes, sir?' The Colonel studied him. 'You are not a fairy are you, Carstairs?' The lieutenant turned red and said: 'Oh, no sir. No.' The Colonel gesticulated and said: 'That's too bad, Carstairs, you won't enjoy Friday night, either.'

1804

A young Irish girl walked into a lawyer's office and complained. 'My husband is a brute. I can't stand any more. I want to be rid of him,

221

that I do.' The lawyer said: 'You mean a divorce?' Then because he wondered about her religion he added: 'Are you of a certain persuasion?' The young woman snapped: 'If you mean do I need encouragement, that depends on the feller.' The solicitor let it go and remarked: 'Has your husband given you grounds?' The girl said: 'You mean has he tried to poison me?' 'No,' said the lawyer, 'I mean has he done anything that would enable you to sue him for misconduct?' The girl said: 'Eh?' The lawyer simplified it by asking: 'I mean has he been having a bit on the side?' 'I don't know,' she answered. The lawyer said: 'If he hasn't given you grounds for a divorce and you want to be rid of him you could let him divorce *you*, you know, by giving him grounds to part from you.' 'I see,' said the girl. 'But won't that cost a lot of money.' Helpfully the solicitor explained: 'Well, in your particular case, considering your financial position, *you* could get legal aid.' The girl thought for a moment and then said: 'Well, all right, if you're not too busy, but it will have to be around half-past-ten on Friday night so that he can catch us properly.'

1805
A young man went to see his doctor and reported a very bad case of persistent nightmares. 'Every night I have this awful dream,' he confessed. 'Lovely exotic girls come crowding into my room trying to make love to me, and there I am, warding them off and pushing them away . . .' The doctor asked: 'Well, what can I do about that?' The young man said pleadingly 'Doc—please—break my arms.'

1806
There was a tragic ending to their love story . . . they got married.

1807
The nice young man began to show his true colours when he proposed to her. She had been going to refuse him, but at the time she was in no position to argue.

1808
He was a kinky sort of feller; maybe that's because his father was a Chinese psychiatrist and his mother used to take in brain-washing.

1809
He washed his hair one night, and after that he couldn't do a thing with it—not even stuff it back in the carton it came in.

1810
She said she had been playing 'Vatican Roulette' and when asked what kind of a game that was she said: 'You play it with with five pills and an asprin.'

1811
A Catholic priest was walking through Dublin admiring the miniskirts when one of the straps snapped on his sandal. As he was just passing

a shoe shop he thought he would go in and get his sandal repaired even though the shop was owned by a Jewish gent named Isaac Goldberg. He thought it might engender some inter-religious goodwill, anyway. So Goldberg repaired the sandal, and as a gesture of religious unity refused payment for the work. Across the road the following day a butcher named Kelly looked out at Goldberg's shop and saw right across the window a phosphorescent placard which contained the wording 'Goldstein & Sons. Cobblers to Father O'Reilly.' So Kelly immediately got out paint and cardboard and daubed a message on it and stuck it in his window, leaning against a leg of pork. It read: 'Kelly for Succulent Sausages, and Knickers to the Chief Rabbi.'

Dubious Definitions

1812 *ABDICATION:* voluntary resignation at gunpoint.

1813 *ANCIENT MONARCH:* having a tendency to falling hair, with the head attached.

1814 *ABANDON:* Running away with someone else's wife, and then running away *from* her.

1815 *ACCORDIAN:* musical instrument invented when an egotistical angler decided to talk about the one that got away.

1816 *ADHERENT:* someone who follows you faithfully until he's got what he wanted.

1817 *ADVICE:* an assault on your intelligence which should be taken with a grain of salt.

1818 *ALIMONY:* post-marital war debts.

1819 *ADAM AND EVE:* an ancient couple who invented green salad without dressing.

1820 *ALCOHOLISM:* a spirited approach to life.

1821 *APARTMENT:* a small domicile where you can be happier with the little woman.

1822 *AIM:* an ambition in life which is all very well if you don't get fired.

1823 *ANTIQUE:* something which you collect after it has collected enough dust.

1824 *APOLOGY:* the only thing that will enable you to have the last word with a woman.

1825 *ALARM CLOCK:* something which scares the living daylights into you.

1826 *ANCESTOR:* someone who shinned right up your family tree.

1827 *ASTERISKS:* plain-clothed four-letter words.

1828 *BACHELOR:* a more intelligent member of the adult species.

1829 *BAIT:* anything that a woman can use to advantage when she's fishing for compliments.

1830 *BALD:* a euphoric masculine condition in which there is no more parting or dyeing.

1831 *ITALIAN BANKER:* The Lone Arranger.

1832 *COCKTAIL BARMAN:* a rich man's pour man.

1833 *BATHING BEAUTY:* something that covets a man's embarrassment.

1834 *SANDY BEACH:* a strip of sandy land over which you make a pebble dash for the sea.

1835 *BEAUTY SPECIALIST:* an expert with so many overweight female patients he considers himself a landscape gardener.

1836 *BIGAMIST:* a man who has a beautiful wife and a good housekeeper.

1837 *BIGOT:* any person who religiously rejects your religious convictions.

1838 *BLONDE:* a sin-thetic girl who could involve any man in a bleach of promise action.

1839 *BATHROOM:* a small tiled cell fitted with hot and cold running infants.

1840 *BORE:* a person who tells meaningless short stories in the form of a trilogy.

1841 *BOTTLE:* a vessel with a cork at one end and a hangover at the other.

1842 *BRASSIERE:* a garment worn by a woman who is both dis-honest and thrustworthy.

1843 *BRAVERY:* the ability to stand up to your mother-in-law when she brings up her big gums.

1844 *BRIDGE:* the ultimate indoor sport favoured by women who have lost their suspension.

1845 *BURLESQUE:* cast-off-clothing show-business.

1846   *BELT:* what a man may get around the head if his wife wears the trousers.

1847   *BEAR:* an animal you should not pat until it's a fireside rug.

1848   *BIKINI:* something which separates the haves from the have-nots.

1849   *BALDIE:* a man who comes out on top but is still a loser.

1850   *BOOK-KEEPER:* someone who refuses to lend from his library.

1851   *BLACKMAIL:* correspondence from the Coal Board.

1852   *BABY TALK:* sex education in primary schools.

1853   —honeymoon conversation.

1854   *BABY SITTER:* a foreign body who falls asleep keeping your infant awake.

1855   *BACHELOR BOY:* an unattached man who steers clear of a semi-detached house.

1856   —a man who believes in his own life and liberty and the happiness of pursuit.

1857   —a man whose home is his castle. A married Englishman's home is his cage.

1858   —someone who stays single to avoid leading a double life.

1859   —a man licensed to pick his *own* trouser pockets.

1860   —a man whose cuff-links are not handcuffs.

1861   *CADDY:* a small motorized golf cart made by Cadillac.

1862   *CALENDAR:* dates which never turn out to be palmy days.

1863   *CAPITAL OFFENSE:* your bank balance.

1864   *CARD GAMES:* pastimes in which you need to be a good player or a good prayer.

1865   *CULTURE:* what you possess if you are a third-degeneration aristocrat.

1866 *COMMERCIAL TRAVELLER:* a salesman for whom nothing ever seems to come off except coat buttons.

1867 *CALORIES:* things which women should watch from a distance.

1868 *COUNTRYSIDE:* where camping enthusiasts are a prime evil.

1869 *CHAFING DISH:* a Society frypan.

1870 *CHANCERY:* a day at the races.

1871 *CHEQUE BOOK:* a small payment scribbler which your bank binds with your own skin.

1872 *CHILDREN:* offspring always springing off the furniture.

1873 *CHIROPRACTOR:* a professional who badly kneads his patients.

1874 *CANDIDATE:* someone who dare not face a candid camera.

1875 *CONSENT:* the thing which familiarity breeds.

1876 *CANNIBALS:* people who take religious missions with a pinch of salt.

1877 *CANNIBALISM:* jungle billiards in which black pots white and when one man's meat is another man's pot-roast.

1878 *CANNIBAL:* a chap who's always fed up with visitors.

1879 *CITY:* a vastly populated environment full of lonely people.

1880 *COMMUNITY CHEST:* the feature that makes Doreen so popular locally.

1881 *CONSCIENCE:* what strikes you if you spot a TV monitor in the supermarket.

1882 *CONFETTI:* small bits of coloured paper made from repulped Sunday newspaper articles about love, sex, divorce and orgies.

1883 *CAPITAL PUNISHMENT:* the only guaranteed cure-all.

1884 *CENSOR:* an official with very little above the ears who worries a lot about things below the shoulders.

1885 *CLAIRVOYANT:* a seer who only has to look in the bottom of a teacup to know that you use teabags.

1886 **DISARMAMENT:** using a disarming manner when you are a munitions salesman trying to sell howitzers and submarines to an overseas nation at reasonable profit.

1887 **DISBELIEF:** the only thing you can fall back on when your wife says something you can't understand.

1888 **DAVID:** the biblical hero who invented the first guided missile.

1889 **DIAMOND:** something often used by a sugar-daddy as a stepping-stone to success.

1890 **DIPLOMAT:** a man who can convince his wife that she would look ridiculously fat in a mink coat.

1891 **DIVORCE:** when one man's mate becomes another man's person.

1892 **DRINKING:** a pastime we indulge in to drown our sorrows only to find that we are irrigating them.

1893 **DESERT:** a vacation centre for people who have saved for a rainy day.

1894 **DICTIONARY:** a useful tome when you want to cast a spell.

1895 **DRAMA:** almost every play these days is a mystery. The mystery is how they ever came to get on a stage.

1896 **DRUGS:** many drugs require considerable research: in the context where research means autopsies.

1897 **DULL:** a dullard is someone who puts purple pep pills to sleep.

1898 **DUEL:** a couple of men, a couple of seconds and it's all over.

1899 **DUTY:** something which the country banned, on which you have to pay contraband fees. They come in three dimensions, small, large and X-size.

1900 **DANCE:** an exercise which shows that there are eighteen inches to a man's foot.

1901 **DEBT:** the first thing you run into when you buy a second-hand car.

1902 **DEDUCTION:** something that you take off. Pursued to its ultimate condition, results in seduction.

1903 **DEFENCE:** taking your own cut-throat razor when you go to the barber-shop, in order to fight back when you are shaved.

1904 *DIPLOMACY:* the art of keeping your shirt on while your wife is getting something off her chest.

1905 *DACHSHUND:* a German word for 'auf weidersehen', meaning 'so long'.

1906 *DAILY NEWSPAPER:* a publication which uses screaming scoop headlines to expose a story which was common knowledge twelve hours earlier on television.

1907 *DETECTIVE STORY:* a novel which ultimately reveals that the author is an unmitigated villain.

1908 *DETOUR:* an inconvenient bypass which proves conclusively that the quickest distance between two points is under repair.

1909 *DOCKER:* a hard-working grappler who is often more loaded than the ship.

1910 *DISILLUSIONMENT:* marital dissolution.

1911 *DOCTOR:* a qualified professional who enjoys bad health.

1912 *DOGAMTISM:* the birth of a litter of pups.

1913 *DUCK:* an amphibious chicken.

1914 *DEMOCRACY:* bludgeonment of the people for the people by the people.

1915 *DEPARTMENT STORE:* a building disguised as a trading station where you go to see your money off.

1916 *DIET:* a slimming regimen with which you swiftly get fed up.

1917 —a clever way of giving your teeth a well-earned rest.

1918 —the food fad of the fat.

1919 —a method of semi-starvation scientifically devised and expensively promoted in that eighth of the world which seems unaware of the fact that in the other seven-eighths it is standard practice.

1920 *EARTH:* a globe that revolves on its taxes. We sometimes wonder what in the world it's coming to.

1921 *EASY:* regular payments which are always difficult to ease out of hire-purchasers.

1922   *ECCENTRIC:* someone who is much too famous or wealthy to be a crackpot, a nutcase or a weirdie.

1923   *EGG:* a suitable place for a sitting pigeon.

1924   *ELEVATED:* (to the peerage) a knight who for too long has wanted to make the Lords.

1925   *ENCORE:* once more with feeling that you've already done more than your whack.

1926   *ENCYCLOPEDIA:* ready? go! get set.

1927   *END:* When *you* are done long before day is.

1928   *ENERGY:* the power used by the man who makes hay out of the grass that other people grow beneath their feet.

1929   *ENGAGEMENT:* an arrangement between lovers after they've been dancing chic to sheik for several years.

1930   *ENGLISH:* the mother tongue of diplomacy because it's often circumspect to keep mum.

1931   *ENOUGH:* what a cockney's wife often goes off in.

1932   *ENTERTAINMENT:* at the very best it generally only reaches a particularly high standard of dubious mediocrity.

1933   *ENTRANCE:* what very few women do to men when they make an entrance.

1934   *EPIGRAM:* a wisecrack, quip or gag which only academics understand.

1935   *ESCAPE:* to get away from it all. Before the government gets it all away from you.

1936   *ETIQUETTE:* social grace which you need when you dine at a restaurant where you must eat with a knife and fork out a 25% service fee.

1937   *EVASION:* dodging the issue by strategic measures: like Dad does when he stays out of the house until the kids are all in bed. (His wife can do it by just staying out of bed.)

1938   *EVE:* the first sex-siren. She was always rooting around for a mini-leaf.

1939   —the first pippin a'peeling enough to make a man say 'Cor!'

1940 *EVOLUTION:* the progression which took Man away from the apes and let him go to the dogs.

1941 *EXPOSURE:* something you get with a camera if your models feel like showing you a thing or two.

1942 *ELEPHANTS:* animals used as labourers in African and Indian forests on trunk-to-trunk calls.

1943 *EAR-PIERCER:* a technician who gives you an ear-ring aid.

1944 *EARWIG:* what you wear if you want to keep your hearing muffled up.

1945 *ECONOMIST:* a man who does his wife's shopping.

1946 *EGOTIST:* someone who is more interested in himself than in you, unless it *is* you.

1947 *ELECTION:* public cross-examination.

1948 *ENTHUSIASM:* faith with a jet engine.

1949 *EVE (2):* a biblical strategist who was the first woman to sew trouser-pockets on a man's figleaf.

1950 *FOREIGN AFFAIRS:* keeping in touch with the right type of overseas secretary.

1951 *FRIDGE:* a kitchen container in which you store leftovers until they are ready to be thrown out.

1952 *FOLK SONGS:* folksy jingles found in most music shops, filed under Criminal Records.

1953 *FOREIGN AID:* the money we drop underdeveloped countries to help them finance our downfall.

1954 *FREE:* when politicians call the peoples of the West free they only mean that a lot of us are not yet in prison.

1955 *FREE SPEECH:* a formula perpetually proclaimed by parliamentarians earning three thousand a year who shut themselves up in luxury flats.

1956 *FLAWS:* things people often come across in new architecturally designed houses if they don't watch their step.

1957 *FLOATING DEBT:* the British fleet.

1958 *FOOTBALL:* the world's pass time.

1959 *FLOOD:* a disaster which Noah didn't give a dam about.

1960 *FACILITIES:* helpful social services provided to meet all contingencies and which proliferate daily. The latest is the Lyons' Rent-a-Loaf service.

1961 *FIREPROOF:* most modern new houses are fireproofed by the builders during construction. Peeling wallpaper pushing down rising damp burns badly.

1962 *FORGER:* a crook whose story ends on a bad note.

1963 *FOOL:* the man who still calls his wife 'dearest' when his mistress is costing him three times as much.

1964 *FAILURE:* what turns a nobody into a nonentity.

1965 —someone who is just able to keep his head under water.

1966 *FAITH:* what keeps you going; sometimes well over the speed limit.

1967 *FAME:* success which is sometimes an overnight accomplishment . . . because it's just a dream.

1968 *FARMER:* a pig-breeder who is constantly adding to his litter through the influx of leaflets from the Min. of Ag.

1969 *FASHION:* when it's from Paris it often looks as though the designer's cutting-room is a guillotine.

1970 *FAULTS:* the things which many a man suddenly finds he has in abundance the moment he gets married.

1971 *FOOT:* an appendage which every motorist ought to keep at braking point.

1972 *FENCE:* a line of sticks which women neighbours never consider a sound barrier.

1973 *GIBBERISH:* the language of Gibraltar, supposedly derived from the famous apes of the Rock.

1974 *GLUE:* the substance used by Eskimos in construction of their ice houses. Hence the expression ig-glue.

1975 *GREAT BRITONS:* proud people dragged into the Common Market to become Euro-peons.

1976 *GOLD:* a non-industrial mineral which would have been of greater benefit to mankind if it had been restricted to dental fillings.

1977 *GRASS:* if the grass is greener on the other side of the fence it is solely because they have a rotating sprinkler whereas your husband is sober.

1978 *GIRLS:* members of the fair sex. Some of them are effeminate.

1979 *GRACE:* what you say before meals. If the meal is not so hot you may sometimes say it's a disgrace, in which case your wife will make it hot for you.

1980 *GLAMOUR:* something which is put on as easily as airs and graces by women who have the requisite chemistry set.

1981 *GOAT:* an animal which will not eat the filmreel if he has already eaten the book.

1982 *GREETING CARDS:* wishes in print which now cost so much it may be cheaper to buy a present, unless you can find a stationer who does hire-purchase.

1983 *GARTER:* a somewhat outmoded elasticated accessory which used to enhance women's clothing. One doesn't see them these days because some girls don't wear any.

1984 *GUEST TOWEL:* part of the bathroom decor, unless you are from out of town.

1985 *GOLF FIEND:* a person who breaks 80, and that's only on the road to the course.

1986 *GOLF FAILURE:* a tee-he.

1987 *GOLD-DIGGER:* if she can find a man with money to burn she'll make the match.

1988 *GOSSIP:* a woman with an excellent memory, and her cheek in her tongue.

1989 *GARAGE:* a lock-up shed which encourages you to exercise because the car can't walk to you.

1990 *GARDEN:* a plot to destroy you. You go there to hoe a row and sow stuff that you know won't grow well enough for the Show.

1991 —a piece of hard ground which takes a lot more out of you than you are likely to take out of it.

1992 *GARLIC:* the essential cooking ingredient for people who nose their onions.

1993 —it's tops for flavour but not for favour.

1994 *GLUTTON:* the gourmet cook who put the greed in ingredients.

1995 *GAS:* a volatile fuel much in demand since the population explosion.

1996 *GENERAL:* an officer with memories who puts a nib on his baton as soon as he retires to marshall his thoughts.

1997 *GEOLOGIST:* a man who studies the earth to find out how old it is, and who would be better employed studying the world to find out how much time we have left.

1998 *HUSBAND:* a man who would rather have a half of bitter for company than his better half.

1999 *HISTORY:* raking up the ashes of bygone mistakes in order to remember how to remake them.

2000 *HONESTY:* a pathological horror of being caught out.

2001 *HORSE-SENSE:* reading '*The Sporting Life*' over your breakfast oats to avoid a running commentary from a nagging mare.

2002 *HAMBURGER:* the ill-bred putting on the dog.

2003 *HITCH-HIKER:* someone who cannot work owing to the disability of a crooked thumb.

2004 *HUMAN NATURE:* the thing which makes some men hewers of wood and other drawers of social security.

2005 *HARD LUCK:* sometimes it's when you make a cable out of a cobweb.

2006 *HALITOSIS:* a social drawback, but at least it's better than having no breath at all.

2007   *HAMLET:* a small town where the payroll can be delivered without aid from Securicor.

2008   *HAPPINESS:* being content with all we haven't got.

2009   *HIGHBROW:* someone who can talk fluently about obscure matters that he doesn't understand, and make you believe it's your fault.

2010   *HOLDING COMPANY:* a corset factory.

2011   *HOLIDAY:* the grim sequel to believing everything you read in the travel brochure.

2012   *HOLY SMOKE:* the padre sneaking a cigarette in the confession box.

2013   *HOME:* dad's hotel; sonny's filling-station; grandpa's concentration camp; eldest daughter's courtroom.

2014   *HOUSEWIFE:* a woman who got off the shelf only to find herself reaching for a dozen others.

2015   *HAPPENING:* where it's all at; instead of being all old hat.

2016   *HASTE:* putting a perfectly lovely day to waste.

2017   *HEAD:* losing it won't prevent you from getting headaches.

2018   *HEALTH:* good health is when you take two *steps* at a time instead of pills.

2019   *HEEL:* some men look down-at-heel; others look up at neckline.

2020   *HEIRESS:* a very chaste girl.

2021   *HENPECKED:* the husband who prays his first child will be a daughter to help him with the washing up.

2022   —A husband who can't even worm himself out of the chores.

2023   *HEROINE:* a spinster who is always dying for a man.

2024   *HINDSIGHT:* watching a woman retreating with a wiggling walk.

2025   *HISTORY:* the saga of the world which its authors have smothered with invention.

2026   —past events coloured by the nationality of the writer whose side lost.

2027   *HOUSE:* an edifice with a long garden, a long mortgage and a laird with a long face.

2028   *HOMOSEXUAL:* a man who eats like a bird.

2029   —a man who is not interested in old wives' tails.

2030   *HORSEWHIP:* what you would like to do to some people if only you could afford a horse.

2031   *ICE:* the only commodity which is exactly what it's cracked up to be.

2032   —the only thing that will ever enable *you* to walk on water.

2033   *ICED LOLLY:* spare cash kept in the deep-freezer.

2034   *ICE RINK:* a place where you can indulge in some invigorating figure-eighting.

2035   *ICE AGE:* something that starts the day your wife begins to get frigid.

2036   *ILL WIND:* the element that blows a saxophone.

2037   *IDEALIST:* a dreamer who is trying to wake everyone else up.

2038   —a person who knows that the world won't be a better place until we can keep politicians out of politics.

2039   *INDIGESTION:* something you get when that square meal won't fit your round stomach.

2040   *IN-LAWS:* what you get through having relations with your partner.

2041   *INJURY:* the result of an altercation with anyone who has gingery propensities, like a hotheaded redhead.

2042   *INTELLECTUAL:* many a high-brow blonde who cannot write owes it all to a pencil.

2043   *INSTRUCTION MANUAL:* information provided by

sadistic manufacturers that produces feelings of incapacity, inferiority and total incompetence in the proud new owner of the equipment.

2044 *INTELLIGENCE:* a department of any Defence Ministry, which encourages an enemy not to worry.

2045 *INTEREST:* what a woman loses in you after she has milked your capital.

2046 *INFERIORITY COMPLEX:* a condition of mind which many a psychoanalyst takes lying down.

2047 *IMPARTIAL:* where the dipsomaniac with a compulsion to wrap things up keeps the spare liquor.

2048 *IMPOSSIBLE:* unlike things that are possible, things that cannot be done never need to be undone.

2049 —putting your best foot forward when you do not have three legs.

2050 *INCOME:* only a really good breadwinner puts his Rolls in the garage.

2051 —if you are rich you can tell any man to go to the devil, and even stake him the fare.

2052 *INFIDELITY:* a pastime that may only be practised legally if there is a prior marriage licence.

2053 *INHERITANCE:* a dead giveaway.

2054 —where the principal beneficiary is an unmentionable lawyer.

2055 —when you are only too delighted with other people's leavings.

2056 *INFATUATION:* increasing your weight.

2057 *INSOMNIA:* a complaint suffered by most living creatures, not counting sheep.

2058 —a condition where the best solution is to go home and sleep it off.

2059 *IDLE:* a person who has loafed and lost.

2060 —anyone with enough spare time to be a busybody.

2061   —the only person who can truly state that his work is never done.

2062   —a man who refuses to have anything to do for you.

2063 *IGNORANT:* being unaware of the fact that you know nothing.

2064 *ILLITERATE:* everybody is born illiterate but some people get over it.

2065 *IMAGINATION:* whenever you fancy that you have seen something good on television, it is probably imagination.

2066 *IMMIGRANTS:* many people who are British-born wouldn't be in the country at all if they had been required to pass the immigration laws.

2067 *IMMORALITY:* behaviour which society frowns upon although people themselves are inclined to be very indulgent.

2068   —a coupling arrangement which might also be expressed as half of one and a bit of the other.

2069 *INTENTIONS:* what necessity is the father of.

2070 *IRONY:* an advertisement for the new Rent-A-Knee Service.

2071 *IRISH STEW:* Bogside goulash for which may the lord have Murphy.

2072 *ITALY:* where female tourists say boo to a goose.

2073   —a country shaped like an old boot, much of which needs souling and healing.

2074   —the breeding station for most of Hollywood's busty big-screen beauties.

2075 *JAZZ:* syncopated music that is beyond words.

2076 *JEALOUSY:* something that would be a cardinal sin if only the cardinal had any option.

2077 *JEWELLERY:* very frequently forgiving presents, or bribes.

2078   —the happiest way for any woman to get stoned.

2079 *JACK:* probably the only way you'll ever get a car in the higher bracket.

2080 *JURY:* a body of people all of average ignorance.

2081 *JOINT ACCOUNT:* the plumber's bill.

2082 *JUNE:* when you know the year has gone off half-shot.

2083 *JONAH:* historical proof that you can't keep a good man down.

2084 *JOURNALISM:* when Sunday newspapers denounce obscenity and pornography by printing detailed examples of it.

2085 *JUDGE:* a man with a wig and a gown who sentences to three years another man for wearing a wig and a dress.

2086 *JEWISH:* something that some of their best friends are, whoever *they* are.

2087 *JUVENILE DELINQUENT:* someone passing through a phase armed with a knife, a cudgel, a pocketful of pot, and a protest banner.

2088 —a youngster who feels so grown up he's youthless.

2089 —the product of a broken home, and often the one who did most of the damage.

2090 *JUICE:* any fruit that has exercised itself to a pulp playing squash.

2091 *KISS:* a cheeky French man-to-man embrace.

2092 —mouth to mouth restitution.

2093 —the dreamiest form of shut-eye.

2094 *KEEPSAKE:* a memento given to you by someone long forgotten.

2095 *KANGAROO:* a giant grasshopper with a built-in playroom down under.

2096 *KEY:* you won't find one in the door of opportunity; you have to pick the lock.

2097 —a musical frequency which ladies sing in very loudly if the bathroom lock is also busted.

2098 *KILLING:* an effective way of taking life easy.

2099 *KLEPTOMANIA:* this is a mental illness which doesn't last long if you keep taking something for it.

2100 *KINDNESS:* the milk of human kindness is found in sour cream more often than in a churn.

2101 *KITCHEN:* a modernistic room where we take stuff out of tins and transfer it to plastic platters. Some modern kitchens are more of a kitsch.

2102 *KNICKERS:* apparel drastically reduced by the makers in a futile effort to stop their sales dropping.

2103   —garments in which the lace round the edge has become the sole ingredient.

2104 *KING-SIZE:* any attractive package which has thicker padding and wrapping around it than the family-economy pack costing half the price.

2105 *KNOWLEDGE:* the more you know the better you are able to reject the persistent persuasions of the encyclopaedia salesman.

2106 *KITTENISH:* any woman who gives herself little pauses between birthdays.

2107 *KNEES:* vital parts of the body. Babies dandle on them; fathers put juveniles across them; people pray on them; girls are petted on them; fiances propose on them; and afterwards you get kneedeep in debt with them.

2108 *LADY:* a genuine lady is a woman who does not leave any bits and pieces uncovered, when she dresses, to ensure that gentlemen are not confused.

2109 *LAKE:* lakes and rivers are protected from the appetites of anglers, and laws exist to prevent them from catching fish at certain times. To many fishermen these laws are superfluous.

2110 *LANDLORD:* a property owner whose heart is as big as the kitchenette which turns out to be a gas-ring screwed to the closet door.

2111 *LAND:* a limited area of space in any populated area where thousands of homeless are expected to stand on each other because those who control it wish to conserve and preserve it for future generations to admire.

2112   *LANGUAGE:* a system of speech employed by many people to replace thought.

2113   —the secret of good language is knowing when to shut up.

2114   *LAP:* if you reckon you are on your last lap, make sure it's the luxurious one.

2115   *LAPP:* a northerner who when he does a good winter days' work is on nights.

2116   *LAS VEGAS:* a Western American gambling resort where pan-handlers now find employment emptying the fruit-machines.

2117   *LATE:* women are traditionally unpunctual. Ever since Eve had to be waited for by Adam.

2118   —when a husband arrives home late from the office with a lame excuse, he turns the key wondering what he's letting himself in for.

2119   *LAUGH:* he who laughs at himself laughs best.

2120   —the ability to laugh is what separates Man from lesser animals. Which is a shame, because animals have far more to laugh at.

2121   *LEAN YEARS:* what a woman hopes for in middle age.

2122   *LAUNDRY:* a place where things are made much whiter now that we have the strength of biological action. The wife.

2123   *LOOK:* if you look at a Traffic Warden curiously it's probably just because you're a nosy parker.

2124   *LAW:* ignorance of the Law is no excuse. But it's not your fault that the Law is ignorant.

2125   —possession is nine points of the Law and most Lawyers talk as if they were possessed.

2126   *LAWN:* you have to mow the grass yourself because your wife is not a maiden all forlorn.

2127   *LAWYERS:* it won't matter if the meek do inherit the earth because the lawyers will still get most of it in fees.

2128   —the Law is an ass, and the judge often adds a rider.

2129   *LAZY:* a lot of people are only unemployed until they can find something better—like a win on the pools.

2130   —the strength of the Welfare State is the power behind the drone.

2131   *LEAF:* epigrams are as old as the pre-biblical era. It was Eve who said: 'Half a leaf is better than none.'

2132   *LYRICAL:* some poet once wrote: 'What is so rare as a day in June?' We can tell him—how about the end of February in a leap year?

2133   *LETTERS:* is a man of letters a postman, a graduate, a sign-writer, a literary genius, a blackmailer, or an estate agent?

2134   *SPIRIT-LEVEL:* a dipso lying prone under the table.

2135   *LIBEL:* something a Cockney finds on a sauce bottle.

2136   *LIB:* Women's Lib. is a movement dedicated to the emancipation of the fair sex. They burn their bras and become dropouts.

2137   *LIBRARY:* a place where the majority of books are taken out—dusted, and put back.

2138   *LIFE:* putting your best foot forward; for someone to tread on.

2139   —one damn thong after another.

2140   *LINGERIE:* what wily women clothe themselves in slightly to give men a frilling experience.

2141   *MARRIAGE:* a coupling of two people of opposite sexes who have proven themselves combatable.

2142   —shared bedlam and board.

2143   —the bonus commandment: thou shalt knot.

2144   *MARTYR:* rambling rose of the wildwoods who didn't really want him to take her there in the first place.

2145   —someone who's been dying, to get an idea off his chest.

2146   *MASTER OF CEREMONIES:* a busy sort of chap who runs things. Like a second-hand car.

2147 *MATCH:* sometimes occurs when a bachelor finds a really striking girl.

2148 *MATE:* the first thing a spinster looks for when she boards a cruise ship.

2149 *MATERIALIST:* someone whose possessions are his buy-word.

2150 *MONKEY-BUSINESS:* a partnership between a hurdy-gurdy man and one of his forbears.

2151 *MANHUNTER:* a girl who wants the whole troth and nothing but the troth.

2152 *MARRIED MAN:* easily recognised on the road because he has a girl in front, and both his hands on the wheel.

2153 *MODERN NOVEL:* a thinly-veiled plot expanded by intermittent bits of tommy-erotic suspense.

2154 *MAGISTRATE:* a notable townie who puts crooked folk straight.

2155 *MAN:* a *homo sap* who spends all his life seeking the perfect woman, without any help from his wife.

2156 —a domestic animal frequently chosen by women with petty minds.

2157 —a virile person who goes around dangling his embraces.

2158 *MISER:* The dough nut with a hidey-hole.

2159 *MODERN WOMAN:* a female who cannot decide whether she wants a career, or only one husband.

2160 *MATHEMATICS:* part of modern education which teaches mankind that there are some you can do.

2161 *MATURITY:* the age at which a woman stops looking for the ideal husband and grabs a man.

2162 *MONOPOLIST:* a person who keeps both elbows on the arms of his theatre seat.

2163 *MONEY:* a fool and his money cannot be soon parted because few fools have any money.

2164 *MEMORY:* if your amnesia bothers you, just forget about it.

2165 *MIDDLE-AGE SPREAD:* a condition which brings people closer together.

2166 —the time when a woman gets thicker on the bottom and a man gets thin on top.

2167 *MINING MILLIONAIRE:* someone who is ore-struck.

2168 *MISSILE:* an expensive object which goes faster than the speed of money.

2169 *MONEY:* the stuff we all used to live on before the era of credit cards.

2170 *MONKEY:* what makes evolutionists think that mankind descended from monkeys? Mankind is still working on it.

2171 *MORTGAGE:* a document which makes you the legal owner of a pile of milestones.

2172 —this provides you with a place of your own where you can have wall-to-wall carpeting and a back-to-the-wall existence.

2173 *MOTION:* perpetual motion is seeking a parking-space.

2174 *MATING:* the least successful marriages are those between men who are mules and women who are nags.

2175 *MURDER:* Casanova had a way with women but Bluebeard was smarter—he *did* away with his.

2176 *MUSIC:* folk music varies in style. It depends upon what your folks were like.

2177 *MOTHER-IN-LAW:* someone who doesn't have to buy her daughter a doormat for a present because she can show her how to make one out of her husband.

2178 —a woman who gives her son-in-law indigestion because she never taught her daughter how to cook.

2179 —someone who is no laughing mater.

2180 —one of the best arguments in the world for avoiding the horrors of a spare room.

2181 —a bridegroom's mother-in-awe.

2182 —a matrimonial merchant of menace.

2183   —the part of a marital union which proves conclusively that it is binding—because she never
stops.

2184 *MENU:* the *a la carte* that lists the horse off which you can
have a little steak.

2185 *MERCENARIES:* many a girl who encourages a man by
running her fingers through his hair is only practising for
the day when she can run them through his wallet.

2186 *MEDIUM:* the happiest medium is one who invariably has a
spiritual list to port.

2187 *MIND:* something that is broadened more by travail than
travel.

2188 *NUDIST:* a chap with no jacket, no pullover and two pairs of
trousers to match.

2189 *NAG:* the sort of woman a man should avoid if he has any horse
sense.

2190 *NEAR BEER:* the place where you will most often find a
disillusioned husband, because he needs a barmaid to lend an
ear.

2191 *NEEDLE:* an implement which was often difficult to find in a
haystack and is now difficult to find in a wife's hand.

2192 *NEURASTHENIA:* pretending to be Nelson so that you can
dodge the column.

2193 *NEWS:* if a dog bites a man it isn't news. If a man bites a dog
it's a hamburger. If an actress bites a dog it's publicity.

2194 *NIGHTCLUB:* too much unrest in the restaurant and too much
din during dinner.

2195   —a rendezvous most frequently used in the early
hours of morning.

2196 *NAME:* a husband gives his wife his name and then puts
everything in his wife's name. This is called the game of the
name.

2197 *NEMESIS:* don't pray now; fry later.

247

2198 *NATIONAL DEBT:* what every individual taxpayer reckons to be personally paying.

2199 *NEW VOGUE:* adopted by girls who live in glass blouses.

2200 *NEIGHBOUR:* sometimes the only way to keep up with the Joneses is to rent a tent next to a dropout.

2201 *NEUROTIC:* a person who not only talks to himself but also answers back.

2202 *NUTCASE:* a person who answers the phone even when it doesn't ring, and then complains to the operator that the phone is out of order.

2203 *NURSING:* an occupation which has hazards, such as trying to measure patients' impulses.

2204 *NEWS:* something which increases circulation and raises blood pressure.

2205 *NEWSPAPER:* a large piece of paper which starts and finishes full of garbage.

2205(a) —a Sunday newspaper is one that gives complete coverage about girls without it.

2206 *NEW YEAR:* New Year's Eve is a time when two years' ends meet; that coincides with the moment you realise that you can't make yours.

2207 —a time when both the bells and us are wrung out.

2208 *NOAH:* the chap who took couples of animals into the ark and was overrun by rabbits within a fortnight.

2209 *NOVEL:* a Victorian storybook published when navels were a novelty.

2210 *NUDE:* a girl not interested in clothes, who makes a man just as disinterested in them.

2211 *NUMBERS:* roulette is the living proof that there is no safety in numbers.

2212 *OBSCURITY:* being the president of an emergent African nation.

248

2213   *OLD MAID:* a spinster who failed to strike while the eyeing was hot.

2214   *OLD FLAME:* one of the lads whom her father put out.

2215   *OLD TIMER:* a seventeenth-century grandfather clock.

2216   *ONE-WAY STREET:* a thoroughfare on which you may only strike a pedestrian fore *or* aft.

2217   *OPPOSITION M.P.:* someone who can sit on the fence and still keep his ear to the ground.

2218   *OPTIMIST:* someone who believes that a free offer through the post won't fill his house with encyclopaedias.

2219   *ORCHESTRA CONDUCTOR:* the smartest man in the audience—he keeps his back to the stage.

2220   *OUTBOARD MOTOR:* an appliance for put-put-putting practice.

2221   *OXEN:* animals who are often the subject of yoke stories.

2222   *OBJECTION:* when a girl says 'no' her objection is not always indicative of her objective.

2223   *OBSCENITY:* the target of a shockproof watch committee.

2224   —something which is even encroaching on off-colour television.

2225   *OBSTACLE:* a stepping-stone disguised as a stumbling block.

2226   *OPPORTUNITY:* some applicants for top jobs could at one time be sure of a post. Now they are more likely to get the gate.

2227   *OIL:* once they used oil for troubled waters; now most of our waters are troubled by oil.

2228   *OLD NICK:* now modernised with hell-fired central heating.

2229   *OVERTIME:* time is pin-money; overtime is for afters.

2230   *OPTIMUM:* any mother running in a sack race.

2231   *OVERWEIGHT:* a woman in bloomers which look like stretch-pants.

2232   —someone who has waisted quite a way.

2233 *OWING:* what you don't owe doesn't worry you. What you are owed by others doesn't bother them. So why all this fuss over debts?

2234 *OPTICIAN:* a practitioner who makes women good lookers so that they can see whether or not men are looking good.

2235 *ODIOUS:* the lyrics of a modern song.

2236 *ORAL CONTRACEPTION:* 'No!'

2237   —a sleeping tablet.

2238   —'I've got a headache.'

2239 *PARASITE:* the person who wants everything on tick.

2240 *PASSPORT:* a folder in which people can see you as you see yourself.

2241 *PATHOS:* a Venetian blind-drunkard looking for a homely gutter.

2242 *PATRIOTISM:* shouting 'foul' when the foreign side scores a goal.

2243 *PHONE BOX:* a miniature gambling casino where the roulette wheel never comes up right, and the fruits are never on the line.

2244 *PONG:* the difference between inexpensive purfume and cheap scent.

2245 *PARENTS:* one malevolent male and one feeble female, according to the progeny.

2246 *PAYROLL:* something shared equally between the workers and the van-snatchers.

2247 *PEACE CONFERENCE:* a battle of words fought out by different nations to kill time while each saves up enough money to kill the other.

2248 *PENTHOUSE:* an apartment in a high-rise block which you cannot approach without permission from the control tower.

2249 *PERSONAL LIBERTY:* what you lose in marriage: you carry her over the threshold and find yourself in a stranglehold.

2250 *PERSONAL MAGNETISM:* what you use on your banker when you're *over*drawn.

2251 *PHILANTHROPIST:* a rich individual who gives some of it back in order to avoid estate duty and supertax.

2252 *PHRENOLOGIST:* an expert at feeling bumps who sometimes gets jealous of chest specialists.

2253 *PICCOLOIST:* a musician who likes to sit around whistling in the dark auditorium.

2254 *PERFUME:* the use of scent is instinctive in women especially odour cologne.

2255 —stuff that is bought for and paid for through the nose.

2256 —men must use deodorants but iron should be smelt.

2257 *PRESSURE:* Atlas once held the world on his shoulders—then he passed it on to the average taxpayer.

2258 *PETTING:* no girl need worry about losing her heart to a man, because he's probably looking for it.

2259 *PHILANDERING:* a bachelor is a man who often has his hands on a girl, but never a girl on his hands.

2260 *PASSPORT PHOTOGRAPHER:* an artist who takes a pretty lousy view of things.

2261 —someone who knows you are a bit thick from the neck up.

2262 *PIANO:* an instrument that usually does its best job as a piece of furniture.

2263 —all works and no play.

2264 *PICKPOCKET:* someone who has the answer to all his problems at his fingertips.

2265 *PICNIC:* an outing that attracts any number of creeping things, especially overladen cars.

2266 *PICTURE:* a picture, they say, is worth a thousand words. But many TV critics don't have that much space to spread their invective.

2267 *POETIC JUSTICE:* the motorist who went into a shopping precinct and got run down by pedestrians.

2268 *POLITICIAN:* parliamentarian who plays both ends against the middle class.

2269 *PAL:* a chap who puts his hand in yours and the other one in your pocket.

2270 *POLYGAMY:* a practice pursued by any nut who is fond of mothers-in-law.

2271 —a man who has six wives and still has to hire a housekeeper.

2272 *POVERTY:* a state enjoyed by the car-owner who can't keep body and engine together.

2273 *PRAYERS:* supplications that most people never offer until they are already almost on the floor.

2274 *PROGRESS:* something that doesn't solve any problems but drastically modernises them.

2275 *PROSPERITY:* the affluence of a farmer who buys new clothes for his scarecrow while his wife is still buying hers at the jumble sale.

2276 *PORNOGRAPHY:* books and pictures that give the public the benefit of the dirt.

2277 —lending money on cast-off clothing.

2278 *PROCESSION:* a young mother walking along with a little girl in front, a little girl by her side and her girdle bringing up the rear.

2279 *PARKING:* a small fortune awaits the inventor who can design a car to look like a parking meter.

2280 *PARTY:* the best thing to do with party leftovers is sober them up and kick them out.

2281 *PATRIOT:* any dictator who is prepared to let his country die for him.

2282 *PLATONIC:* in love from the neck up.

2283 *POET:* someone who is born, not paid.

2284   —a song-record writer is a poet who lyrics waxical.

2285 *POLL:* where people are expected to come to their census.

2286 *POPULATION:* to heir is human.

2287 *PORN BOOK:* a novel with a zip fly-leaf.

2788 *PORTRAIT:* approximately £30 a case for vintage.

2789 *POVERTY:* being down on your uppers without a crust.

2290 *PREGNANT:* the result of the patter which led on to his little feat.

2291   —the outcome of a courtship that turned out to be a short kip.

2292 *PROMISCUITY:* going on a sex drive without a licence.

2293 *PRESS AGENT:* a doorbell-to-doorbell salesman.

2294 *PRIZEFIGHTING:* canvas-ing for rights.

2295 *PROPORTIONS:* any woman who wishes to be presentable should aim for more spick and less span.

2296 *PASSPORT PICTURE:* convincing evidence that you are badly in need of that holiday abroad.

2297 *THE PRESS:* if you are awakened every morning to the sound of the baby yelling its head off, tell your wife not to let the kid read the morning papers.

2298 *POSSESSION:* a beautiful girl in your fond embrace is better than two in some other place.

2299 *QUESTIONS:* if they are on an official inquiry form it's invariably a nonsensus.

2300   —answers to most official questions merely serve to prompt three further questions.

2301 *QUEUE:* playing patience, but not solitaire.

2302 *QUIP:* a comment employed sometimes by someone who should be gagged.

2203 *QUIT:* what you should try, try, try to do if you don't succeed at first.

2204 *QUOTATION:* getting a pre-arranged costing for a modern haircut; if the barber will give you one.

2205 *REPUTATION:* what you find you had, when you lose it.

2206 *RESORT:* a place where the weary get tired.

2307 *RABBIT:* a small quadruped of singular unimportance which provides the fur that other animals get credit for when made into a coat.

2308 *RECKLESS:* a motorist who has lost his vehicle.

2309 *REDUCING MACHINE:* an apparatus which slims you because you can't afford food while you are paying the instalments on it.

2310 *RADIO PLAY:* an entertainment which always has a happy ending if you switch off half way through.

2311 *REDSKIN:* a sunbathing lady who has no reservations.

2312 *RAKE:* a man who gets his kicks painting the town blue.

2313 *RACETRACK:* a place where you can get soaked on a hot, dry summer's day.

2314 *REAL ESTATE:* that's your lot.

2315 *REVELATIONS:* the modern Book of Revelations is a male mag with affrontal nudes.

2316 *REVENGE:* going to a wife-swapping party and getting your own back.

2317 *REFEREE:* foul pest.

2318 *REFUSAL:* where she's got a will there's a won't.

2319 *REFUSE CART:* something that's always down in the dumps.

254

2320 *RUGBY:* a wild game played by rugged he-men who go back to the dressing room and get very dirty.

2321 *REPAIRS:* what the carpenter does to the kitchen cabinet you mended.

2322 *RESISTANCE:* men who meet too much resistance, keep such women at a distance.

2323 *RESTAURANT:* every wife should know her husband's favourite dish, and which cafe she works at.

2324 *RESOLUTION:* when hope springs eternal in the human breast, the ardent hopes he'll get the rest.

2325 *REUNION:* a repeat performance.

2326 *REVOLVING DOOR:* an ideal apparatus for pushing other people around.

2327 *REWARD:* getting what's coming to you, as long as it isn't your mother-in-law for a fortnight.

2328 *SALESMANSHIP:* the man who broke in to rob the safe at an insurance broker's office and got sold a with-profits life-endowment policy.

2329 *SANATORIUM:* a hospital where you have a rheum with a view.

2330 *SEAMAN:* Captain Hook who was retired from the navy because he wasn't a wholesailor.

2331 *SAINT:* farewell, and halo.

2332 *SACKED:* shiftless.

2333 *SHOE-HORN:* a hooter used by motorists to shoo people away.

2334 *SALAD:* mounting greenery, with mayonaise.

2335 *SANTA CLAUS:* someone who comes annually down the chimney, after the stork.

2336 *SATURATION POINT:* any pub.

2337 *SCANDAL:* the result of spreading your roomer.

2338 *SCIENTIST:* someone who can differentiate between a virgin metal and a comon ore.

2339 *SCULPTOR:* an artist who can be found in 'Who's Hewing Who.'

2340 *SINCERE:* a sexy soothsayer. Also a clairvoyant voyeur.

2341 *SKIER:* an athlete who's rapidly going downhill.

2342 *SEAT BELT:* academic method of corporal punishment.

2343 *SEXY BRA:* almost a hold-all.

2344 *SECRET:* untold stealth.

2345 *SPAGHETTI:* food which should not be cooked longer than eighteen or twenty inches at the most.

2346 *STRAP-HANGER:* the hook where you keep the children's chastisity belt.

2347 *STILL:* petrified like stone, while illicitly making the hard stuff.

2348 *STORK:* maternity winger.

2349 —a bird of a feather which starts father flapping.

2350 *SEASICK:* a hangover primed by non-alcoholic provisions.

2351 *SECRETARY:* just because a girl has shorthand doesn't mean she's completely armless.

2352 —it isn't always the girl's typing that gets the boss all keyed up.

2353 *SEDUCTION:* human sofering.

2354 *SERVE:* there are some people who even complain about the self-service.

2355 *SEX APPEAL:* 'all right; how about it?'

2356 *SEXOLOGY:* a science interested in high fidelity and high frequency but not connected with stereo-gramophonic aspects.

2357 *SHAME:* what people shrink away with when dirty washing is ironed out in public.

256

2358 SHAPE: sometimes a girl likes to be shipshape in Bristol fashion.

2359 SHOW BUSINESS: if it's a girlie show it can be sure of a long run if the chorus line has good legs.

2360 —there was a time when a take-off was an impression or impersonation. Now it's mere titillation.

2361 SHREWD: obtained a wife.

2362 SAILOR GIRL: one who likes the strong, Solent type.

2363 SPINSTER: someone not tried and found wanting.

2364 SUPER-BRA: the bust that money can buy.

2365 SLUM: a place where if opportunity knocked it would demolish the door.

2366 SMILE: in these days, if you see someone smiling it makes you wonder who he's been doing.

2367 SMOKING: statistics prove that more and more people are giving up giving up smoking.

2368 SOCIETY: society people are often the bluebloods who take their coffee in the library; and keep their books on the telephone table.

2369 —the people who know their station, have the right training, and court the upper-birthed.

2370 SOLITUDE: if you find solitude boring, don't talk to yourself.

2371 SOPRANO: a lot of sopranos are built like battleships, which explains their ability to cope with high C's.

2372 SPORTSMAN: a house-doctor who wouldn't grudge a nurse.

2373 SPRING: the only chance most of us get to make a clean-up.

2374 STOCKS & SHARES: investments that go up and down almost as dramatically as their purchasers' blood pressure.

2375 STOMACH: the size of your paunch can be what you chews.

2376 SUBURBS: moving into the suburbs these days usually means putting yourself on the outskirts of the next town down the line.

2378 *TABLOID:* a small format newssheet containing stories which substitute for comic strips.

2379 *TOUT ENSEMBLE:* eighty-eight cars blocked behind a motorist stuck at the traffic lights.

2380 *TACT:* making your visitors feel at home when both they and you wish they were.

2381 *TANNED:* a beautiful girl with nicotine fingers all over.

2382 *TAPIOCA PUDDING:* crepe-suzette melba, boarding house style.

2383 *TAXI DRIVER:* a wheeler-spieler.

2384 *TAXES:* the penalty paid for the privilege of working your fingers to the bonus.

2385 *TEARS:* a method of torture invented by women for wearing you down, drop by drop.

2386 *TEETH:* Gnashers for gnoshers.

2387 *TELEPHONE BELL:* an exchange operator: or a call girl.

2388 *TELEVISION:* one of the best sellers as an advertising tedium.

2389 —gripping entertainment, if you know how to grip the off-switch.

2390 *TIME:* something that waits for no man although it will loiter a little for women.

2391 *TOASTMASTER:* the M.C. who pops out to butter up the guests.

2392 *TODAY:* today it may be puppy-love, but tomorrow it's the doghouse.

2393 *TRADING STAMPS:* a shopper's method of filling up a little book with stamps while emptying two cheque books.

2394 *TRAFFIC:* highway throbbery.

2395 *TRANQUILLISERS:* some people take little pills to quiet their nerves, but others are calming through the rye.

2396 *TRIANGLE:* two spouses with a little added spice.

258

2397 *UGLY:* what you must be if even the music won't let you face it.

2398 *UMBRELLA:* a foul-weather appliance which spends more time in the lost-property hall than in the hall-stand.

2399 *UNDRESS:* a state in which a stripper earns her living, sometimes without even anything on her mind.

2400 *UTOPIA:* the place where there will not be any Joneses.

2401 *VARIETY:* this was invented in order that we do not need to make the same mistake twice.

2402 *VENUS DE MILO:* the goddess of disarmament who couldn't even cover up her embarrassment.

2403 *VIRGINITY:* nothing ventured, nothing lost.

2404 —keeping away from the straight and narrow.

2405 *WAGES:* take-home pay is what you have left after stoppages, such as you at the bar, en route.

2406 *WAITRESSES:* the bill-of-fair sex.

2407 *WALLET:* a bulging folder filled with notes, mostly finals.

2408 *WAR:* the 4th World War will have to be fought by people throwing rubble at each other with their teeth.

2409 *WATER:* nobody ever drowned their troubles in water.

2410 *WEAKNESS:* many a girl has been weakened on strong liquor.

2411 *WEDDING:* marriage starts with 'I do,' but from then on, it's 'You didn't . . .'

2412 *WEEPING:* sometimes the person you call a cry-baby is a full groan woman.

2413 *WORM:* sometimes we have to wonder if the worm in the apple in Eden's orchard wasn't blown up into a snake.

2414 *WATCH:* be careful that the watch you buy doesn't have a Swizz movement.

2415 *WHISKY:* whisky can make it a great life if it isn't weakened.

2416 *WISDOM:* remembering your wife's birthday present but not her birthday.

2417 *WOMEN:* the sex that came out of man's rib and divorced him from his backbone.

2418 *WINK:* what a girl does when she has someone in her eye.

2419 *WORD:* what's all the fuss? Even 'word' is a four-letter word.

2420 *WORLD UNION:* the United Nations has the sorry task of trying to put the last peace into the jigsaw puzzle.

2421 *WORM:* don't worry if you find a worm in the apple. The time to worry is when there's only half a worm.

2422 *WRESTLING:* if you want to wrestle with your conscience you must start with a submission.

2423 *YAWN:* the person who is listening to you with open-mouthed wonder may only be yawning with boredom.

2424 *YEARS:* the woman who seems to be carrying her years well probably dropped a few of them some time back.

2425 *YES GIRL:* one with beautiful ayes.

Terse
Verse

2426
The indolent vicar of Bray,
His roses allowed to decay,
His wife, more alert,
Bought a powerful squirt,
And stiffly remarked: 'Let Us Spray.'

2427
My girl Millie with the false eye-lashes,
Fell into the fire and was burnt to ashes.
Now, when the room gets damp and chilly,
I haven't the heart to poke poor Milly.

2428
A statistics expert in Djakarta
Had gone there to gather fresh data
On how many Djakartans
Wear short Stuart tartans,
And, under them, something much smarter.

2429
Rich Sheik Ab owns a private oasis
Where young girls go to learn the Ten Graces,
In the pool each one sploshes
In yashmak and goloshes
And a chastity belt with loose laces.

2430
A dark maiden from old Samarkand
Danced a nude native-dance in the Strand,
The policeman on duty
Cried: 'Now, me proud beauty,
Cover up there! I'll lend you a hand.'

2431
There was a young lady of Bude
Who was known to be chillingly prude;
She pulled down the blind
When changing her mind,
So the neighbours would not think her lewd.

2432
There was an old maid in Bermuda
Whose family name had been Tudor;
Descended no less

From the Virgin Queen Bess,
She bore sons although nobody dood her.

2433
A powerful young madam in Brussels
Was renowned for the size of her muscles;
No man was nonplussed
By the thrust of her bust
Unless he had rich red corpuscles.

2434
They retail every fashion at Barkers,
From sweaters to sheepskins and parkas;
But they do little trade
With Miss Katie Kincaid,
'Cos she likes to run around starkers.

2435
As a young artist Toulouse-Lautrec
Had a bed-sitter near Tooting Bec,
On a piece of stretched canvas
He etched Dodie Danvers—
Who returned him to Paris a wreck.

2436
There was an old man in Uttoxeter
Who cursed his poor wife and threw rocks at her,
And when she complained,
Contritely he aimed
A large box of hard-centred chocs at her.

2437
Our coloured photos show that we
Saw many foreign spots:
We even brought some back with us:
On baby's face, there's lots.

2438
When you are sweeping autumn leaves
They go their own sweet way.
Up they fly,
And around,
Or down;
But never fly away.

2439
The ladies inhabiting Venus
Have signalled to say they have seen us.
They state: 'There's a yen here

To transport some men here
And start a completely new genus.'

2440

God's design made a hopeful beginning,
But Man spoiled the pattern by sinning.
We trust the end story
Will salvage the glory,
But it looks like the other side's winning.

2441

There was a young couple in Kent
Whose TV antenna got bent;
When they both lovey-doved it,
The neighbours, too, loved it,
For instead of receiving, they sent.

2442

There once was a maid with such graces
That her curves cried aloud for embraces;
'You look,' observed Sid
'Like a million quid,
Invested in all the right places.'

2443

There was a young girl, but the catch is
Her garments were always in patches;
When comments inquire
Re the lady's attire,
She says 'When I itches, I scratches.'

2444

A young single girl born in York
Complained she'd been scared by a stork;
Some neighbours believed
That was how she conceived.
But others continued to talk.

2445

Breathes there a man
With soul so dead
That to some lass
Hath never said
'Let's go to bed?'

2446

Whichever way you reckon it
Nature's rather rum;
Flowers smell so sweet
And yet the bee can only hum.

2447
A man met his girl friend in Brussels
And charged, 'You are wearing two bustles!'
She declared 'That's not true;
It's a thing I don't do.
You are merely observing my muscles.'

2448
A tremor shook her lovely form,
Her eyes began to blink,
Her pulse rose to a hundred and
She cried: 'I think—I think—.'
He sighed: 'You think you love me?'
For his mind was on that track.
'Oh, no!' she yelled; 'I think a bug
Is crawling down my back!'

2449
A deathwatch bug married a lugworm
An accident cut her in two.
They charged the bug with bigamy;
Well, what else could they do?

2450
A silly young man from the Clyde
In a funeral procession was spied;
When asked, 'Who is dead?'
He giggled and said,
'I don't know; I just came for the ride.'

2451
Said an envious, erudite ermine,
'There's one thing I cannot determine:
When a dame wears my coat,
She's a person of note;
When I wear it, I'm nothing but vermin.

2452
There was an old man in Nantucket
Who hid all his loot in a bucket.
His daughter Michaela
Ran off with a sailor;
And as for the bucket, Nan took it.

2453
There was an old sculptor named Phidias
Whose knowledge of Art was invidious.
He carved Aphrodite
Without any nightie,
Which affronted the frail and fastidious.

2454

There once was a sailor called Cripps
Who married on one of his trips,
A widow named Block;
But died of the shock,
When he saw there were 10 little chips.

2455

There was an old lady named Brewster
Who was often annoyed by a rooster.
She cut of his head
Until he was dead,
And now he's quite sorry he goosed her.

2456

A lusty young wench in Toledo
Had a very inflated libido.
When a couple of Finns
Made her mother of twins
She got them a job at the Lido.

2457

A gent who was weak-willed and weird
Declared, 'This is just what I feared.
Please pass me the Lux
For a flock of wild ducks
Have established a nest in my beard.'

2458

Little Willy, with a grin,
Drank up all of Daddy's gin.
Mummy said, when he was plastered,
'Go to bed, you little basket.'

2459

A scraggy old spinster in Bude
Said 'Young men are exceedingly rude,
When I go for a swim
They pull my left limb,
But the rest of me's never pursued.'

2460

Egotistic is Monty Montrose,
An amorous beau among beaux;
Indiscreet in the street
He will kiss his own feet
And address them as Myrtle and Rose.

Trees (A Golfing Parody)

2461
I think that I shall never see
A hazard tougher than a tree;
A tree o'er which my ball must fly
If on the green it is to lie;
A tree which stands that green to guard,
And makes the shot extremely hard;
A tree whose leafy arms extend
To spoil the mashie shot I send;
A tree that stands in silence there
While angry golfers curse and swear.
Niblicks were made for fools like me
Who cannot even miss a tree.

She Was Poor But She Was Honest

2462
She was poor but she was honest, victim of the squire's whim;
First he loved her, then he left her, and she lost her honest name.

Then she ran away to London for to hide her grief and shame;
But she met another squire and she lost her name again.

See her riding in her carriage in the Park and all so gay:
All the rich and nobby people come to pass the time of day.

See the little old-world village where her aged parents live,
Drinking the champagne that she sends them, but they never can forgive.

In the rich man's arms she flutters, like a bird with broken wing:
First he loved her, then he left her. And she hasn't got a ring.

See him in his splendid mansion entertaining with the best,
While the girl that he has ruined lies discarded and distressed.

Standing on the bridge at midnight says she: 'Farewell blighted love.'
There's a scream—a splash—Good Heavens! What is she a-doing of?

Then they drag her from the river, water from her clothes they wrang,
First they thought that she was drowned, but the corpse got up and sang:

'It's the same the whole world over,
It's the poor what gets the blame,
It's the rich what gets the pleasure,
Isn't it a blooming shame?'

2463
We had a dachshund, one so long
He hadn't any notion

267

How long it took to notify
His tail of his emotion.
And so it happened, while his eyes
Filled up with woe and sadness,
His little tail went wagging on
To show his former gladness.

2464

A young Hippie nit from Bavaria
Met a girl in a nearby Nudes area;
She said 'Here among us,
You'll need much more fungus.
To be fair, we like men who are hairier.'

2465

There was a fair maiden in Malta
Whose wanton ways no one could alter
Till a priest in Coblenz
Had the very good sense
To get her a Cross and a psalter.

2466

Life had pretty Paula quite soured
'Cos her Howard was a cautious young coward
But she set things in motion
With a strong potent potion
And was soon overpowered and deflowered.

2467

We know of a spinster in Neath
Whose purity beggars belief;
She opined that a chair
Looked lewd with legs bare—
So she knitted each leg its own sheath.

2468

The knot was tied; the pair were wed,
And then the smiling bridegroom said
Unto the preacher, 'Shall I pay
To you the usual fee today,
Or would you have me wait a year
And give you then a hundred clear,
If I should find the married state
As happy as I estimate?'
The preacher lost no time in thought,
To his reply no study brought,
There were no wrinkles on his brow;
He said 'I'll take £3.00 now.'

2469

A Hawaiian lovely, Minoa,
Swirled her grass-skirt and whispered 'Aloha'
I gave her, besides
A short back-and-sides,
Two rides on my motorised mower.

2470

I remember, I remember,
As my childhood flitted by,
It was cold then in December,
And it was warmer in July.
In the summer there was sunshine
In the winter people froz;
But the weather isn't now at all
Like what it used to was!

2471

Have pity on the poor Hindu,
He does the best that he kindu;
He sticks to his caste from first to last,
And for trousers he makes his skindu.

2472

The owl and the pussycat went to sea
In a beautiful pea-green boat;
The cat had the bird and greenpeas for his tea;
'Sad!' said puss, with a lump in his throat.

2473

The curfew tolls the knell of parting day
The lowing herd wind slowly o'er the lea;
Its perfume holds the smell of rotting hay,
And puts the visiting townsman off his tea.

2474

There was a young lady named Hester
Who wore clothes made of clear polyester;
And to give life a boost,
She induced to her roost.
A bailiff who twice repossessed her.

2475

A feminine dentist called Joan,
Treated all her male patients alone;
She was eager and willing
To attempt any filling,
And, my, how her practice has grown.

269

2476

A highwayman came riding;
Riding through the dales;
He'd had his oats in John O'Groats,
And was after more in Wales.

2477

Mary had a little pram
She hated every minute;
Till Sam, who didn't give a damn,
Helped her put something in it.

2478

Methuselah ate what he found on his plate,
And never, as people do now,
Did he note the amount of calorie count;
He ate it because it was chow.
He wasn't disturbed as at dinner he sat,
Devouring a pizza or pie,
To think it was lacking in granular fat
Or a couple of vitamins shy.
He cheerfully chewed each pellet of food,
Unmindful of troubles or fears
Lest his health might be hurt
By some fancy dessert.
And *he* lived over nine hundred years.

2479

She was leaning on the rail,
And was looking deathly pale.
Was she at a bargain sale?
Or did she fall?
She was daddy's only daughter,
Casting bread upon the water,
In a way she hadn't oughter,
That was all.

2480

With Violet cuddling in his arms,
He drove, quite willy-nilly.
Where he once held his Violet,
He now holds just a lily.

2481

A beautician who's never been lonely
Is the much-admired Millicent Stoneleigh,
An unusual fitment
Above her equipment
Is a sign reading 'Standing-room only.'

2482

A worthless young man born in Kent
Always leased out his wife for the rent;
But as she got older
The landlord grew colder:
And they finished their years in a tent.

2483

An anaemic young lady from Stoke
Who in favour of chastity spoke,
Was asked by her doctor
In words that quite shocked her,
'Did your parents have you for a joke?'

2484

'Men seldom make passes
At girls who wear glasses,'
(As Dorothy Parker has said.)
She said it quite rightly,
She's very unsightly;
The lass who wears glasses to bed.

2485

In a cheap simple cassock of satin
The Pope made a trip to Prestatyn,
He prayed to the Lord
Who looked happy, but bored,
For the Lord knew no Gaelic or Latin.

2486

Miss Vera Tremaine, the young vamp,
On the golf course would play, dry or damp,
With the scores added up
She won rose-bowl and cup
As the amateur inter-course champ.

2487

There was once a pious young priest
Who ate loads of poisonous yeast,
For he said: 'It's quite plain
We must all rise again,
And to rise I must first be deceased.'

2488

There was a young man, name of Strauss,
Who was surely a man, not a mouse,
He could play, play could he,
In any old key,
If the key fitted some friend's wife's house.

2489

A tic-tac man worked in Calcutta
With a very unfortunate stutter;
For a week they held up
The Calcutta Gold Cup
As his hands went split, splat, splutter-splutter.

2490

A greasy-haired maid in Vienna
Made gallons of tea out of senna;
Many people were rude
As they watched what she brewed,
So she scrubbed it. And rinsed it in henna.

2491

'Icka caffa a-a comp
Google gurgle googoo glump . . .'
'What *can* that stupid infant want?'
'The vicar's dropped him in the font!'
'He'd better name him, pretty fast!'
'He has, *you fool*. It's Dammon Blast.'

2492

The boy stood on the burning deck
Whence all but he had flown.
There he was, all by himself,
Alone, and on his own.
The lousy lot of cowards
Had scuttled, one and all,
The thin ones and the fat ones,
The long, the short, the tall.
The boy stood on the burning deck,
So brave, much more than most;
And as the flames licked round his neck
He made himself some toast.
So now he knew why they had fled.
He was more doughty. Better bred.

2493

Half past five and all is rush;
Against each door the thick throngs crush;
Peter saw a door marked 'Push'
And pushed it right in someone's mush.
After a brief and pregnant hush,
The victim softly murmered 'Tush,'
Then, gee, how the gore began to gush.
They swept up Peter with a brush.

2494

Always conscientious
Is that model maid Miss Merke;

272

When artists need a wench, she's
Always in the nude for work.

2495
Trim size, king size,
On the shelf,
Fags and panatellas;
Susan doesn't smoke herself,
But she sure makes all
The fellas.

2496
In Prague a young maid from Quebec
Was outraged by a slav, Ivor Schlek;
A doctor named Winnick
From Colmunster Clinic,
Expensively cancelled her Czech.

2497
A geography mistress in Goa,
Did a favour for me, which Iowa:
I sail north, south and west,
As you've probably guessed,
So I might even go for Samoa.

2498
A traveller called Mortimer Beatty
With a cannibal King signed a treaty;
With a jungle gin-sling
Beatty toasted the King
Then the King toasted Mortimer Beatty.

2499
To be at Mamma's apron strings
Was one of childhood's roots;
But now it's just the laces of
Their mother's kinky boots.

2500
To his wife living in Nicaragua
Hubby said: 'What an 'orrible nag you are'
Yet when she passed her test
He was very impressed
So he bought her a car—(nivorous Jaguar).

2501
A fearful aspect is Lydia's,
Her face and her figure are hideous,
And yet Percival Scott

273

Married her like a shot,
Because she was rich and fastidious.

2502
A young fashion model in York
Has a scraggy form, lighter than cork;
She has to be fed
On pure wholemeal lead
Before she dare go for a walk.

2503
So often did Jock's elbow tilt,
On his clothing four whiskies were spilt,
But he had to refuse
To dryclean his trews
'Cos he wore them the same as a kilt.

2504
Fiercely the fire's flame flickers;
It is washing day, down at the vicar's.
The door's barred and locked,
The vicar's unfrocked,
And the organist's airing her knickers.

2505
Rub-a-dub-dub
Three men in a tub
It might not be healthy, but it's that type of club.

2506
She was only the neighbour's daughter;
She rarely came to call.
And so I never saw much of her
Till I made a hole in the wall.

2507
The Dean undressed with heaving breast,
Her loveliness, to pry on;
He thought it lewd
To practise nude,
So he kept his old school tie on.

2508
There was a young man from Skegness:
He got a young maid in distress;
For sad to relate
He thought it too late,
So they spent the whole night playing chess.

2509
Christopher Robin is saying his prayers:
His skates on the stairs
Caught Dad unawares.

2510
I remember, I remember, the place where I was born;
There were eighteen children in the house and ten more on the lawn;
I quickly learned the meaning of the comment 'barren wastes,'
It seems that both my parents had very catholic tastes.

2511
The boy stood on the burning deck
When all but he had fled;
'But for the rain
I'd examine his brain'
A passing doctor said.

2512
By Class Economic went Monica
On a love-seeking cruise to Salonika
But despite gin and tonic
The first week was chronic
And the second one even platonicer.

2513
He that loves a rosy cheek
Goes where the liquor flows;
To drink to the renowned physique
Of the waitress, Cheeky Rose.

2514
Of all the knights in Appledore
The wisest was Sir Thomas Kincaid;
None of them did grapple more—
For he had his own daily maid.

2515
They told me, Heraclitus,
They told me you were dead;
But you've caught me in the actlitus:
In Mrs. H's bed.

2516
A peculiar beast is the glow-worm.
Each night you'll hear him cursing;
'Cos everywhere he has to go
He has to go, reversing.

2517

The Calif of Lower Cadiz
Stayed in bed when he ought to have riz.
His wife banged on the door
To ask him what for,
And he shouted 'It's none of your biz.'

2518

There was once two dogs in Kilkenny,
Who both thought it was one dog too many;
So they bit and they clawed
And they split and they gored;
Till apart from their tails
And a few odd entrails
Instead of two dogs there weren't any.

2519

How fierce my wild heart flutters
At the picture my wife makes;
She's also quite an expert
On ferro-concrete cakes.

2520

An intruding mouse roused Miss McLeod,
Who reacted with screams fairly loud,
When no rodent inspector
Arrived to protect her,
She just lay on her front and meeowed.

2521

No more will hungry hordes of Yanks
Rebel to vent their hate;
For now dear God's Own Country
Has a fifty-second state.
We understand the Sandwich Isles
Were bought by Uncle Sam
Because its fields are made of bread
And its roads are paved with jam.

2522

A cowardly husband in Fife,
Watched a sassenach kissing his wife;
The brute saw him vexed,
Said: 'You can be next,'
But the husband said: 'Not on your life.'

2523

There was a young girl from Genoa
Whose neckline could not have been lower,
She displayed with great zest

276

Twelve tenths of her chest,
And her parents just don't wish to know her.

2524
When she'd finished her studies, Louise
Was replete with MA's and MDs.
Her exhaustion was sheer,
Her GP said, 'It's clear
That you're killing yourself by degrees.'

Miscellaneous
Meanderings

The Gentle Art of Giving a Speech

2525

The first thing about giving a speech is to talk with your mouth, which is a gaping hole just below your nose, and contains a few teeth, several gums, and a thing that flaps up and down and is usually coated with cigarette fuzz and liquor fur. To stop it fraying at the edges, you will also find two labia, or lips; one above it and one below it, to form a red gash in the shape of a beach ring. You also require a throat, a uvula, some voice chords and plenty of breath. Don't worry if you suffer from halitosis because halitosis is better than having no breath at all.

Remember to breathe from your stomach and should you find that air is escaping, plug up your navel with a blob of plasticine or quarter pound of cotton wool.

When you start to deliver your speech, don't talk a load of rubbish but try to interest your victims. Most of the people awaiting your sermon will be a captive audience, especially if you have bolted and barred the exits and pasted the seats with impact adhesive. Some speakers talk a lot of tripe; one whom I know talks so much tripe he was recently awarded the Golden Milkpail by the Association of Guernsey Cows. He probably talked tripe because he is married to an old faggot; and in any case he is in a privileged position because he's a Member of Parliament and every time he opens his mouth the Speaker of the House falls off his woolsack with hysterics.

It is always policy to prepare your talks well in advance because you cannot give a speech off the cuff even if you have written it there for reference. In any case, some fool might have obliterated your cues: it happened to me not long ago when I forgot I'd made notes on my shirt and sent it to a Chinese laundry the day before my appearance. When I went to collect it I realised that the speech had been cleaned off, and instead there were some Chinese characters written on the cuffs. I asked the laundryman, a chap named Shanghai Charlie, if the words represented my name and he said: 'No, just descliption—fat slob with small eyes and big nose.' No speech can be created suddenly—the average talk takes at least three or four minutes to write, especially if you are calling on previous experience. If you really want to give an effective address, try 28 Dorchester Towers, Park Lane, or something of that stature. I know the girl who lives there, and she won't mind you using her address at all. She doesn't mind anything.

It is essential to arrange the main body of the speech into several parts, so you need a body that is fairly flexible and not too gross. Get your facts right, be precise and if you have any personal feature that you wish to enlarge, don't hang it out.

It is always expedient to keep to safe subjects that you know your audience will understand. Never talk down to people unless your audience consists of pigmy Rotarians squatting on the floor. You should keep to cultural matters if possible. For instance, when talking to all male audiences, stick to topics like, beer, women, horse racing, the dogs, football and more women; and throw in a few rugby songs or some limericks about the bishop and the actress. The successful speechmaker goes into action well-armed. You could wear chain-mail and a space-helmet if you are working at a place where there may be a lot of rowdies and leftist militants, such as the Lord Mayor's dinner. Occasionally, (or every two seconds according to the locality and how you put yourself over) there may be reactions from an audience such as people throwing questions at you—or lumps of coal, or chairlegs, or hand-grenades . . . and it is quite admissible for you to defend yourself. Keep an adequate supply of stink-bombs, cotton-wool balls and housebricks in your pocket in readiness for retaliation.

Talking is very thirsty work, but one cannot line up a dozen beers or a bottle of Scotch on the rostrum. The smartest trick is to have a glassbowl filled with gin or vodka, and a soup ladle which you can dip in to the bowl when your mouth dries up. If you need a drink and your mouth hasn't dried, dry it yourself on your coat sleeve or the guest-towel. Nobody will blame you. In fact it has been known for some audiences to throw bottles to speakers who look dehydrated.

The worst enemy of public speakers is the heckler; the person who knows better than you. Since most audiences consist entirely of people who know a *lot* more than you, the situation is fraught with disaster. It is essential to knock down hecklers instantly because any success they have will strengthen their desire to silence you. The answer is to have a vast assortment of ready-to-wear rejoinders with which to slap hecklers down. Examples that spring readily to mind, and which you may employ at random are:

'Why don't you go home and get some kids to mind?'

'I wouldn't have known you were a lady if I hadn't seen you come through the door with the nude silhouette on it.'

'I remember when you wanted to join the Committee of 100 and they said you were too old.'

'You may be one of the jet-set, sir, but kindly don't break the sound barrier.'

'Shut up, you stupid old cabbage-head.'

'Is that your own face, sir, or did you have a transplant?'

'Please Madam, go and see if anyone's pinched your broomstick from the carpark.'

'You sound as if you got up from the wrong side of the floor this morning.'

'For an encore would you like me to cut your throat?'

'You're in bad shape madam, you look like a slag heap.'

'You appear to have been using the soap that gives you B.O.'

'Why are you spitting like that; have you got a weak bladder?'

'Is it true that your wife has bought a new bike and is peddling it all over town?'

'Where do you fancy going to convalesce?'

Such comments are always effective. Our local vicar swears by them. You may also occasionally get interruptions from the rostrum. The chairman of the conference or whatever barmitzvah you are working at may sometimes come out with a violent comment just to show how important he is, or to prove that he's still awake. He may well shout out: 'Order! Order!' This is not an invitation for you to say you'll have a pint of mild and bitter. He's only trying to start a riot.

If you have any sense, which is debatable in itself, you will shy away from all subtle invitations to address large civic assemblies. Affairs like that are always crammed to the bogs with highfaluting dignitaries— councillors, sheriffs, town clerks, and other local criminals. This gathering of the élite demands that you start with a long speech that sounds like giving the runners in a steeplechase: 'My Lord Mayor, Lady Mayoress, honourable Aldermen, Bishop Scabbclock, Mr. Chairman, Mrs. Chairman, little Stools, Lord Lieutenant, Convenor of the National Fish-Finger Board, assistant Sewager, Auntie Fanny, ladies and gentlemen...', etcetera, etcetera and Mrs etcetera... It goes on sometimes for well into the night before you even start to announce the subject of your talk. It is obligatory to address important assemblies in this vein and you can do one of several things:

(a) You can pre-record the line-up of important guests and play this over the amplifier-speakers before you even enter the building. Bribe the nightwatchman to start the tape at a certain time. Allow sufficient leeway and then walk in as if you own the place.

(b) You can state quite baldly (since you are bald) that you have no intention of introducing all the visitors to each other because you are against capitalist protocol and as a fully-paid up anarchist you protest against the system. Then all you need do is wave your banner a few times, and get on with what you came to say.

(c) You could hire a stand-in to take over the introductory nonsense. This will not only simplify your job, save your breath, and cost you a few pence in wages, but it will also spotlight you as a famous speaker who can afford to have individuality, and no further bookings.

(d) You could pretend to be stricken with acute amnesia and claim that you don't remember anyone in the entire building except yourself.

(e) You could shout 'Fire' and make a run for it. Be careful, however, that your shout is not misinterpreted, or someone may loose off a fusilade of grape-shot at your retreating rear.

Some of the meetings you have to address will harbour people only too glad to harass you with stupid questions—which you are unable to answer either because you do not know the answers or because you don't even understand the query. Dealing with these louts is quite difficult but there are a few evasive stratagems which you can adopt. You can for instance pretend that your hearing-aid has gone on the blink. Or you could smile in the vague direction of the offender and say through your teeth: 'I'm sorry? Did you say something or is your lunch repeating?' This gains you a little time. Or you can answer: 'Well, yes or no depending upon what you mean, exactly.' Or you can say: 'I'd like to answer your question personally; can you meet me in Athens in three or four months time?'

Alternatively you could squash the interrogator most effectively by screaming at him: 'Any idiot knows the answer to that! 'I'm surprised at you parading your complete ignorance by asking such a ridiculous question. You only make yourself look a fool.' This always goes down well at political meetings, particularly if the questioner is the Prime Minister.

Now there are occasions when you are invited to make a speech and when you get to the place you are surprised to find that only two or three people have managed to raise enough courage to hear your silver tonsils vibrating. This sort of situation could drive anyone to drink, and you are no exception. A couple of quick slurps and you feel better, but even if you see *double* it still won't make much of an audience. How to cope with this calamity? You may well ask. Here are the obvious steps to take:

The first thing to do is offer them their money back. But this presents side-issues. On the one hand the meeting is free; and on the other hand, the few people who did arrive have only come to get out of the rain. You could of course bribe them to go away by giving each of them a few coppers (or a handful of rice if the assembly is in Brixton, Bradford or Saigon). The reaction of your small audience will be to demand that they get the speech you promised to deliver or at least as much of it as they can bear until the monsoon stops.

Since they are determined to make you work, the next step is to keep a watchful eye on them by making them sit as close together as they can, directly in front of the rostrum. There is only one other thing you can do now, if you resent spending the night making a speech to a duet or trio of cold, saturated morons. You can gather them together and take them home for supper. If you really like people you may find that they taste delicious.

That takes care of all the main points to watch. The one thing I would stress about talking to large numbers of people who are complete strangers to you, is to keep them amused with witty little anecdotes and plenty of vague statistics. The ideal method is to talk honestly about yourself and your family, and give your measurements.

Because all public speakers are like birds of the air. They don't like to be shut up.

Confessions of Liberace

2526

I've been playing the piano since I was three years old and all I've got to show for it is stubby fingers . . . My neighbours love my playing. Only last night they sent their little lad round with something for me to try on my piano . . . a hatchet. Some pianists can't read a note of music, but I'm different. I can't even read the lyrics. Until I was nineteen I also played the violin, but I had to give it up. There was nowhere to rest a pint of scotch.

At a concert last year I brought the house down with 'Sleigh Bells in the Snow' . . . they encored it twelve times and in the end I caught pneumonia. This piano, by the way, was made by an Italian firm. If you look inside the machinery you won't see any strings, just taut spaghetti. Since I appeared on T.V. many more television sets have been sold. My mother has sold hers, my cousin his and the neighbours theirs.

My landlady has a wonderful piano, a boudoir grand. How I admire those big bulbous legs—and her arms are pretty fat, too . . . It was her mother who taught her the five-finger exercises, and she's been doing them for so long that she has the healthiest five fingers in show business. You'll notice that when I play pianissimo, my right hand is fitted with a silencer—my left hand isn't even loaded. I know that the audience tonight is filled with music lovers, nevertheless I still intend to play.

Don't imagine that you only use your fingers when playing the piano, you have to use you feet as well. There's a lot of pedal work in some of these longer rhapsodies . . . fortunately I've had a lot of training on the pedals. I used to peddle dope. By the way, next time I play some twiggy bits notice that my fingers never leave my wrists. Here is one of the latest piano scores: Winifred Atwell 5, Russ Conway nil; rain stopped play. This keyboard is made of real elephant ivory. When there's a draught blowing into the cracks the keyboard still gets a toothache. The other day I opened the lid of the stool to get some music out and what do you think I found inside? A stool pigeon! After the last concert the audience clapped and stamped their feet . . . all over my face.

Lecture Time: Standing Room Only

2527

The subject is that most abused section of the anatomy, the lower end of the spine or backbone, commonly referred to as the cocyxine posterior. With more than eleven tenths of the population now engaged in work of a sedentary nature, the Government has asked me personally to examine the situation and get to the bottom of it.

This is not the first time I've been called in to postulate posteriors for posterity. Last month the Duchess of Darlington consulted me, saying: 'I am giving a Hunt dinner on Saturday and I'm a bit worried about my seating arrangement.' I advised her to go on a crash diet or else invest in a more affectionate girdle. Too much sitting around tends to increase adipose tissue, which is why so many white-collar workers get so much behind with their work.

Last week, Sir Bernard Bottomley was offered a seat on the Board of the British United Metals company, whose initials are, as you know, very uncompromising. Being so very flabby, Sir Bernard refused to take the seat on the Board until they had the board foam-padded and upholstered.

His first job was to study the office staff, most of whom were desk-bound. He discovered that two of the top directors had swivelling seats, and these were sent to the infirmary for treatment. The other fourteen directors were sitting pretty. With secretaries on their laps, dictating letters in such ungrammatical terms that every sentence ended with a proposition.

Among the junior staff, fifty per cent spent at least eight hours a day sitting, and forty per cent spent ten hours sitting, and this did not include tea breaks or visits to the lift-up seats where they spend 1p. An identical state of affairs is common to many commercial concerns. My report to the Prime Minister will suggest the banning of chairs in offices so that everyone works standing up, for which purpose table tops and desk tops will have to be raised and female tops lowered.

During my early probing I visited the manageress of a Marriage Bureau and this presented a rather awkward situation. The only chair in her office was a love-seat. We were somewhat cramped, especially as she had outsize hips. I asked her if she was herself married and she said: 'No, but I have got a little bottom drawer.' I hate to think what she had in her little-bottom-drawer unless it was a dozen pairs of super-stretch panties. She told me that most of her trousseau consisted of hunting clothes. 'Horses and I get on very well together' she told me, and I could see the remarkable resemblance. She also said: 'My fiance, the Master of the Hunt, says I am a very good ride.' There was no answer to that, and she was slowly edging me off the love-seat.

Some very interesting facts about seats came to light while I was doing my very early researches. When I was invited to the Annual Athletics Meeting of Rowhampton Girls' College, the games-mistress, Miss Rhoda Kammel made a very good showing in the hundred yards hurdle handicap. The higher she jumped the more she showed. It was a very warm day, as I remember it, so Miss Kammel was not the only girl there who had rosy cheeks. That same afternoon I got stuck in a hammock on the lawn. I've always had a deep-seated horror of ham-mocks. There was nowhere else to rest that afternoon, and the games-mistress did not wish to stand, for anything.

We must not forget all the seats that local and national politicians stand for. Many politically-minded businessmen develop a leaning towards standing for seats as they grow to maturity. In Parliament there are two lots of seats. Front Benches and Back Benches. The total number of sitting-places in the Commons is two hundred short of requirements, but fortunately MP's never attend the House in one solid mass. For casual debates about matters like declaring war or putting the Transport Minister in his place, only half a dozen Members show up, leaving plenty of empty benches. Seats in the Upper House, or as it is jokingly called, The Gods, are more numerous and mostly remain unused.

In Ireland the Stormont Parliament is short of 45 seats and when their debating chamber is full, half the Members have to sit on each other. Usually there is quite a lot of rear-guard action as those lucky enough to find a seat search hopefully around for companions who are not too heavy for their laps. Such Members of the Irish parliament are known as 'the little people,' and often have names like Shaun Shorthouse or Patrick O'Heck.

Seats in general are becoming more pronounced nowadays and people are more conscious of them. To distract attention from the feminine nether regions, fashion designers in Paris and London have cunningly tried to emphasise the other end of people, with such unusual diversions as topless modes, but generally speaking there has been no swing to this idea. The eminent Italian designer Sophia Lollobodega even went so far as to design a new style of glass-fibre bloomers but she used such inferior fabric, the bottom fell out of her market. I discovered while I was in Naples that crime is on the increase in Italy. Now that the tourist Season is in full swing, despite numerous warning notices in Restaurants and Hotels which state: 'Watch Your Figure,' the number of bottoms being pinched is on the increase. Nevertheless a few English women visiting the area are protesting heatedly that they are not feeling the pinch. A week ago eighteen Italian bumnippers were arrested in Milan and fingerprinted; for some of them it was touch and go.

The medical profession is stepping into the breach with many new products and ideas to reduce the size of seats. One appliance now available claims to reduce the hips by several inches: it consists of a series of rubber rollers. A demonstrator used this apparatus for a fortnight. Her thighs gained an inch and the rubber rollers lost six inches all round. A doctor in Prague suggests that another method of reducing the hips is to lay off rump steak. Diet is an important factor. Margery Broadbeam went on a diet of green salads and Vichy Water for a month and reduced her 52 inch hips by only 1 inch: She had only consumed three lots of salad and Vichy Water daily, but had been eating large cream cakes between meals. A man in Manchester was advised by his doctor to reduce his seat by using large quantities of Epsom Salts. A week later the patient died. Drinking a bath full of Epsom Salts daily for a week had proved unwise.

Despite all the unhappy data which was uncovered by my investigations, I can at least report one measure which has been satisfactory in reducing the embarrassment of people who suffer from a hangover when they squat. It is a preparation called 'Sitwell's Soothing Seat Solution,' or known colloquially in the pharmaceutical trade as Bum Balm. Sitwell's Soothing Seat Solution comes in three sizes, Large; Extra Large; and Large-Family-Economy-King-Size-Giant-Double-pack. This astonishing substance, applied to the afflicted area as directed, is guaranteed to bring instant relief. At the same time it has a mild hypnotic effect which convinces you that your behind has vanished. This phenomenon is technically known in quasi-medical spheres as 'numb bum'.

Among the neurotic letters we have received from users all over the world but mainly from Chipping Sodbury is one that reads: 'My husband and I could not sit down for meals watching television in comfort but after applying Sitwells S.S.S. can sit through *anything*.' It is signed 'Mother of Eight.' The second letter is from a Miss Fanny Danglin: 'Sitwell's saved my life! What is more, it is excellent for growing rhubarb.' The third letter is from a big Rear-Admiral (Sir Joshua Maxibutt) and says blandly: 'Sitwell's Soothing Seat Solution has put all our ships on beam ends! England salutes you.' It was sent from the Portsmouth arsenal.

Why not dash right down to your local garage at once and lay in a supply of Sitwell's Soothing Seat Solution? Or even two supplies? (Two supplies will give you sufficient to lay in it all day). So I leave you with this thought: 'It may be destiny that shapes our ends but anyone can make a mistake.'

Good Queen Bess and all that

Lizzy the First's Diary

2528
'All day long, Francis Drake is playing bowls. Bowls before breakfast. Bowls before lunch. Bowls before supper . . . It's a lot of bowls.

Yesterday Sir Walter was so obliging. It was raining hard and a puddle barred my way from the coach. Raleigh stepped forward and placed his cloak across the puddle for me to step upon. If only some anti-monarchist hadn't removed the man-hole cover from the sewer I should have reached the pavement safely.

Mary Queen of Scots attacked me again yesterday. She swore at the Chamberlain and said I had no ethics . . . yet everyone knows how much I love the Duke of Ethex.

How well I remember my debutante days. My coming-out ball. Verily I was an emergin' virgin.

I have appointed household suppliers under a Royal Warrant. Only the best tradesmen in the country shall provide my wants. Henceforth appointed tradesmen may use the Royal Arms. Except when they are around Essex. And beneath the Royal Arms they are permitted to put their slogans, such as 'Tailors to the Queen,' 'Costumiers to the

Queen,' 'Grocers to the Queen' and mayhap, 'Wine Merchants to the Queen.' I am not very happy about Mr. McTavish, who is the appointed boot mender. I object to his sign which reads 'McTavish & Company—Cobblers to the Queen.'

Raleigh came to the palace yesterday with some new discovery he made in the New World. A great seed which he calls the potato. He had me bending over the hot stove all evening, cooking this wretched vegetable, sliced up in hot fat. I fear that Raleigh has had his chips.

Walter has also brought back from Virginia some strange plant, the leaves of which he has dried, shredded and rolled into a cylinder of paper . . . A long cylinder which he calls Queen Size. And the fool sticks these things in his mouth and sets them alight. No wonder he was giving me burning kisses all evening. Then he tried to make me smoke one. I coughed and the thing dropped down my bodice. He leapt to my assistance, saying 'With your Majesty's permission?'—and then he squirted a full siphon of soda down my neck.

Drake sent me a message this morning to tell me that a Spanish ship sneaked into harbour, and a band of Spanish sailors crept ashore and seized ten young girls from Plymouth. I asked him if they were frightened and he said 'No. They were delighted.'

Sir Francis is such a sloppy sailor. When the Spanish Armada was sailing into British waters, there he was still in his hammock . . . and the landlady's daughter banging on his door like mad . . . Trying to get out.

William Shakespeare came to see me yesterday. He has written a new play. He spent hours alone with me in my drawing-room, trying to draw me to him. We went right through his sonnets and his new play. Eventually I picked up the new manuscript from the floor as he sprawled on the sofa and asked him: 'Is this, then, "As You Like It"?' and he he said, 'It's exactly as I like it.'

Tonight the minstrels will be playing again for me during supper . . . They're not a bad group, but they should get their hair cut, and stop trying to plug their ukeleles into the oil-lamps.

Soon I shall be fifty, the blush of maidenhood faded from my cheeks. But that is no reason for Raleigh to send me such a cheeky Christmas present. What would I want with a Do-It-Thyself-Book?

I must have a word with young Shakespeare about his conduct. He is carrying on with that young girl in whose place he writes most of his works these days. I really must stop him dipping his pen in Ann Hathaway's cottage.

Essex is full of brilliant ideas. He has just invented a new cow-cake
288

for my farm herd. It's supplied in square cartons, each with a free coupon for a harpsichord candle, and he's called it Tudor Cud.

I shall never forgive my father Henry for having so many wives. No wonder I can't get anyone to marry me. What man would want a wife and six mothers-in-law?'

How to Present a Cheap Opera

2529
An economical method of presenting opera is to stage a production without music. This cuts down the cost considerably since you only have to pay the cast. No chorus, orchestra, composer or conductor.

Many operas, especially Italian musicals, do not make sense if you listen to the words. Most of the story is obvious from the acting, and the music is nothing but a background irritant.

When you have a long-haired conductor standing in front waving a baton around in the air it distracts the audience. Not that the musicians are watching the baton. They know that it *never* follows the score that they are playing.

A typical opera doesn't have much plot and what story there is, is usually needlessly complicated. We all know that in the end the boy will get the girl and the villains will make a profit.

In a typical Italian opera, love plays a major part. Real, honest love. Like seduction, rape and perversion.

Opera without music simplifies the mechanics of the entertainment and swiftens the action. When you divorce an opera from its music you realise that *all* operas have the *same* plot and that the only difference between them is the music. So if you do an opera without music you are providing a capsuled summary of every opera that has ever been staged. One single typical story enables you to know and understand every opera that was ever written, or performed.

Casting is easier because you don't have to worry about getting the right actors and actresses to match the music. The operatic leading lady has to have a sweet soprano voice, but if you do it without music, any good-looking doll will do. Even a female-impersonator. You don't need a fat, jolly, bejowelled contralto with a voice that can crack a crystal champagne glass at forty paces. Any old actress will do, as long as she has a billowing bust. You don't need a brown-voiced baritone nor a suave mustachioed tenor. Nor a plump, paunchy, treble-chinned bass with a voice like gravel being swept over an acre of broken glass with a lavatory brush. All you need is a bunch of cheap, healthy, actors and actresses who need the work. Provided they can read the script.

The Basic Story of all Italian Light Operas

The opera I will demonstrate is the standard romantic story, 'The

Barbarian of Seville Meets Count Dracula,' which is written in three flats. Two in Milan and a penthouse in Turin. The whole thing works much better without music because too much noise in the sequel invariably distracts attention from the big orgy scene, when one wants to use eyes and not ears. In brief the plot is as follows:

Sylvano, the Countess of Eurania is the illegitimate daughter of a poverty-stricken spaghetti manufacturer, who is living with his mistress in a converted Chianti warehouse somewhere near the Po. Sylvano falls madly in love with a captain of Hussars in the Italian Vice Squad. This officer, Roberta D'Orsay, is actually a plainclothes secret agent who was born in a slum in Seville where his father was a well-known procurer of fallen women for the Court of Rome and the *dolce vita* set.

D'Orsay keeps sending passionate love-letters to his beloved Countess, which are confiscated by the Italian Postal Authorities because of their interesting obscenities. The Countess, receiving no mail from her lover begins to suspect that he is deceiving her with the whores of Padua. She disguises herself as an orange-seller and takes the next sedan-chair to Rome, where she believes D'Orsay is having secret assignations with Floria Ciano, a disreputable club hostess who works as a belly-dancer in a Greek antique shop in her spare time. She reaches Rome and pauses at the sedan terminus to sing a long aria. This runs for half an hour, with an augmented chorus of middle-aged transvestites, and is entirely superfluous to the story.

Sylvano is picked up by an itinerant guitarist who plies her with adulterated biancos and talks her to his underground bunker. Under the influence of a potent drug, Sylvano surrenders to the vicious, perverted guitarist. In the middle of her song 'Pluck My Heart-Strings Gently, Lover' the naked couple are surprised by the dramatic appearance of Count D'Orsay who has been keeping an eye on the guitarist, known to be working for the Leftist group of the Federated Gondola Union, a militant body anxious to overthrow the Chinese exiled Government, controlled by the disreputable former mandarin, Dr. Hu Fu Char-Lee, a member of the secret sugar Tong in Chunkow.

There is a tremendous fight scene in the underground station as the protagonists struggle to the death. Sylvano defeats the Count by two Boston Crabs and a submission in the fifth round. As he lies dying on the dusty dry-rotten floor, the Count raises one head and sings: 'As I Die My Love Takes Flight.' He expires with his lips tightly fixed on Sylvano's as he cries unconsolably and pushes the guitarist's hands away from her right breast.

As the song dies away on the damp Roman air, the Italian Naval Captain, Bruno Fellini—a cheerful rogue who nonchalantly smuggles hashish into Turin harbour on his four-masted clipper *Chiavaria Vaticanus*'—breaks into the cellar with a patrol of midshipmen and apprehends everyone in sight. Including the conductor of the orchestra who has only gone on stage to retrieve his baton which had flown from his hand during an exciting twenty-bar movement in C-sharp major. Even the dead Count D'Orsay resuscitates and struggles to his feet, regardless of the dagger in his breast and the four gunshot wounds in his bleeding head. Then they sing the concerted oratoria, 'We Shall Be

Overcome' about which Stravinsky wrote an extremely disconcerting review on the music page of that ill-fated French Communist newsmagazine *Veni-Vedi-Vici-Water*.

Act 27 opens with the state funeral of Count D'Orsay including a comique aria from Sylvano, a duet with the dead Count, and the massed choir of the Italian Scala State Pensions Board. This entire act is in music and a complete waste of highly-trained tonsils.

Eventually we reach Act 35 when Sylvano's adventures come finally to a tragic end in a pitiless saga of salacious insincerity . . . For the first time we meet the Barbarian of Seville himself in the parchment flesh. This grossly overfed manic-depressive Italian moron had made a fortune forging Stradivarius bass-cellos in a disused sewer at Cremona. He is a sado-ornithologist with a reputation for being cruel to Blue Tits as well as a grim genius for stuffing other birds in his lair. Sylvano meets him half-way; on the road to Venice. She was hoping to meet an agent who had promised to make her a postwoman if he could only find an aqualung to fit her.

The Barbarian takes one look at Sylvano and immediately bursts into a lovesick song, treating us to fifty-five-minutes of cacophonic bass-baritone agony. An aria that rocks the auditorium with sonic booms and leaves a significant crack down the proscenium arch. After that, the Barbarian sits down for twenty minutes, regaining his breath with furious asthmatic inhalations. He then grabs Sylvano around the waist and makes romantic love to her for 25 minutes while she sings the hit song from the opera, 'Take Your Hands From My Heart.'

He is just about to drag her to his hide-out when on comes the variety agent who had promised to find work for Sylvano at the Doge's Palace or the Vatican Grillroom. The agent, a suave Italian macaroni roller, sums up the situation and attacks the Barbarian with an outsize Toledo cutlass. He cuts off the Barbarian's head which rolls to the side of the stage and immediately starts to sing 'I Ain't Got No Body' in a shrill soprano voice. Sylvano falls into the agent's arms. The curtains fall at the same time, landing with a thud in the pit. As you will readily understand, the whole production looks and sounds more impressive without music. That goes for *all* operas, with the possible exception of 'Waiting for Godot.' It's quite reasonable to enjoy a little music while you are waiting for someone.

A Sailor's Farewell: The Log of Able-Seaman Smith

2530
I should like to tell you a little story—a sad little story—a true little story, about an adventure that happened to me recently. I'd just got back to Liverpool on my last voyage; the first time I had been back in England for well nigh twelve years.

It was so good to be home again, even though I'd lost track of all my old mates, my family, my friends, and didn't know a soul in the place. But I'd picked up all my back pay, and I was pretty well fixed for cash. Yes, indeed, there must have been as much as three hundred and twenty-seven quid in my wallet; it was stuffed out like a fat little pig in my pocket, and very comforting, too, I might tell you.

I hung around one or two pubs and had a few drinks . . . It was like being with a lot of strangers. I began to feel sorry I'd left the ship—at least I'd had a few shipmates to talk to and plenty of work to do . . . I mooched around the town, visiting some of the old haunts I remembered. I even found my old home in the slums . . . but they were knocking the place down. What memories that brought back to me.

I had a sister living somewhere in Liverpool, but she'd left the old address, and I'd been told she'd gone to live down South. I didn't know where. I didn't know anyone. I felt lonely as hell. I went into a cafe and had a bite to eat, and then started another round of the pubs. Folks didn't seem to want to talk to me. Maybe they didn't like the look of me. I passed another old slum building on my way to look for a kip for the night. Suddenly I saw a little urchin lad sitting on a doorstep. He was a grubby little arab, skinny and frail, with a dirty face and clothes tattered and torn. He put his tongue out at me and when I went nearer to him he cringed away in fear. I told him I wasn't going to hurt him and asked him who he was.

The building was deserted; workmen had left their tools lying around and it was obvious they were pulling the place down. The kid said he didn't have any folks and had been spending the last few nights sleeping in the old derelict building on sacks. I felt sorry for him, and started to talk to him, telling him some of my adventures. He seemed to like me. He kept asking me questions. Then he said he was hungry and hadn't eaten for three days. So I took him to a little place at the end of the next road; a scruffy old transport cafe where he nearly made himself sick tucking into sandwiches and cakes and tinned fruit . . . He kept asking me if it was all right, and if I had enough money to pay with. He ate until he was fit to burst, but he looked a lot happier then.

We left there and walked across town and out into the country. The sun was setting now, and a grey gloom was settling over the area. I said to him that we'd better find somewhere to spend the night, so we both kept our eyes open for a likely spot. All the time we walked I told him about my life at sea and how I'd only just got back to England, and that I didn't know anyone. He said he'd like to be my friend, and I said that would be fine. So hand in hand we walked on, and I felt like a new man. I wanted to father the poor kid and promised to get him some clean clothes in the morning.

Soon we saw a barn in a field. There was no one around so we clambered over the fence and went inside. There were some bales of straw. We made ourselves comfortable, and while he lay there I sang him a song or two of the sea. He started to nod, so I hummed a lullaby to him and he fell asleep. I'd really got to like him now; he was someone to talk to, someone to share my hours with—almost a pal. I fell asleep, dog tired. Then when I woke up in the morning . . . the place where he'd been lying was empty. I got worried and went to look for him, thinking he must have gone to wash himself in the stream nearby. I searched for half an hour without finding him. Poor kid, all alone in the world . . . I was almost on the point of tears . . . I pulled out my handkerchief to blow my nose hard . . . my wallet came out with it . . . I grabbed for the wallet . . . and found it. Empty.

Press Section

The News Behind The News Behind The News Behind. . .

2531

Everyone is familiar with the local type of newspaper which bends over backwards to mention the names of people in the town and its immediate environs. Weddings are scrupulously covered, complete with pages of insipid pictures recording the moment of impending disillusionment. A year or two later the divorces are covered, but without pictorial evidence.

But one provincial weekend newspaper, at least, treats the journalistic scene with more realism . . . It ignores the disasters, the crimes, the pillaging and the inconsequential tittle-tattle so beloved by the provincial newssheets. Instead it gives its readers the full low-down on the activities of the little people, the plebs of society; those who might never achieve recognition but for the courageous reporter who probes their private perambulations.

We refer of course to Peter Kneecap, the intrepid newshound attached (by close family ties) to the sensational weekly newspaper *The Brighton Clarion*. (For the information of foreign explorers, Brighton is a sprawling metropolitan seaside holiday venue lying low on the South Coast; not far from Ford prison; in one of Britain's most salubrious provinces—Sussex).

The following random selections from past copies of the 'Clarion' are reproduced despite the objections of the late owner.

Thereby Hangs a Tail

While fly-fishing off Beachy Head last Friday, Mr. Barry Crabbuck, a former councillor and retired master campanologist, aged 43, of Livingston Lane, Southwick, was astonished to find that he had hooked a full-grown attractive 22-year-old mermaid. The bait he used was a mature force-fed Moravian bluebottle.

With commendable initiative and baited breath Mr. Crabbuck, who is married and has eight or nine children, covered the mermaid with his biluminal whelking net to avoid embarrassment. He then returned

293

speedily to Snoreham in his home-made sampan, the *Katy Moran*, class three, and anchored offshore while he swam to Cobham's, the well-known High Street ligerorium where he purchased a 38-cup bra.

Eventually he got his catch home and concealed her in the garage. When he speechlessly tried to explain the situation to his wife by miming an eggtimer with wild gesticulations, his wife became hysterical and went out to the car, where she found the mermaid combing her long blonde tresses with a rusty fishfork.

She did not remonstrate with Mr. Crabbuck at that time, but went to the bedroom and threw all his clothes out of the window. Mr. Crabbuck was wearing some of them at the time.

Mrs. Crabbuck, an attractive 29-year-old redhead, in curlers, then telephoned the police who arrived in eight patrol cars and transferred the mermaid to the Dolphinarium, two abreast. The event has created quite a sensation all along the South Coast and armadas of boats from yawls to kyaks have been seen heading out to sea manned by men between the ages of 14 and 67 who were born under Pisces.

Hard Times

A visitor from Birmingham complained last week to the secretary of the Hotels Association because of overcrowding at the Crab and Salmon-Paste Hotel in Kings Road.

The man, Mr. Edward Grottby, 34, a part-time gynecologist and sheet-metal worker from Edgbaston stated that the hotel manageress, an inactive 32-year-old brunette, Miss Phoebe Sprought, living at the hotel, had charged him and his wife £5 each a night, and had provided only a well-worn Chinese rug on the landing of the sixth floor.

He was annoyed because guests had kept waking him up by treading on him to get to the bathroom. His wife, Nora, also of Birmingham, could not corroborate his statement because, she said, she had been given another rug on the seventh landing, and had spent the night searching for her husband without success. Their holiday had been completely ruined.

The manageress insisted that this sort of thing will never happen again. She is fitting every landing with twin rugs.

Crime Increases by 12½ Per Cent

There was another robbery at the West Street branch of the Sussex & Halifax Merchant Bank yesterday. The manager raised customer charges by another fifteen per cent, and increased overdraft interest to 12½ per cent.

Thespian Corner

A young Hove actor who was given a part in a play had a severe disappointment on Friday when the producer sacked him at rehearsal. The man, attractive blond Arthur Drabcackle of New Church Road, had been selected for a part in the touring production of 'Hair.' He was to play the role of Dan Druff. When he attended for rehearsal, however, he admitted that on Wednesday he had joined the skinheads.

Hurrah for Our Side

The calming influence of Jack Dimstock, a director of Portslade Amateur Rugby Club, saved a desperate situation from developing into a fracas last Saturday, when the visiting fans of the opposing team from Maidstone protested about the referee's decision on the winning try. Jack explained to them that it would not have happened if the referee had not accidentally left his seeing-eye dog in the refreshment tent at half-time.

Blooming in the Spring

Two young Hippie flower-people, Alfred Augustus Nuttle, aged 19, and Mavis Gorlston, aged 31, were arrested in West Street late on Monday night for causing a disturbance outside the Odeon Cinema. They were taken to Brighton police headquarters and found to be without visible means of support, after the matron had searched Mavis. The police watered them and sent them back to their homes in Macclesfield by Interflora.

More Sheep Gambling in the Meadow

Following the opening of a betting-office at the Hove Country Cricket Ground, applications for similar privileges have been received by the court from: Steyning Youth Club Bowling team; the vicar of All Saints, Trueleigh Hill; The Preston Park Yoyo Association; Miss Constance Cunningsby, secretary of the Conway Luxury Council Flats Residents' Committee; her lodger, Guiseppe Cerlliani; Withdean Grottle & Morris Dance Troupe; and Ginny Silvera Hu Chu Kow, proprietress of the St. Isaac Chinese-Italian Coffee Kitchen in Blatchington Road. Any objections to these applications should be sent to the Harold Wilson Disaster Fund, c/o Coutts Bank Ltd., Scilly.

Champion Wedding Belle

Mrs. Delilah Norich, a plain-looking woman of 36, gave a big party at the Kingfisher's Claw Hotel in Wivelsfield last night, to celebrate her sixth wedding anniversary. All her former six husbands were present.

Her *fiance*, thirty-one-year old Ethelred Plunkfitch gave her a brand new off-white wedding-gown in broderie-anglaise and midnight-green chiffon, decorated with solitaire sequins and zodiacal motifs.

Mr. Plunkfitch, who lives in a basement flat in Holland Road, Hove, claimed that her old one looked a little shoddy.

A Pier of the Realm

New plans have been revealed for West Pier. The dilapidated extremity is not, after all, to be demolished. Structural engineers from the Devil's Dyke Agricultural & Fisheries Research Hut Annexe have conceived a method of re-building the pier as an oil-rig and towing it out into deep water so that the South Eastern Gas Board can drill for high-speed gas.

The pier, in its new guise, will still have amenities open to the public, including a Fun Palace, Open Air Cinema Club showing the latest continental nudity films, and an underground hovercraft park. As the pier will be outside the three-mile limit, and beyond government control, whist drives will also be held on each Friday evening throughout the winter.

To simplify travel, Bovis Ltd. have been commissioned to build a ten-mile-long gangplank, linking the oil-rig with the shore. Seeboard have offered to donate coloured fairy lights along the entire planking area.

The lights will be switched on at a massive ceremony on the 5th October, 1976 by Commander Leopold Abercorn, the first man to walk solo across a gangplank from the Khyber Pass to St. Moritz (*Guinness Record of Books*). For this special occasion, the commander will wear his best switchgear.

Chequing Off

The failure of the Brighton and North Hove International Finance & Banking Corporation has produced some interesting repercussions. The chairman, who was not available for comment, stated that it was an imposition for the Board of Trade (23, Fish Market Underwalk) to send an investigator to examine his books, which in any case were not forthcoming as they had been loaned to the Roedean Archivists' Society's Antique Library of Eastbourne Erotica.

The investigator for the BOT, pretty $17\frac{1}{2}$ year-old Felicity Hoffmeyer, daughter of the Brighton philatelist and part-time clairvoyante Mrs. Maria Zodiacus, explained that her brief was to probe the financier's fiscal state, for which purpose she called at his home in Lower Market Street Mews to study his liquid assets and located four magnums of Irish champagne, a jeriboam of Scandinavian cooking sherry, three cases of apricot saki, two splits of Malawi zakumatu-tyuyu (whatever that is) and a half-emptied bottle of coca-cola marked 2p off. The chairman, Jocelyn Reddish is still convalescing.

Let it all Hang Out

Members of the Adelaide Crescent, Hove, Women's Liberation Front, flying the Liberian flag of convenience, are planning to start off next year's Brighton Festival with a massive demonstration of bra-burning and scantie-scorching.

The procession will move off from Topless Rank, West Street and march militantly along Kingsway to Grand Avenue, with drummers beating time by hammering on manhole covers and wrought-iron chastity belts. They will all be wearing the official uniform of nylon see-through mandarin blouses, tweed midi-kilts, bikini briefs, pantie-girdles and kinky mules.

Next year's Grand Mistress of the Order will mount a rostrum set on the lawns and deliver an ovation as she wields the official banner in her hands—a pair of long johns embroidered with the flags of all nations and the appropriate sex-symbol, a circle surmounted by an arrowed interrogation mark. The international president, Madame Yvonne D'Avignon-Armentieres, from Brest, will then lead the delegates in community singing around a camp-fire in the middle of the road as the flickering old flames turn the burning lingerie to embers. Praises will be chanted to their patron saint, St. Michael, and champagne will be handed around in nylon cups.

The meeting will end with a local reporter being burned at the stake, after which the exhausted women will return to their families' bosoms. Further information may be obtained from the Loins Club. Please be sure to send a stamped and undressed envelope.

Doggone it!

Two women were involved in an altercation on Thursday afternoon on the grass verge near the dog toilet in Hove. Mrs. Leonora Prunk, 32, an attractive strawberry blonde of Wellington Mansions, Grand Avenue, was exercising her dog Bruno when the other woman, Miss Violetta St. Cyr-Guerard, an au pair girl from Latvia, now working part time as a masseuse in St. James's Street, arrived on the scene with an atracrive toy poodle and attempted to make use of the amenity.

Mrs. Prunk immediately objected on the grounds that the amenity was a Men's, and that it was therefore out of bounds to a female poodle. She was inordinately rude and gave Miss St. Cyr-Guerard directions to another dog toilet in Preston Park.

While the two women were scratching each other an alsatian named Rover, attached to the Blatchington CID, and in plain-clothes, inter-vened by chasing the poodle all the way to King Alfred Baths.

In a very excitable state, the Latvian girl then attacked Mrs. Prunk and bit her St. Bernard in the nearside rear leg, evidently with hostile deliberation. At that juncture Policewoman Alice Veronica Fairbrother, an attractive 23-year-old ex-beauty queen and karate expert separated the two squabbling women and was joined by her patrol-car officer,

Chief Inspector Lionel Branchfoster, on loan to the Sussex Constabulary from New Scotland Yard. As he tried to calm down Miss St. Cyr-Guerard, he, too, was bitten in the left leg. Policewoman Fairbrother then arrested the two women and cautioned the St. Bernard. The arrested couple were taken to Holland Road.

The RSPCA officer for Grand Avenue Lawns asks anyone who saw a tired police alsatian and an exhausted French poodle in the vicinity of Hove Lagoon to mind their own business.

Press Section Advertisements

(Special Offers and Typeslips)

2532
130 MENS WOOL SUITS
£3·50 each
At this price they won't last a day!
We Will Try It On.
SAUNDERS, 56 Stepney Street.

2533
PROP. WHISKY—ONLY £1·85
Drink It Straight
Staggering Offer
Carlson Wines Co.

2534
Champton's Patent
ALLOY WIDOWS
Large and small.
Cannot Fall Out.

2535
GIRLS WANTED FOR SOWING
Ideal conditions
60p per hour.
Ring: ATLAS TAILORS
56889

2536
FOR SALE. Six goldfish in large round owl.
'Phone FIN 4644

2537
FOR SALE. Chaste-longue and other furn.
Owner a broad. Offers Box No. GH566

2538
LADIES BRYLON PANTIES
All sizes from 34-cup up.
75p
Table Covers to Match 80p.

2539
FU CHOW CHIN RESTAURANT
offers chickens dressed to order
Also nudles
(to take away)

2540
FOR SALE: Violin and cow in decorated case.
No strings attached.
Best offer. Andrews
4 Culper Avenue, Honnington.

2541
THE NEW BRINCK AUTO-TOASTER
Stainless Model
No side burns.
Shoots up when done. Only £4·25.

2542
ADD
FISH BALLS
TO YOUR PARTY.
Wholly mackerel.
No cod.
OLIVIA'S DELICATESSEN SERVES YOU.

2543
Kingsford Newtown Restaurant
LOOK! TRY OUR SPECIAL FOUL DINNER.
£1·25 inc. ½ bot. of wine.

2544
KAD GLOVES (EXPORT ORDER)
Feel very smoothe.
Felt liners.
£3 a pair, all sizes.

Classified Clangers

2545
Front room to let. Suitable two elderly ladies. Use of kitchen. Or two
gentlemen. (*Harford Times*).

2546
Employment sought by semi-retired bank clerk. Honest. Loyal. Will take anything. (*Jarrow newspaper*).

2547
Commode wanted by lady antiques exporter with Heppelwhite legs.

2548
Small boarding house offers comfortable all-in terms, breakfast and other tasty males drom £4·75 weekly.

2549
Widow offers comfortable home to working man, flat and share bath. 'Phone any evening. Mrs. R. Watford.

2550
Chauffeur/handyman wanted. Beautiful country home, titled director. Good conditions. Preferably familiar Rover. Kind treatment, could also use a wife. Box P46647, Argus.

2551
Wanted. Young lady for general sousework, and take care, no children. Ring Worchester Keynes 456.

2552
Fulbright, near Shottsby, 4-room bath and kitchen with water, heat, garbage free. £8·25. Box 6613.

2553
FOR SALE: Fast, attractive 1968 model, top gear 80s, with humorous accessories. (*Birchford newspaper*).

2554
People who suffer from arthritis, rheumatism, sciatica, lumbago and other ailmants can be eliminated in hours with new Floyd's Linament. Aston, Chemists.

2555
Part time teacher required by private school. Must be able to speak fluent French and Italian. Also Algebra. Mostyn College, Morbank.

2556
Large well-upholstered antique love-seat £18·50 or exchange two Knoll occasional chairs or small pouf. Wilson, 'Phone 44598.

2557
Wanted urgently experienced night nurse, male ward, preferably mature and used to bedding down. Cowper Nursing Home, Whatley.

2558

For sale. New-laid eggs, top quality, any quality, call at Scott's Curiosity Shoppe.

2559

Woodworm? Termites? We exterminate all home pets, also dry rot and other fungus by mail order. Write today: Homecare, Gillingham.

2560

Bungalow for sale, with two beds., dng.rm., and combined study/loving room. Kit. & bth. Greenhouse and lean to up the garden. 'Phone BOS 776.

2561

What can you offer for a really well-trained wire-haired female? House-trained. Loveable. Or £21 cash. Anton Gale, Pitt Road, Salford.

Slips that Pass in the Type

2562

'WILD-WIFE PROTECTION LEAGUE'
'Forest Husbandry to be Investigated'

TRANSPLANT SURGEON LEAVES STERILIZED INSTRUMENT AT AIRPORT.
Operations Curtailed.

LYING-TERM WEATHER FORECAST.

YACHTSMAN FLOUNDERS IN FORCE NINE ALE.

CHURCH MISSION FLIES IN FROM SCOTLAND.
Tribesmen Had Not Eaten for 15 Days.

ARMY OFFICER ACCEPTED BRIDE.
Confined In Quarters.

NAVEL PROBE AT PORTSMOUTH.
Secrets Case. Girl Held.

RAPE VICTIM UNDER DOCTOR'S CAR.

SUNDAY SCHOOL FETE TO BE HELL IN VICARAGE GARDEN.

MAN FATALLY MURDERED.

COMPREHENSIVE SCHOOL TO GET SEX-STORKS.

PRISONERS BREAK JAIL AFTER EXECUTION.

BRIDE OF FOUR MONKS FOUND DEAD.

HOTEL FIRE.
145 Guests Escape, Half-glad.

BELFAST MINISTER CONFESSES SUICIDE.

INFANT MORALITY DECLINING.

BRIDE COLLAPSES OVER MOTORWAY

BREATHALYSER TESTS TO STAY
Prime Minister Upheld.

ENRAGED BULL INJURES FARMER WITH PAIL.

BRADFORD POLICE BEST BANK BANDITS.

DOCTOR SAYS MEN PREFER MARRED WOMEN.

JACKSON LOSES UNION SUIT.
Support Drops.

BRISTOL GRANNY CHARGED WITH WRECKLESS DRIVING.

THIEVES EAT THEN ROB CAFE OWNER.

BRIDE OBJECTED TO DOG IN BED.
Judge's Submission Rejected.

PEACE OR WAR?
Yes, says General Mannering.

TAXI IN COLLISION WITH LORRY IN GLASGOW.
24 Passengers Hurt.

PAKISTANIS ALL OUT.
Army Leader Blacks Powell.

WEST INDIANS WIN BY ARROW MARGIN.

RIOT AT WIFE-SWAPPING ORGY.
Disgruntled Husband Gets His Own Back.

MILK BOARD STRIKE.
Hundreds of Gals Thrown Away.

FARMER AND WIFE IN LOVE TRIANGLE.
Farm Hands on Wife's Side.

100 ROSEBOROUGH STUDENTS ON POT
Judge Holds Inquiry in Chambers.

BEAUTY QUEER OPENS VICAR'S FETE.

WHISKY LORRY OVERTURNS ON MOTORWAY.
Driver Badly Loaded.

Capsuled News Reports

2563
'For her wedding Miss Angela Roberts has asked the organist to play "Fight the Good Fight".' (*Calthorpe Express*)

2564
'On Friday there was a meeting to debate "The Human Nude", which was held by the Loverdale Women's Missionary League.' (*Dalkeith Mirror*)

2565
'A resolution "that the working man would be better off or worse off under a 30-hour a week system" was passed by the Women's Federation of Labour at their meeting yesterday.' (*Cardborough Weekly Sentinel*)

2566
'She protested that her husband, a professional entertainer, had told her some abusing stories on their wedding night because he hoped to tickle her fancy.' (*Edinburgh Mail*)

2567
'Dairy farmer Harry Hastings of Valentine Hill Farm has now added a cow to his stock and supplies many of his neighbours with butter, cream and eggs.' (*Fairfield Advertiser*)

2568
'Mr. Orwell had been in bed with a throat defect due to his job as Town Crier. The doctor decided to cut off the cause at source and Orwell was away from work for many weeks.' (*Mansfield Courier*)

2569
'Out of 38 guests, more than 20 had been married to the same man for over 11 years. After the speeches, Mr. Carl Downdley was congratulated by envious colleagues.' (*Smedley Vale Times*)

2570
'The hostess was attired in a charming old creation of jade-green crepe trimmed with ecrue lace all around her punchbowl.' (*Tipton Herald*)

2571

'Vera Sprogg and Evelyn Chambers, who are both 25 years old, have opened a joint enterprise at 38 North Street Crescent selling remodelled fashions. They have discarded clothing of all types and are open for business from 9 a.m. to 5.30 p.m. They are prepared to entertain only married men seeking gifts.' (*West Whitley Mirror*)

2572

'At the annual meeting, Joe Coleman, this year's secretary, delivered a paper on "The Benefits of Modern Democracy". He spoke for two minutes and was enthusiastically applauded for tackling such a difficult subject.' (*Ovingdean Literary Review*)

2573

'Mrs. Georgina Holmes of 45 Harbour Close accidentally let a can-opener slip at her home on Friday and cut herself severely on the back porch.' (*Webbington Gazette*)

2574

'The opening music of the Minderbridge Symphony orchestra under the direction of Vladimir Verbrugghen will be "The Battered Bride". This will be followed by "The Firefry".' (*Solihull Church Reporter*)

2575

'Police Inspector Roland CJK Townshend stated that he could find no possible reason to suspect that the murdered man could have committed suicide after knifing his wife and mistress because the note that he left behind had never been found and the gun was stuck up his chimney. The coroner returned a verdict of justifiable incompetence.' (*Stuttley Courier, Colour Supplement*)

2576

'After the wedding ceremony there was a reception after which the bridegroom left for a honeymoon in Scotland taking only one small baggage for use on the night sleeper.' (*Lands' End Free Press*)

2577

'The accident victim was taken to St. Luke's Hospital, Kenilworth Road, but left there in the morning fortunately with no bones broken. He stated that the house surgeon had done his best.' (*Mid-Wessex Evening Standard*)

2578

'66-year-old Paul Vardner of Basement Flat, 23 Lake Heath Drive, a candidate for the forthcoming ward polls was born on a farm in Wiltshire 45 years ago and has been married six times.' (*Nottingham Notebook*)

2579

'A woman who admitted being present at the Grey Witches Annual Orgy on Calsblane Heath on Tuesday night said that there were at least seventeen girls but only one man present and that the whole coven had been exercising the devil.' (*Morriston Star*)

2580
'The Garden Club met for two hours on Wednesday to hear a talk on "The Conservation of Hothouse Pants". Andrea Fitchley covered her subject with palm leaves as the main feature to start with and the chairman showed great interest. Owing to the size of her project, it was difficult to deal with, but she pulled it off in the end.' (*Georgeton Night Mail*)

2581
'At the Carnival celebrations on Sunday afternoon in Southbeach, the biggest donkey market in the country, there was also an impressive parade of mules led by the mayor and the town clerk.' (*Jeferson Clarion*)

2582
'Our Answers expert states that it is not advisable to use sodium di-flouride for cockroaches at this time of the year because small children and pets may swallow the sodium di-flouride instead of the cockroaches.' (*Malling Magazine*)

2583
'Worthing has always been an interesting holiday resort. Visitors find it particularly inviting because the town is known for its intemperate climate.' (*Bognor Mail*)

2584
'The lifeguard gave evidence. He is Peter Leonard Pooleby of 29 Clarence Mansions, and agreed that he was considered very strong and virile. The waves, he said, had been particularly fierce, but he had succeeded in getting Miss Hacker ashore where he covered her with a borrowed towel because he had lost the top of her bikini. He revitalised the half-drowned girl with kisses of life and she came round about a week later. To thank him. She stayed for about two days to ask his advice about getting into deep water, and also asked him to demonstrate a few survival tactics. She did not have her swimsuit on for that visit. Pooleby gave her some useful tips, and again she thanked him. He has since lost his job with the council's Emergency Service.' (*West Bromwich Bulletin*)

2585
'The town clerk stated that the employee, Arnold Featherby of 2344a Sentinel Street East, had worked for the council for two years as a Social Services visitor. His job was to deal with homeless teenagers, unmarried mothers and fathers, deserted wives, and teenagers on withdrawl treatment. Although supplied with a furnished house rent-free he found it impossible to love on his wages of £18·50 plus supplementary benefits. The council voted a salary raise of fifty pence and the memorandum was recorded.' (*Falstone Bridge Gazette*)

2586

'A gang of young town hooligans on chopper bikes went to the college and got over the wall without much difficulty. They threatened to molest the girls in the East Wing dormitory block. The police were called and also the fire-brigade who turned their hoses on them. While the police dried out the school matron supplied refreshment. Two of the boys, part of a musical group, had previous records, but none had sold very well. The probation officer said it was probably just a case of high spirits getting out of hand and the magistrates confiscated the crate of which only two bottles remained. Ten of the boys were sent to remand homes, four to probation houses, six to an open prison, ten were find £5 each and the other forty-nine were found to be in need of care and protection. Their knives, chains, knuckledusters and airguns were taken from them and they were sent to a reception centre which has since been demolished.' (*Fobford Examiner*)

2587

'While the farmer and his two sons were thrashing in the long meadow a party of girls from the Rangers' Camp joyfully climbed the fence and went to their assistance, and put their backs into it.' (*Dartford Times*)

2588

'One of the bank clerks told the police that the intruder menaced the staff with a monkey wench.' (*Towley Times*)

2589

'Mr. and Mrs. Eric Darbley are giving a Thanksgiving Dinner after the wedding of the only daughter, attractive 43-year old Doreen, to Dr. John Hormon.' (*Grantham Visitor*)

2590

'The Vicar of St. Angela's has now returned from his extended stay in Bournemouth to take up his usual cuties.' (*Stapleford & District Weekly News*)

2591

'The Inspector warned that he was determined to catch the elusive shoplifter even if he had to put eighteen of his best men on her tail.' (*Sunday Monitor*)

2592

'The Council has announced that all nudity on the Teascoombe Cliffs Underwalk will be bared from the end of May.' (*Perriporth Mail*)

2593

'Making her statement to the judge, Miss West added that the accident had completely put an end to her serf-riding activities.' (*Law Gazette*)

Classified
Alphabetical
Index

Classified Index

Notes

To simplify the location of comedy items suitable for your purpose, most subjects have been cross-referenced under two or three categories. It is advisable to check as many associated theme headings as possible to ensure complete coverage of your main subject. For example if you are seeking material under the general heading of MARRIAGE, look under such allied subjects as Husband, Wife, Couples, Women, Men, Children, Wedding, Vicar, Housing, and so forth. It should be borne in mind that even these subsidiary topics are capable of further expansion so that you may find funny comments and joke stories useful to your needs in relation to the principal theme. 'Marriage', for example, might also be the subsidiary subject of items relating to Holidays, School, Travel, etc. MOTORING, as another example, may offer associated humour under headings such as Garage, Tourist, Hotels, Driving, and others.

Broadly speaking it is helpful to pursue your main theme through as many associated possibilities as you can think of, if you require a speech or talk of fair length. Although the index has been carefully and comprehensively devised it is obviously difficult to classify a joke story which has varying situations and characters in it. If, for instance, an item concerns a widowed duchess travelling in a second-hand car to the Continent via cross-channel ferry in the dubious company of a retired salesman of toilet requisites, and the couple lose their way in a French forest and have to be rescued by a midget monk from a Trappist monastery during a violent thunderstorm in which the duchess loses her pet poodle and they have to make inquiries at a local farmhouse, owned by a Pakistani spy who only speaks Yiddish . . . how do you index it?

A wide variety of subjects are also covered in some passages of patter under one heading, and these are not separately indexed.

You can also find a wide range of items in the alphabetically arranged Definitions section: these have not been separately indexed.

A

ABODE 754
ABSENCE 1703
ACCIDENT 27, 1134, 1275, 1560
ACTOR 165, 1482, 1499, 1643
ACTRESS 39, 44, 118, 552, 687, 688, 745, 767, 1435, 1592, 1503, 1754
ADAM AND EVE 196, 210, 399
ADULT 456
ADULTERY 1296
ADVERTISING 160, 181, 182, 306, 422, 577, 627, 628, 629, 654, 679, 862, 1057, 1288, 1522, 2532–61
AFRICA 1297, 1301
AGE 313, 580, 633, 1050, 1454, 1494
AID 326
AIR LINE 161, 248, 332, 475, 741, 1103, 1179, 1317
ALASKA 1147
ALIMONY 338, 1559
AMERICA 143, 161, 325, 453, 693, 856, 1629
AMBITION 339
ANAESTHESIA 301, 1442
ANATOMY 1221
ANGER 296, 404, 1573
ANIMALS 1443
ANIMOSITY 56
ANONYMOUS 56
ANNIVERSARY 1362
ANTIQUE 51, 90, 1258
ANTICIPATION 1777
ANXIETY 946
APARTMENT BLOCK 1608
APPEAL 1261, 1424, 1508, 1614
APPRECIATION 1580
ARCHAEOLOGY 859

ARISTOCRACY 656, 746, 1080
1129, 1366, 1396, 1544
ARCHITECT 380, 842, 187, 1495
ARMY 127, 394, 444, 735, 814, 896, 1068, 1122, 1151, 1483, 1538, 1547, 1610, 1735, 1803
ART 275, 875, 1056, 1113, 1254, 1544, 1638, 1647
ARGUMENT 903, 1059, 1256
ASPIRIN 1810
ASSAULT 791
ASSIGNATION 1256, 1713
ASYLUM 530, 1195
ATHEIST 1087, 1704
ATOM BOMB 205, 857, 950, 951, 1193, 1220
AUCTION 691, 1414
AUDIENCE 1161, 1197
AUDITION 1326
AU PAIR 476, 1461
AUSTRALIA 1213
AUTHORSHIP 199, 237, 432, 449, 512, 829, 1148, 1280

B

BABY 231, 543, 759, 869, 1020, 1078, 1242, 1266, 1639
BACHELOR 79, 557, 826, 870, 908, 1416, 1466
BALDNESS 98, 104, 1717 (see Hair)
BANKER 139, 239, 689, 943, 1356, 1505, 1568, 1635
BANKRUPT 1267, 1381, 1597
BBC 794, 795
BARBER 1142, 1511
BARGAIN 416, 1041
BARMAID 1140 (see Drinking)

313

314

317

319